Disorders of Desire

Sex and Gender in Modern American Sexology

HEALTH, SOCIETY, AND POLICY
a series edited by Sheryl Ruzek
and Irving Kenneth Zola

Disorders
of Desire

*Sex and
Gender in
Modern
American
Sexology*

Janice M. Irvine

Temple University Press
Philadelphia

Temple University Press, Philadelphia 19122

Copyright © 1990 by Temple University.

All rights reserved. Published in 1990. Printed in the
United States of America

The paper used in this publication meets the mini-
mum requirements of American National Standard
for Information Sciences – Permanence of Paper for
Printed Library Materials. ANSI Z39.48-1984

Library of Congress Cataloging-in-Publication Data

Irvine, Janice M.

Disorders of desire: sex and gender in modern American sexology / Janice M. Irvine.

p.   cm. – (Health, society, and policy)

Includes bibliographical references.

ISBN 0-87722-689-X (alk. paper)

1. Sex – Research – United States.   I. Title.   II. Series.

HQ60.I79   1990

306.7'0973 – dc20   89-36961   CIP

For my mother, Elvera Siket Irvine

Contents

Preface

This book is the culmination of a decade of work on this topic. During this time, I have explored many of these themes in papers, a dissertation completed in 1984, articles, conference presentations, and a class I taught at Tufts University in 1986 entitled "The Sex Expert in American Culture." These ideas, then, have been shaped in many different contexts and from numerous discussions. Yet since my own experiences in sexology have been a powerful source of these arguments, they rightfully deserve mention.

I have been a sex educator since the early 1970s. In 1975 I attended the summer training program at the Institute for Sex Research (now the Kinsey Institute), and I began a professional affiliation with sexology. I have been AASECT certified as both a Sex Educator and a Sex Counselor. Many who read Chapter Eight will be surprised to know that I worked for five years at Gender Identity Service in Boston as a therapist for individuals engaged in the process of sex reassignment. Currently I consult on issues of sexuality education and training at several community-based organizations. In many ways, this book is a critique from the "inside," written to encourage institutional and structural change for a more comprehensive, representative, and progressive sexual science.

Despite my own experience as a sex educator, this book does not explore the historical development of sex education in this country. Although, of course, there is some overlap, the history of sex education follows a different trajectory and thus requires a separate project. Rather, my emphasis here is on scientific sex research and its clinical applications.

Acknowledgments

I might never have actually written these ideas without the help of Rosemary Taylor, who generously advised and supported me through the completion of my dissertation. Several years later, Ellen Herman persuaded me to pull it out from under my bed and revise it for a book. I am extremely grateful to the following people who read various sections and drafts, in some cases several times, and provided invaluable suggestions, corrections, and insights: Michael Bronski, Lisa Duggan, Ellen Herman, Liz Keeney, Zella Luria, Jade McGleughlin, Carolyn Stack, Rosemary Taylor, and Carole Vance. Special thanks to Lisa Duggan and Carole Vance for support through those enormous changes at the last minute.

Thanks to the following people, who discussed various issues with me, provided supporting material and references, or otherwise helped with the many aspects of book production: Laura Benkov, Lee Edelman, Jim Harrison, Ruth Hubbard, Nan Hunter, Freada Klein, Donna Penn, Michael Shernoff, and Charlie Shively. I am also grateful to the many women working in sexology who encouraged me to develop and publish these ideas.

At Temple University Press, thanks to Irv Zola for his longstanding and enthusiastic support of my work. Janet Francendese has provided editorial insight and witty commentary. And I am extremely appreciative of the thorough and painstaking copyediting of Jane Barry.

I am grateful to my father, William A. Irvine, for his vision of the importance of work. And, in more ways than I imagined, the work of Jon Goldman has made this writing possible.

Special thanks and love to Carolyn Stack, for clarifying my ideas and reviving my spirits. Her support has made this book better in all ways.

Finally, I could not have completed this work without the exciting and courageous scholarship from feminism and the lesbian and gay liberation movement. I am grateful to all who have contributed to it, with their writing and their lives.

Disorders of Desire

Sex and Gender in Modern American Sexology

Introduction

> My goal is to make people
> take our field seriously, so
> that, when we say we are
> sexual researchers, people
> will no longer laugh.
>
> DONALD MOSHER,
> *former president, Society for
> the Scientific Study of Sex*

On May 23, 1983, the sixth World Congress of Sexology convened in Washington, D.C.[1] For one week, more than a thousand delegates considered the history and future of the complex field of sexual science. The diverse group of conferees at the Washington Hilton—educators, physicians, biologists, psychologists, and others—participated in an array of workshops while erotic films ran incessantly in adjoining rooms. Official Washington looked the other way; both the White House and the mayor's office refused to send their routine welcoming message, saying that it would be "inappropriate."[2] The *Washington Post* covered the conference in an article entitled "Only One Thing on Their Minds." It featured a picture of sex researcher Shere Hite standing in front of a blackboard with SEX scrawled across it in huge letters.[3] Some conference speakers alluded to the aura of disrepute surrounding sexology and acknowledged the difficulty of securing funding for sex research in a conservative political climate. Overall, however, the mood of the World Congress was one of celebration for the growth and progress of the controversial science of sex.

"Sexology" is an umbrella term denoting the activity of a multidisciplinary group of researchers, clinicians, and educators concerned with sexuality. With a history of persecution and a somewhat controversial presence in contemporary society, sexology is attempting to develop fully as a profession. This book examines the efforts of sexology to prevail—both as a viable profession and as a science that would wield "cultural authority" over issues of sex and gender.[4] As American sexology develops a professional identity, one sees a strong emphasis on biomedical science both as a methodology and as a historical legitimation for the study of sex. This emphasis is, however, at odds with the complex nature of this field in which scientists, pornographers, feminists, transvestites, therapists, and others uneasily share the podium. This book is concerned with the myriad social and political factors that have converged to create an identity crisis within sexology, and a turf war over the control of cultural definitions of sexuality and gender.

The Congress

The sixth World Congress can be seen as a microcosm of the field. Professional identity was a central theme. The program notes welcomed participants, declaring "a new pride in the progress of our science" and exhorting them "to lead sexology into a richly deserved bright future."[5] Keynote addresses focused on the history of sexology from the 1900s to the present and chronicled current successes and new directions in the field. As the professional identity of its practitioners depends largely on sexology's identification as a true science, the proceedings consisted largely of a paean to scientific theory and method. Historian Edwin Haeberle pointed out the distinction between erotology—the practical study of sex (for example, the early Hindu love manuals or more contemporary works such as *The Joy of Sex*)—and sexology, the scientific study of sex.[6] Haeberle noted that, for sexologists, scientific objectivity is not merely an ideal, but the only justification for their existence. Shirley Zussman, past president of the American Association of Sex Educators, Counselors, and Therapists (AASECT), stated that the real sexual revolution involves the application of scientific method to achieve the objective study of sex.[7] A glance through the schedule for the congress confirms the appeal of science and technology for sex analysts: "A Telemetric Method for Registration of Vaginal Sexual Response," "Failure of an Attempt to Differentiate Psychogenically from Organically Impotent Males (by Arterial Lesions) by Means of a Standardized Questionnaire and MMPI," and "An Update on the Neurophysiology of the Clitoris." The same can be said of the substance of the proceedings. For example, the male presenter of a paper on women's orgasms cautioned, "We must not politicize sexual response and become pro-clitoris or pro-vagina, but we must be good sexual scientists."[8]

Walking through the exhibits lobby, however, participants encountered a variety of conflicting representations of sexology. For example, Dr. Haeberle's scholarly pictorial display on the birth of European sexology was flanked by the booths of major drug companies, which displayed recent technical innovations such as Flexi-Rod (a penile implant with "natural concealability") and the Clinical Perineometer (a biofeedback instrument that trains women to strengthen the pubococcygeus, the muscle that tightens the rectum and vagina). Sexology's professional meetings are certainly the only ones at which academic texts are marketed alongside dildoes, vibrators, and sex toys (some endorsed by sexologists or, like the new "G-Spotter" attachment for the Hitachi vibrator, "designed in conjunction with a Certified Sex Therapist"). Booths representing major sexological organizations sat side by side with Magcorp, publishers of "The Rolls Royce of swingers' magazines," and with *Forum* magazine, published by Penthouse.

The conference presentations reflected the diversity of a field whose enterprises range from the staid and scientific, to the politically controversial, to the mildly fetishistic. Throughout the week gender scientists debated the efficacy of sex reassignment surgery, and sex physiologists from around the world disputed the existence of the G-spot. Celebrity sex researchers presented their work, among them sex therapist Helen Singer Kaplan, gender sexologist John Money, and sex researchers William Masters and Virginia Johnson. In a slightly unorthodox presentation, a couple from California spoke on amelotatism (the erotic attraction to amputees) and displayed copies of a newsletter they publish, containing articles such as "A Young Lady with One Pump and One Stump." On the first evening, the "media extravaganza," which featured pornographic movies and the live appearance of some of the stars, prompted some controversy. One sex educator from Australia noted, "I have never in my professional life been eye to eye with people like that. We are all liberals and more comfortable with ourselves than other people, but some of us feel that the adult film scene is almost totally destructive."[9]

There were moments of tension between sexual science and sexual politics. At an open discussion of women's issues and concerns, some women charged that although sexologists typically espouse an encompassing definition of sex as an aspect of one's total personality, in actuality conference presentations reflect what these women considered a male preoccupation with genital expression. Other women asserted that gender politics permeate the very institution and practice of sex research. Most participants in the discussion, however, focused on how women practitioners could achieve equality and better representation within the field. A more radical critique was offered by local feminists. D.C. Feminists Against Pornography passed out leaflets urging sexologists to eliminate male bias in sexual science, and a review in the Washington-based feminist newspaper *Off Our Backs* criticized the "sexist sleaze" at the conference, such as a presentation that focused on the "loving nature" of "most" father–daughter incest, a finding that is at odds with contemporary feminist and therapeutic opinion.[10]

Such criticisms notwithstanding, the optimism expressed about the future of the controversial science was striking. Helen Singer Kaplan stated that as recently as ten or fifteen years ago, an individual with a simple sexual problem was "doomed to a lifetime of sexual inadequacy. Today . . . a patient with a sexual problem is fortunate indeed."[11] Since sexologists have largely grounded their professional mandate in the alleged ubiquity of sexual dysfunction and the ever-increasing efficacy of their treatment techniques, progress in sex therapy is indeed good news for the profession. Many sexologists, however, see themselves as pioneers fording a murky river of sexual ignorance and repression. As

Wardell Pomeroy, a Kinsey team researcher, assured those attending the congress, sexologists "would ultimately prevail, if not in two years, then surely in twenty."[12] Such qualified optimism, even doubt, is a result of the difficulties that have beset sexology in its first century and have impeded the formation of a professional identity.

The Birth of Sexual Science

After almost a century of sexual science, it is possible and appropriate to assess both the nature and value of its achievements. Although this analysis begins with the Kinsey era and proceeds to the present, sexology has a longer history that provides clues to the field's development. The scientific study of sex arose indirectly in Europe from public concerns about such issues as prostitution, venereal disease, and eugenics. By the beginning of the twentieth century, Richard von Krafft-Ebing, Havelock Ellis, and Sigmund Freud had already written major works on sexuality. The formal conception of a specific sexual science is attributed to the German physician Iwan Bloch. In his major work, *The Sexual Life of Our Time* (1907), Bloch asserted the need to study the sexual life of the individual within the context of medicine and the social sciences. It was Bloch who coined the term for this composite endeavor—*Sexualwissenschaft*, or sexology. In these early decades, the science grew rapidly, with the founding of a journal and two sexological associations.[13] In addition, several major studies of sex were published, and sexologists collaborated on films on topics such as syphilis and homosexuality.[14] The organization of several international scientific congresses on sex led to the founding of the World League for Sexual Reform in 1928. With the establishment of journals, institutes, and collaborative research projects, sexology began to acquire the trappings of a scientific enterprise.

Early sexology was centered in Germany. In addition to the two professional organizations, Berlin was the home of the first sexological institute, the Institut für Sexualwissenschaft, founded in 1919 by Magnus Hirschfeld. It housed over twenty thousand volumes, thirty-five thousand photographs, and an abundance of archival material. By the early 1930s, approximately eighty sex reform organizations, with a total membership of about three hundred fifty thousand people, exerted a considerable force in German life.[15] Composed of doctors, laypeople, and various professionals who staffed clinics, these groups provided medical and sexual information and counseling.[16] This flurry of sex reform activity was short-lived, however. In May 1933, only months after Hitler's rise to power, Nazis raided Hirschfeld's institute and removed books and papers, which were later burned in the street. Within a short time, sexological journals folded, institutes were closed, and many sexologists were arrested or went into exile. Most were Austrian or German Jews, so that anti-Semitism, as well as Nazi opposition to the sex reform movement for its own sake, fueled this attack.[17]

Some commentators portray early German sexology as a monolithic, scientific enterprise directed by progressive scholars.[18] A closer look reveals the presence of many of the same internal tensions and controversies that plague contemporary sexology. Early European sexologists were a disparate group with conflicting professional and political agendas. Magnus Hirschfeld and Wilhelm Reich passionately advocated sexual science as a tool to effect social and political change; Albert Moll called for academic rigor and the rational pursuit of scientific sexual knowledge. Moll and his colleagues eschewed activism or the use of sexual science to develop social policy. German sexology was also strained by the tension between "natural" and "cultural" science. An emphasis on biology, and later biomedical science, was regarded as crucial in achieving legitimacy and was linked to scientific solutions for such problems as venereal disease and prostitution. In fact, the consistent bias of sexologists from Bloch and Reich to Kinsey, Masters and Johnson, and the sexual scientists of the 1980s has been toward biology and physiology as fields from which "objective" facts can be mined. Social science, to the extent that it relies on a rigorous scientific method, is accepted, but primarily as a complement to natural science.[19]

Building a Profession

E ven after a century of sexual science, sexology is relatively obscure as a profession and is as likely to evoke blank stares, or snickers, as nods of respectful recognition. The "sex expert" is often the object of parody or the butt of off-color jokes. Yet thousands in this country count themselves as professional sexologists. They work as therapists, educators, researchers, or administrators in settings that range from universities and social service agencies to religious institutions and private practice. Because of the multidisciplinary nature of sexology, practitioners usually identify with another field of study, such as medicine or psychology. For many, however, the very invisibility, isolation, and disreputability of sexual science galvanize their commitment to a larger professional identity as sexologists. For the sexologist, who might be the only sex researcher in a university, or the only sex therapist in a town, conferences such as the sixth World Congress are more than a forum in which to network and discuss the latest research; they provide a vital connection to a larger vision. More than individual support is at stake, however. Ultimately, the claim to unique expertise and authority in the area of human sexuality depends on the successful consolidation of sexology as a field of inquiry within which designated groups of specialists operate.

In the United States, the profession of medicine is considered the prototype of successful professional consolidation.[20] Throughout the century, modern medicine has exercised enormous control over policies, economics, and cultural ideas of health and illness. As sociologist Paul Starr notes, "In America, no one group has held so dominant a position in this new world of rationality and power as has the medical profession."[21] Since sexology aspires to similar control over both scholarship and the professional market with respect to issues of sexuality and gender, it is useful to ask how a group manages to accrue such power.

Classic research focuses on such characteristic elements of a profession as a systematic theory and cognitive base, authority over this knowledge, the sanction of the broader community, development of regulatory ethical codes, and a culture of associations and organizations.[22] In this view, a profession's exclusive claim to an internally consistent body of theory is contrasted with the comparative ignorance of the layperson. If sanctioned by the community, this claim bestows on the profession a degree of power and privilege; an example of such power might be autonomous control over the training and regulation of the profession.

Successful professionalization has been attributed by some to a particular social or economic development that sweeps a profession to power. The rise of science and technology, for example, has been suggested as a major factor in allopathic medicine's establishment of a monopoly over healing. Yet this idea implies a determinism that simply does not hold true. For example, a strong alliance with science has not secured professional dominance for sexology, and, as Starr notes, medicine's scientific underpinnings might just as easily impede the consolidation of power.[23] It is not sufficient simply to examine a group's strategies or overarching social influences. Professionalization is an internal process, but it is also a dialogue and often a struggle. The status of a profession, Eliot Friedson notes, reflects "society's *belief* in the dignity and importance of its work" (emphasis in original).[24]

A profession, therefore, must respond to external social, political, and economic influences. It must also establish credibility with the public, who must be persuaded to consult it. The profession does not simply impose its demands upon consumers, but must seek a market. Consumers can, and do, actively resist. Moreover, the area of expertise of the would-be profession has an impact. The case of sexology strikingly illustrates that content is not neutral, but can exert an enormous influence over social willingness to accede to professional claims. The ultimate success of professionalization depends, then, on how well, within a particular sociopolitical context, the field negotiates its internal tasks and its relationships with the status quo and a diverse group of public consumers, on the level of resistance to its claims, and on its subject area.

The quest for professional ascendancy raises questions about sexology's content and the nature of the power it would command. French historian Michel Foucault has asserted that the proliferation of public discourse on sex is itself a primary mechanism for sexual manipulation and control.[25] As a social institution actively engaged in questions related to sex and gender, sexology has developed interpretive systems and a language to describe sexual experience. Sexual scientists are integrally involved with issues concerning sexual functioning, sexual variation, and gender development and dysfunction. The field is vast, with myriad enterprises. Sexological practice ranges from biomedical laboratory work investigating hormonal determinants of sexuality to nude therapy sessions for people seeking better sexual relations. "Multiple orgasms," "gender dysphoria," "ejaculatory incompetence," "sissy boys," "sex reassignment," and "disorders of desire" are among the concepts integral to the discourse of modern sexology. One of the ways in which sexology could achieve hegemony is through the assimilation of these images into our cultural lexicon; once internalized as moral and normative, they would eventually assume the power of the "natural." Sexology would serve, virtually unchallenged, as the arbiter of culturally normative sexual behavior and gender relations. This has not yet occurred.

The few systematic critiques of the field that exist for the most part view sexology as a bastion of sexual liberation, an enemy of women, or a plot by physicians and/or communists seeking mind control.[26] Modern sexual science must, however, be understood as an amalgam of theoretical and philosophical systems that have evolved within a particular social and political climate. This book explores the professionalization of modern American sexology, addressing four salient aspects: the major enterprises of sexology and their underlying ideologies; the role of sexology in the historical construction of sexual disease and a biomedically negotiated sexuality; sexology's internal process of professional consolidation; and the field's relationship to shifting political, cultural, economic, and demographic variables.

Strategies for Professionalization

Sexology's role in the cultural discourse on sex and gender has been to a large extent shaped by the tensions involved in sexology's efforts to establish itself as a profession; and that attempt is itself constrained by the subject matter sexology addresses, by dominant social groups and sexology's competitors, and by factors specific to the development of a sexual science.

First, sexology's process is unique because its subject matter is so culturally charged. The erotic terrain in Western societies has become the site of social and political conflict, which is often highly symbolic. Critics have noted that erotophobia—an irrational fear of the erotic—is common in societies where pleasure is rigidly controlled and defined.[27] This Western mistrust of sex both advances and hinders the attempts of sexology to professionalize. It must often tread softly or risk the wrath of social conservatives and religious fundamentalists for whom sexual science is anathema. Funding for sex research is subject to political winds, and usually dries up in times of sexual backlash. Over the decades, many sexologists have been personally harassed by the public or by governmental bodies such as the postal service (under obscenity laws), the House Un-American Activities Committee, and the Federal Bureau of Investigation.[28] And, as we will see, many decisions about what sexual issues will be studied and how are made with an eye toward achieving respect and legitimacy for the scientific study of sexuality.

On the other hand, that sexology deals with issues of immense personal importance is certainly an advantage. In this century, sexology has both benefited from and contributed to social values that increasingly regard sex as vital to personal happiness.[29] One consequence of erotophobia is a dearth of sound information and advice on sexual matters, and the phenomenal success of books by Alfred Kinsey and by Masters and Johnson suggests widespread interest in such information and a vast market to be tapped.

A second influence is sexology's relationship to dominant social groups and institutions. Since the mid-nineteenth century, religion is no longer the major authority in issues of sexuality, but there has been no single successor. Certainly sexology has not achieved uncontested control over sexual ideas and definitions. Indeed, it still struggles to establish itself as a reputable enterprise and achieve legitimacy with respect to mainstream social institutions. Sexology's strategy involves both methodology and the direction of research and practice. First, attempting to bask in the cultural approbation accorded to science, and particularly biomedical science, sexologists consistently contend that scientific research will vanquish troubling sociosexual problems. The mystique of science has been invoked by sexologists from Iwan Bloch to Kinsey and Masters and Johnson in the hope that scientific methodology will render acceptable their research into issues that mainstream society often considers unacceptable. This affinity for logical positivism, while no doubt sincere, furthers sexology's quest for respectability; as Sandra Harding comments, "Neither God nor tradition is privileged with the same credibility as scientific rationality in modern cultures."[30]

Concurrently, however, sexology's professionalization strategies involve specific choices about the focus of research and practice. Attempts to establish a market and exert cultural authority in matters of sexuality involve complicated relationships with potential clients and certain sociopolitical movements. Sexology has had some success in serving a market defined by sexual ignorance and sexual problems, and it aims to expand this market and achieve cultural legitimacy by responding to prevalent cultural crises. Sexological research and practice consistently address anxieties about normative sexuality and gender development. Specifically, sexology has responded to cultural fears about the survival of heterosexuality and the institution of marriage by claiming to improve heterosexual and marital relationships through better sex. Additionally, many sexologists have sought to define and channel gender roles and "gender-appropriate" behavior in a social and historical context in which traditional notions about these roles have been challenged. Throughout the century, sexology has attempted to define what it means to be a man and what it means to be a woman, and to enhance the compatibility of both.

Yet professions do not simply impose language, ideologies, and interpretive strategies on a passive public; social movements may defy professional claims to knowledge as true and timeless. Sexologists' claims to market, legitimacy, and expertise have been challenged by the feminist and lesbian/gay liberation movements, both of which have been strong forces in the rebellion against the traditional cultural institutions of marriage, heterosexism, and stereotypic gender roles. Sexology is thus placed in a complex ideological position. While many individual sexologists define themselves as liberals and feminists, the profession often aligns itself with a conservative ideology to achieve legitimacy and stake out a market. At the same time, it attempts to accommodate the radical challenges of feminism and lesbian/gay liberation as a means of broadening its authority and market. These tensions result in contradictory ideologies and render sexology exceedingly vulnerable to conservative drift. (Part Two of this book explores the complex relationship between movements of sexual politics and the field of sexual science.)

Lastly, internal struggles of self-definition within sexology have influenced its attempts at professional consolidation. In the development of professions, splinter groups often emerge with their own identity, history, and interests. Although they operate within the boundaries of the profession, they largely oppose the more established segment.[31] Until the late 1960s, sexology was primarily concerned with developing a scientific base of expertise. By the late 1960s, however, sexology was becoming more active as a business that marketed such commodities as sex therapy and sex change. Market potential affected the direction of sexology as well as the types of people drawn to the profession. Sexology has always been multidisciplinary, but the 1970s and 1980s introduced a new source of fragmentation, as two major ideological groups within the field competed and often contradicted each other. I have labeled them the orthodox scientific sexologists and the humanistic sexologists. Although both claim the authority of sexology, they have different theoretical origins, different methods, and different philosophies.

Sexology in Context

P rofessions evolve in a particular web of social and political relations. One goal of this book is to examine the impact of such relations at each stage of sexology's development, paying particular attention to the political systems of capitalism and patriarchy, the rise of science in the United States, sociopolitical changes in the 1960s that led to the emergence of social and countercultural movements, and changing sexual and gender roles throughout the century.

Historians have detailed the complicated relationship of capitalism and the wage labor system to marriage, the family, and sexual communities.[32] Of significance for sexology are the ways in which the gradual shift to a free labor economy over the last two centuries has effected widespread transformations in the nuclear family, gender relations, and the meaning and expression of sexuality. Central to this process was the decline by the nineteenth century of the household economy, in which the family, with men and women working together in a role-specific, patriarchal arrangement, was the unit of production. The nuclear family gradually lost its economic centrality but increasingly became the site of interpersonal connection and emotional sustenance. At the same time, the wage labor system permitted men and women to move to developing urban areas and live away from their families. A number of changes in sexual and gender relations became possible with the growth in the number of economically independent single people. Sexual expression became less tied to reproduction and more centered on intimacy and pleasure. And as nonmarital, nonprocreative sexuality grew more commonplace, individuals were freer to recognize and act on erotic attractions to those of the same gender. Such changes in economic and social conditions allowed for the development of gay identity and community.

Capitalism also expanded opportunities to buy and sell objects, activities, and ideas associated with sexuality. Over time the use of public space for sexual expression and transactions increased. Brothels, dance halls, and pornography afforded men the opportunity to purchase wider sexual options. For women, the sword of sexual commerce cut both ways. With less earning power, women found themselves vulnerable to prostitution, rape, and sexual harassment at the workplace. Yet even a semblance of economic autonomy brought with it freedom from family scrutiny and the possibility of increased sexual experimentation and pleasure.

The ramifications of sexual commerce—the purchase and exchange of sexual pleasure—have been widely debated. Some critics have seen it as ultimately repressive, yet another way human expression is turned into a commodity that can be controlled, cheapening sexuality and weakening the human spirit.[33] In both the nineteenth and twentieth centuries, feminist critics argued that women are inevitably victimized by practices such as prostitution and pornography.[34] In contrast, some recent analyses explore how the marketing and exchange of sexual commodities loosen some of the traditional, oppressive values of sexuality for women. In a society that is deeply ambivalent about pleasure, eroticism and sexual agency can achieve wider social currency through the acceptance of sexually explicit imagery and advertising. Many feminists have noted that pornography can rupture stereotypes by depicting women as powerful sexual agents pursuing erotic pleasures. In such cases pornography serves as a radical renunciation of sexual socialization. Similarly, sex industry workers have begun to speak out about how the exchange of sex for money can offer important economic and sexual options to women.[35]

Sexology has clearly been affected by the economic changes that expanded sexual commerce and altered notions of family and sexuality in the nineteenth and early twentieth centuries. The field has certainly benefited from the emergence and viability of the sexual marketplace. The development of sexual science required a shift of sexual discourse to the public arena: research and publication are possible only in an era in which sex can be spoken and written about. An increasingly public vision of erotic satisfaction has generated a willing group of consumers readily enticed by promises of more and better sex. In addition, the disruption of traditional gender and family structures has produced anxiety, instability, and a ready focus for sexology. Changes in social and economic arrangements have thus created optimal conditions for sexology to take root, expand, and ultimately market interventions such as sex therapy and sex reassignment surgery.

Like capitalism, patriarchy complicates sexology's social context. A historical referent to the "rule of the father" in the household economy of the family, the term has become a shorthand designation for a male-dominated hierarchical system. Patriarchy is the source of social arrangements and an intellectual environment that oppress women: man is subject, woman is object; men and their designated activities are associated with privilege and with concepts such as truth, divinity, and authority, whereas women's tasks are seen as insignificant and femaleness is a devalued category associated with illusion, mortality, and submissiveness. To the extent that patriarchal values underpin sexology, traditional assumptions concerning the roles and sexual behavior of men and women permeate research and clinical interventions. The male sexual experience is universalized as the model for healthy human functioning. Sexology's categories of sexual dysfunctions are based on departures from this norm. While privileging male heterosexuality, sexology has largely masked sex and gender biases in its research and clinical practice—for example, by substituting an allegedly objective, biomedical lexicon for the generally male-identified street language of sex: "frigidity" is translated as "inhibited sexual desire" or "orgasmic dysfunction," and "faggots" and "perverts" reappear as "sissy boys." Within sexology there have been many claims and sincere efforts to challenge stereotypic expectations for men and women; many sexologists are genuinely committed to equality, reproductive freedom, and women's sexual liberation. And, as we shall see, sexologists have professed to erase the gender hierarchy by claiming the similarity of men and women in sexual anatomy and functioning. Yet, historically, the field in fact has tacitly supported traditional gender roles, the nuclear family, and patriarchal assumptions.

We have already noted, in connection with sexology's professionalization strategy and internal tensions, the cultural idealization of science and sexologists' efforts to portray their field as a biomedical discipline.[36] Yet science, as an institution and a set of social practices, has itself been challenged. The two world wars, for example, raised questions about the military application of what had been promoted as socially neutral scientific research. In the last two decades, social scientists, historians, and feminists have examined science with respect to its social context and impact, its systems of knowledge production, and its cultural biases. In particular, feminists have criticized institutionalized discrimination against women and minorities within the scientific community, as well as uses of science and technology that further sexist and racist social projects. Science, such critics argue, is a social construction masquerading as "pure truth." Objectivity, a characteristic supposedly immanent in the scientific enterprise, is simply an attractive fiction with roots in the social and political context of the seventeenth century;[37] scientific process is a set of social relations, values, and beliefs that largely reflect the political and professional interests of scientists themselves. Implicit assumptions and sometimes explicit self-interest determine the kinds of questions scientists ask, their methods of research, and their interpretations of data.

Ignoring such challenges, many of the scientists and physicians who perform the work of sexology claim objectivity as their method and truth as their goal. Yet, as we shall see, many internal conflicts in the field revolve around attempts to keep sexology scientific and thus "pure and value free." And the application of the scientific method to issues of sexuality and gender has not gone unchallenged by those outside the field. The protests and social upheaval of the 1960s encouraged people to question traditional ideologies and institutions, including sexual science. Within sexology, a humanist influence emerged, in concert with wider influences such as the human potential movement, as an alternative to orthodox scientific sexology. Together, humanistic sexology and the feminist and gay liberation movements challenged the field's narrow scientific focus. Conflicts about the best approaches to issues of sexuality and gender, and about appropriate methods of research and therapy, persist into the 1990s.

As a construct of prevailing social, economic, and political conditions, the sex/gender system is by its very nature subject to change. Social and demographic upheavals in this century have wrought profound changes in marriage, the family, love and heterosexual relationships, and gender role expectations. Science has provided new interpretive schemata, while capitalism has altered family relations and the terms of sexual identification and negotiation. The two world wars accelerated changes already occurring in family structure and gender.[38] Furthermore, economic advance and then retrenchment, the emergence of social change movements such as feminism and lesbian/gay liberation, and the subsequent backlash from a powerful religious right wing have all contributed to the definitions of sexuality and gender in our culture. A rapid redefinition of norms and competition between various forces for cultural authority have created an amalgam of traditional values, progressive themes, and a healthy dose of uncertainty—a climate conducive to the development of sexual science.

This review of the work of major sexologists and trends and paradigm struggles within the field will be grounded in an understanding of the content of sexology not simply as a factor in its professionalization, but as a source of popular images, expectations, and organizing beliefs about sex. We shall analyze the ways in which sexology attempts to structure and negotiate our sex/gender system, for only by understanding the material circumstances of their construction can we demystify sexual belief systems that are accepted as either moral or biological imperatives.

Sex and Gender in American Society

Gender relations and sexual behavior are commonly viewed as natural and even instinctual in our culture. Tradition or biology allegedly dictates social roles for both men and women, and sexual practices trail behind. "Boys will be boys," the popular wisdom has it, symbolically encoding for us the supposed inevitability of male insensitivity or aggression. And whether or not we support such expectations, we all learn to solve the equation in which masculinity equals strength, aggression, certainty, power, and wisdom. Conversely, defined by both opposition and inferiority, femininity signifies passivity, confusion, weakness, and silliness. Although these individual gender expectations are increasingly being challenged, they still inhere in the collective consciousness; depending on one's frame of reference, they may appear as either powerful cultural imperatives or vestigial irritants. Part of their power derives from the strength and persistence of the dualistic expectations that make up what philosopher Sandra Harding terms the "symbolic gender system."[39] These roles are structurally translated into institutional and social life: the workplace, for example, is highly gendered. On the individual level, our cultural anxiety about gender confronts us in exhortations that can be traced over decades regarding what "real" men and women do and don't do. Perhaps the phenomenal success of Boy George and Michael Jackson, *Victor/Victoria* and *La Cage aux Folles*, reveals that rigid gender stereotypes have relaxed; more likely, however, it shows that anxiety is often the source of humor and entertainment.

As with social behavior, gender is also viewed as the organizing principle for sexual behavior. Gender-based sexual expectations are so accepted that they are generally considered to be biological in origin. In his book on male sexuality, sex therapist Bernie Zilbergeld summarizes the stereotypic male model of sexuality with its focus on anatomy: "It's two feet long, hard as steel, and can go all night."[40] The female continues to be trapped in a web of competing expectations: she is, for example, to be sexy but not a slut; autonomous but not aloof. More recently, these ideals have been called "scripts," in recognition that they are culturally taught and highly stylized models of behavior.[41] Sex therapist Wendy Stock refers to women's traditionally passive role as that of "Sleeping Beauty."[42] Men, on the other hand, are the "Rambos" of sex. It is no coincidence that mythic characters can be invoked as the referents for these expectations, since the media delineate sexual scripts with great clarity. In the late 1980s, as in the past, there is no precise correlation between individual styles of sexual expression and symbolic gender expectations about sex—one of Kinsey's major contributions was to chart the gap between cultural expectations and actual behavior. Yet gender-based sexual stereotypes persist, despite evidence that attitudes themselves changed somewhat during the 1970s.[43]

The theories we use to analyze the sociosexual order are significant, since our actions and interventions are shaped by the terms in which we frame an issue. The traditional mode of analyzing sexuality and gender treats prevailing arrangements as normal and natural. This essentialist analysis implies the inevitability and universality of traditional gender and sexual behaviors. It traces sexual and gendered behavior to an immutable biological impetus, suggesting, for example, that male violence is endemic because of males' high testosterone levels. Women's capacity for childbearing will, depending on the perspective, either confine them to the home or render them ideally suited for nurturing and peacemaking activities. Sex and gender are thought to be stable categories of meaning seamlessly unfolding over time. This is the dominant ideology of sexuality and gender in this culture, so powerfully entrenched as to be unspoken and often unacknowledged.

In the area of sexuality, essentialist thinking suggests an insistent, internal force or powerful biological drive that must be expressed, but only in certain normative patterns. The male heterosexual is considered the universal subject, the yardstick of evaluation. Gender identity and gender role, along with sexual preference, are cast in a particular configuration that signifies normality. Male gender identity, for example, is expected to generate masculine behavior and the choice of a female sexual partner. Conversely, women are expected to behave in characteristically feminine fashion and to choose male sexual partners. Ideologically, this "principle of consistency" is a cornerstone of our sex/gender system.[44] Sexual activity other than heterosexual intercourse is suspect. And although masturbation has, throughout the century, become more acceptable, homosexuality, cross-dressing, and fetishistic behavior are still considered violations of normal sexual expression.

Essentialist analysis of sexuality eschews complexity. At best it has been used, typically by sexologists, to wrest control of sexual definitions from moralists by insisting that sex is natural, not dirty or sinful or even sacred. Sexual expression is compared to eating, or even sneezing—a

biological impulse, the fulfillment of a natural drive. At worst, essentialist theorists seek out biological causes for atypical sexual behavior and
attempt to prevent it. This enterprise is reflected in the upsurge of research on the biological determination of homosexuality during the last
decade. Controversy has focused, for example, on the work of Gunter
Doerner, who has posited that maternal stress during wartime alters the
prenatal hormonal environment and results in an increase in homosexuality. In an argument that some have described as advocating "endo-
crinological euthanasia of homosexuality," Doerner has concluded that
"prevention of war and undesired pregnancies may render possible a
partial prevention of the development of sexual deviations."[45] Although
not all essentialist thinking is so extreme, an analysis that views sex as
the transhistorical unfolding of an immanent drive is severely limited in
scope and imagination.

Over the last two decades, scholarship by social scientists, feminists,
and gay activists and scholars has challenged the notion that sexuality
and gender are essential, internal, and universal forces. Some pioneering
critics have begun to investigate the ways in which sexuality and gender are products of historical and cultural mediation.[46] The influence of
social movements was crucial in redirecting research. By the late 1960s,
activists and scholars were providing a framework for understanding
the interaction of sexuality and gender. In 1975, anthropologist Gayle
Rubin developed the concept of the sex/gender system to describe the
set of social arrangements by which biological sexuality is molded into a
human product.[47] Rubin later disentangled sexuality from the context of
gender relations to argue that, although related, sex and gender "form
the basis of two distinct arenas of social practice."[48] Sexual activity and
sexual oppression, she argues, are not inevitably derivative of gender,
but may follow their own trajectories. Historically, however, sexual ideologies and gender roles have been woven into highly codified systems,
even though the symbolic systems and material conditions underpinning
the sex/gender system undergo tension and transformation.

This new literature is characterized by a social construction theory
that views the sex/gender system as a product of human activity, much
like religion, the family, and other social institutions. Sex and gender
are seen not as inevitable products of biological difference and internal

drive, but as fluid constellations of meaning. This theory allows for an understanding of the historical and cultural mediation of sex and gender, and also examines the issue of power and privilege. When we explore how certain constructs change over time and across cultures, we can start to understand the role of certain groups and organizations in establishing new ideas and expectations. We can begin to ask, "How does the meaning of certain activities change historically?" and "For whose benefit does this operate?" We can examine conflict over language, definitions, policy, and legislation. Whether we are discussing stereotypes about men and women, teenage pregnancy, the emergence of a gay community, or the medical discourse on sexually transmitted diseases, social construction theory acknowledges human agency in sexuality and gender. And it becomes increasingly clear that sexual and gender differences are not simply variations but delineate important dimensions of political activity and conflict.

As Doerner's research illustrates, essentialist theory, with its belief in normal, stable categories of sexuality and gender, can easily support a dominant ideology that views some behaviors and identities as privileged and others as inferior. Differences in gender or sexuality are not neutral; rather, there are sharp differentiations among behaviors in Western culture. As Rubin notes:

> Most of the discourses on sex, be they religious, psychiatric, popular, or political, delimit a very small portion of human sexual capacity as sanctifiable, safe, healthy, mature, legal, or politically correct. The "line" distinguishes these from all other erotic behaviors, which are understood to be the work of the devil, dangerous, psychopathological, infantile, or politically reprehensible. Arguments are then conducted over "where to draw the line," and to determine what other activities, if any, may be permitted to cross over into acceptability.[49]

The reification of gender and sexual norms and the stigmatization of difference are serious endeavors that maintain a social hierarchy of power, of good and bad. An ideology of gender oppositions underpins human thought and social arrangements, Tucker Farley points out: "If behavior is not gender-determined, then all the systems of knowledge and all the social systems built on the assumption of heterosexuality and inherent male-female differences are inaccurate."[50] Given the related systems of power and privilege, theories and research concerning sexuality and gender are not simply academic but highly political in nature.

The question of sex/gender differences is crucial to understanding the nature of such research—including that performed by sexologists—throughout the century. Lines of inquiry and the direction of research projects frequently are related to issues of power and privilege. Biologist Ruth Bleier, for example, has examined the heightened research interest in biological differences between women and men in the 1970s and 1980s.[51] Historically, political struggles concerning relations of gender, race, or class have been played out in research projects that attempt to prove one group different, and therefore inferior.[52] A primary task of feminism has been to elucidate the ways in which notions of "difference" have not been neutral. As critic Nancy Miller says, "Western culture has proven to be incapable of thinking not-the-same-as without assigning one of the terms a positive value and the other, a negative."[53] In patriarchal culture, then, the binary opposition of male and female forms the basis of the central organizing hierarchy. Phallocentrism enforces the notion of woman as deficient because of her lack of a penis. Similarly, sexual differences like homosexuality, transsexualism, or transvestism are considered deviations that pose a threat to the heterosexual imperative.

Yet simple awareness of gender and sexual inequity and oppression has not brought with it a clear political agenda for change. Since "difference," for women or sexual minorities, is typically read as "inferiority," the temptation is to push for similarity and to expose the fictive nature of alleged and exaggerated differences. Diminution or abolition of difference was seen by many feminists in the nineteenth century and the early 1970s as the only route to feminist revolution.[54] With the mid-1970s, however, came a renewed emphasis on women's experience and women's uniqueness. Feminist scholarship began to detail the ways in which women differed from men in areas such as psychology, moral development, intimacy, and sexual behavior. Such research produced a celebration of women and women's culture and a renewed emphasis on difference as a positive quality. Yet the issue is far from being resolved, either for feminists or for gay activists, because the pursuit of equality through the legal system has led to explosive differences over strategies for opposing discrimination. As currently framed, the question is whether to advocate for "sameness," and hence equality, or protective legislation based on real differences, which could leave a historically oppressed group vulnerable to discrimination.

Strategies that emphasize "sameness" and those which stress "difference" both function within a culture that devalues and oppresses women and sexual minorities. Both approaches are therefore problematic as strategies for social change. As we shall see with regard to sexuality, stressing the sameness of men and women ignores or trivializes historical differences in sexual socialization, making a leap that is too rapid and acultural. For example, the claim of some sexologists that men who are sexually assaulted experience the same emotional reactions as women who are raped ignores the impact of the culture's tacit approval of male violence against women. And the claim that gay and straight people are the same because they have the same physiological sexual responses is the most reductive biologism. The "sameness" strategy ignores differences of power and privilege based on gender or sexual status and suggests that people can be equal only when they are exactly the same.

Yet the opposite strategy has its own set of pitfalls. Stating that women are more sensual or romantic has the interim advantage of elevating female sexuality from its historically despised status. What is gained in the short term, however, is ultimately lost in the risk of entrenching a politically lethal essentialism that locks women and men into a set of ideals and expectations about who they "really" are. No matter how the lines are drawn, a strategy that emphasizes difference is closely allied to either a biologically or a culturally based essentialism, falsely universalizing a set of historical and social relations.

Sexology has played a complex role in identifying, challenging, and perpetuating cultural imperatives about sex, gender, and difference. The field is deeply implicated in the political controversy over sexual and gender difference, though its agenda seems contradictory. It staunchly espouses the similarities of men and women while spending vast resources to search out the differences between gay people and straight. Sexologists have timed contractions and measured secretions with the goal of quantifying maleness and femaleness. Through hormone research, they seek information about physiological nuances that might distinguish male and female sexuality, homosexuality and heterosexuality. In the clinical realm, they teach "gender-appropriate" behavior to children and "gender-inappropriate" behavior to sexually dysfunctional women, in the hope that women who behave more like men might enjoy sex more. Indeed, positing precise scientific answers to questions about masculinity and femininity has been a major strategy in the struggle to achieve professional legitimacy.

Through an analysis of the professionalization of modern American sexology, this book explores the ways in which modern sexual science has participated in the cultural discourse on sex and gender. The story is a complex one with numerous voices and subplots because the field encompasses so many contending forces: different research directions and conflicting interpretations of data, market demands that hinder efforts to establish a scientific identity, a biomedical conservatism at odds with the impulse to defend sexual freedom. The ultimate professional goal, the achievement of cultural legitimacy and control over sexual knowledge and the sexual marketplace, remains elusive. It is a goal that, for some sexologists, is framed in increasingly simple terms: they hope that when they say they are sex researchers, "people will no longer laugh."[55]

Part One: The Emergence of Scientific Sexology

T he period from the 1930s to the mid-1960s was a time of steady, if incremental, growth in modern American sexology. It was an era of paradox: the drama and conflict attending the publication of the Kinsey reports coincided with the virtually unnoticed proliferation of sex researchers and therapists. Fundamental changes in roles for men and women elicited a few sighs of relief and more than a little insecurity about the loss of traditional models.

Sexuality's shift from a private, marital, and familial context toward an increasingly commoditized status marked it as a public issue and a potential social problem. With scientific and technological rationality heralded as the solution to social ills, the stage was set for a more public role for sexual scientists. Although sex researchers and theorists such as Sigmund Freud, Havelock Ellis, Katherine Davis, Clelia Mosher, and

Robert Latou Dickinson had produced a sizable literature, it was Alfred Kinsey who both captured the popular imagination and provoked cultural conservatives with his investigations into the social patterns and individual sexual behaviors of American men and women. Kinsey, the biologist and taxonomist, consistently stressed the transformative potential of the scientific study of sex. Sexual science, he believed, could supply the data that would promote greater understanding among groups of people whose relationships have been historically fraught with tension because of different sexual patterns and systems. Both marriages and class dynamics could be improved if only people had this information. The social context and the style of Kinsey's research fostered the pragmatic, empirical enthusiasm characteristic of the field at this time. This was a key moment for the emerging profession of sexology, as the confluence of striking cultural changes with Kinsey's pioneering research helped create a climate favorable to the acceptance of the scientific study of sexuality. The adulatory reviews accorded to Masters and Johnson upon the publication of their first text in 1966 signified the distance sexology traveled in these years.

Throughout this period, as we have seen, sexologists were intent on consolidating the profession through scientific achievement, accruing data, and developing a canon. Kinsey's empiricism dovetailed with the later biomedical research of Masters and Johnson, and by the mid-1960s professional aspirations soared as sexologists sought to present themselves as staid scientists in pursuit of sexual truth. The implicit ideologies of sex research located scientific sexologists in this period among the major promoters of sexual modernism.[1] Sex, they assured the public, was not a suspicious or inchoate impulse, but rather a natural drive. For males and females alike, sex was a biological birthright, and "more is better" was assumed. This normalization of the sexual drive was a further step away from both moralism and the Freudian mystique of sexuality, supporting the growing cultural importance of sexuality while locating it as an appropriate object of scientific scrutiny.

Yet the advocacy of sex as a natural phenomenon raised nagging questions about what kind of sex was natural. Kinsey seemed to suggest that any behavior, by its very existence, fell within the normal span of sexuality. On the other hand, Masters and Johnson's early work virtually ignored anything other than marital sexuality. Marital ideology to varying degrees characterized the work of most sexologists during this period, a function of both traditional belief systems and a desire for mainstream acceptance. Modern sexology's strategy during these decades—rigorous scientific consolidation combined with an emphasis on issues of cultural importance for the white, heterosexual majority—was moderately successful, but by the late 1960s its content and its relentless empiricism had opened the field to charges of bias and exclusivity.

Chapter One

Toward a "Value-Free" Science of Sex:
The Kinsey Reports

I hardly ever see him
at night any more
since he took up sex.

CLARA KINSEY

The development of sexology in the Kinsey era is best understood in light of widespread changes in sexuality and the family early in the century. The social and economic changes that reshaped marital ideology and gender roles in the wake of World War I form the cultural backdrop for the emergence of the scientific study of sex. Increasingly, women were moving into the cities, living on their own, and working in the public sector. Having achieved a sense of independence in college or in jobs, women were less content to settle for the exclusivity of wife/mother roles.[1] Sociosexual mores for women changed rapidly in the 1920s. Smoking in public vied with sexual adventure as the epitome of female licentiousness. An official of the National Reform Bureau noted that smoking "is the beginning of the end" and prophesied, "Virtually all the male vices will be feminine vices, too."[2] Much later, Alfred C. Kinsey would document that public anxiety about loosening sexual morality was based in reality. The generation of women born in the first decade of the twentieth century showed twice the incidence of premarital intercourse of those born earlier. And more of these women were having sex with men other than their intended husbands.

Throughout the 1920s and 1930s, traditional sexual morality was increasingly at variance with people's actual behavior. Discussion of sexual matters was becoming more acceptable, and with the confidence and authority of all popular magazines, *Fortune* proclaimed, "Sex is no longer news."[3] The era moved toward an attitude that Estelle Freedman and John D'Emilio describe as sexual liberalism—an emphasis on erotic pleasure as an integral part of personal and marital satisfaction and a rejection of the belief that sex is inevitably oriented toward reproduction.[4] Heterosexual relations outside marriage became more normative, amid popular cries that the family was in peril and home life was disintegrating.

Yet sexual ideology was merely one arena of the more widespread shift in gender roles. As the Victorian sociosexual boundaries of separate spheres blurred, it was becoming harder to define what it meant to be a man and what it meant to be a woman. A popular poll in the *Ladies Home Journal* in the mid-1930s reflected the ambivalence about men's and women's traditional roles. Of the women polled, 60 percent objected to the word "obey" in the marriage ceremony; 75 percent believed that husbands and wives should make decisions together; and 80 percent believed an unemployed husband should perform household duties. Yet 60 percent of the women added that they would lose respect for their husband if they earned more than he did, and 90 percent stated that a woman should quit her job if her husband demanded it.[5] The tension between traditional demands and the emerging order was palpable.

This flux in gender roles was accelerated by World War II. Women were propelled even more dramatically out of traditional roles by the war mobilization. And, since definitions of appropriate gender roles are inextricably related, historians have noted how the increasing liberation of women precipitated a crisis of masculinity among men.[6] Gender insecurity during the war led to an idealization of images of women and the family that were invoked with a vengeance in the postwar era. Heavy-handed propaganda called for the reinstitution of gender polarities along traditional, conservative lines. The celebration of heterosexuality and marriage led to the baby boom of 1946–1964, a cohort of 75 million whose movement from phase to phase of the life cycle has had a profound effect on U.S. culture at each stage.[7] Yet one can discern the signs of intense cultural anxiety about sex, gender, and marriage in this period. The witchhunts of the early fifties, directed against communists and homosexuals, spoke to a pervasive fear of Otherness. The crisis of gender was reflected in fears that our men weren't man enough (to protect us from the red scare) and our women were too strong and overbearing (which would lead to a decline in the moral fabric and subsequent communist takeover). As journalist Michael Bronski has observed, such films as *The Incredible Shrinking Man* and *The Fifty Foot Tall Woman* capture the gender anxiety of the era.[8]

It was in this context that Kinsey published his work. Sex and gender, both socially constructed concepts, were heavily influenced by the changes of the early to mid-twentieth century. Thus, while Kinsey documented and verified the quantitative dimensions of sexual behavior, he also tapped the public's ambivalence about fluctuating sexual mores. For some his work was reassuring and for others outrageous. Yet Kinsey spoke to the cultural confusion about sexuality by offering the hope of scientific solutions to the crisis of gender and heterosexuality. He presented data that he hoped would help men and women understand each other and thus improve both the marriage contract and the marriage bed. It was a vision in which he deeply believed, and which simultaneously functioned as a strategy to secure acceptance of sex research.

In the thirties, as issues of birth control, sexuality, and marriage were increasingly dealt with by professionals, as opposed to feminists and sex radicals, the professionalization of sexology appeared logical.[9] Science and medicine had established themselves as the mechanisms for solving social problems, and elite institutions dedicated to preserving the traditional social order, like the Rockefeller Foundation, funneled millions of dollars into hard, scientific research. Until the sixties, when political movements once again organized around issues of sex and gender, scientific sexology was a major option for individuals who needed information or help with sexual problems.

The Kinsey Era

To most people the name Kinsey is evocative of the emergence of scientific sex research in the United States. Alfred C. Kinsey was undeniably a pioneer and indeed a landmark figure in the scientific study of sex. Other scientists in Europe and America had conducted research before Kinsey, and J. M. Exner, Katherine Davis, Clelia Mosher, and Robert Latou Dickinson had in the early 1900s conducted sex surveys in the United States that foreshadowed Kinsey's empirical methodology. Yet none approached the magnitude of the research Kinsey produced.

By Kinsey's time, a number of factors had converged to loosen traditional religious strictures on the secular approach to sexuality in the United States. The work of Sigmund Freud had achieved wide currency in the early decades of the twentieth century, providing new paradigms for understanding the social and emotional significance of sexuality. Other writers such as Havelock Ellis and Theodore van de Velde had produced popular books and marriage manuals, which were available to the general public. Several empirical sex surveys had been published, and "health" issues such as birth control, venereal disease, and abortion provided a forum for discussing sex. Widespread demographic changes triggered public concern about marriage and sexuality. In this context, sexual behavior was being widely discussed by groups as varied as physicians, clergy, eugenicists, feminists, radicals, and social reformers.

By 1910 the Rockefeller Foundation had already committed over $5 million to the study of prostitution and the "white slave" trade, convinced that sexual biology, then a fledgling science, was the means by which social "problems" of sexuality would be solved. Breakthroughs in endocrinology at the turn of the century fueled this belief. Hormones, and their relationship to certain sexual characteristics, had just been discovered, and many physicians were hoping that questions about sexual "problems" such as homosexuality would be answered by research on the sex glands.[10] Chemicals extracted from the ovaries and the testes had been labeled "female" and "male" sex hormones, reflecting the underlying ideological hope that research would explicate the essential differences between the sexes. Although later research revealed the presence of both hormones in both sexes, the labels stuck, and these biological interpretations were directly used by some scientists to imply that gender differences, and by extension women's "inferiority," were inborn.[11]

Two prominent sex endocrinologists persuaded the National Research Council to establish the Committee for Research in Problems of Sex in 1921. The stated intent of the committee's founders was that "by their concerted effort and with the prestige of the National Research Council, they could raise to scientific favor in the United States a subject which up to that time had remained in relative dispute, and that they could stimulate and coordinate research in all the related sciences that bear upon human behavior."[12] The committee was funded by the Rockefeller Foundation and from its inception until the late 1940s was both umbrella and impetus for much of the scientific sex research conducted in the United States. The research that the committee funded reflected the ideological agenda of the officers of the Rockefeller Foundation. Some were opposed to the direct study of sex; others were interested in "backing brains" in order to solve "the social and moral problems of sex behavior in the community"—divorce, illegitimacy, prostitution —all reducible, in the opinion of the Foundation, to some biological or psychological etiology, and thus amenable to "objective" empirical analysis. The research funded consisted of "the kind of morphological, functional studies that appealed to the sexologists for their scientific definition of the socially normal, and to the biologists for their mechanical insight into the animal organism." From 1922 to 1949, the Foundation gave the committee between $60,000 and $75,000 a year, most of which, until 1934, was allocated to hormonal research.[13] At that point, the committee broadened its focus and took the risk of funding what would prove to be the most pivotal sex research of the century.

It was to the Committee for Research in Problems of Sex that Alfred Kinsey, the quintessential scientist, turned for funding in 1941. After a nominal grant the first year, the committee increased its funding to him exponentially over the years, so that by 1947 Kinsey's Institute for Sex Research was receiving half of the committee's entire budget. His rigorously empirical approach to the study of sex mirrored the Foundation's intents. But in 1954, prompted by a congressional investigating committee, the Rockefeller Foundation completely terminated his funding. The Foundation was apparently unwilling to weather the moral and political outrage engendered by Kinsey's research.

Kinsey's research was a logical outcome of his own evolving interests and professional predilections. He was a professor of zoology at Indiana University whose area of expertise was the gall wasp. A taxonomist and collector par excellence, he had amassed over four million wasps during the course of his fieldwork. Kinsey's shift to the study of sexuality can be traced to his involvement with a marriage course instituted at Indiana University in 1938. As coordinator of the course, he was dismayed by the dearth of scientific literature on sex and his consequent inability to answer his students' questions. He was critical of all previous sex research as methodologically unsound or, in contrast to his own penchant for collecting, too narrow in scope. Thus he began compiling his own data, initially by taking the sexual histories of his students.[14]

The cultural idealization of science in American society was Kinsey's inspiration as well as his validation. He was convinced of the relevance and necessity of the application of the scientific method to the study of human sexuality, and he devoted considerable space in his texts to arguments for the viability of sexual science. Any increase in knowledge, he believed, would increase "man's capacity to live happily with himself and with his fellow men."[15] Kinsey squarely faced challenges to the right of scientists to conduct research in the area of human sexuality. Psychology and philosophy, he said, "ignored the material origins of all behavior"; only direct observation could provide reliable information on material phenomena—and for Kinsey, sex was essentially a material phenomenon. A true son of science, Kinsey was committed to the value-free objectivity of his research. In his first volume, *Sexual Behavior in the Human Male* (*SBHM*), he wrote,

The present study . . . represents an attempt to accumulate an objectively determined body of facts about sex which strictly avoids social or moral interpretations of the fact. Each person who reads this report will want to make interpretations in accordance with his understanding of moral values and social significance; but that is not part of the scientific method, and indeed, scientists have no special capacities for making such evaluations.[16]

From the purview of the 1980s, when science has, at least in some circles, been removed from its pedestal, Kinsey's naiveté is obvious. Radical critiques of science emphasize that, far from being value-free, science embodies a white, middle-class, heterosexual imperative. And, as we shall see, Kinsey's work is grounded in this dominant ideology. Yet, in that particular historical era of sex research, Kinsey's claim to objectivity was, in some respects, quite radical. The scientific study of sex was still suspect in a climate where discussions of sex were typically conducted under the aegis of religion and philosophy. The work of the early sexologists such as Krafft-Ebing and Ellis categorized forms and classes of behavior as "abnormal" and "perverse." When Kinsey proclaimed his "objectivity," he was eschewing both the moralism of religion and the pathologizing tendency of the social sciences. It was essentially, for Kinsey, a claim that he would make no negative judgments, point no fingers, and condemn no behavior.

But though scientists may avoid explicit moral judgments, research is implicitly striated with values and biases. In fact, Kinsey's values permeate his work. Kinsey conveys his belief, cloaked in the rationale that what is "natural" is right, that sex is good and more is better, thus effecting an important ideological shift for sexology. His prosex stance inheres in modern sexology and accounts for some of the field's ideological complexity, particularly with respect to female sexuality.

Kinsey's belief in scientific objectivity had another consequence that persists within modern sexology: his refusal to take public stands on political or social issues of the day. Wardell Pomeroy, one of Kinsey's research associates, cites Kinsey's dogged continuance of his research during World War II as if he were untouched by it. "He never joked about politics," Pomeroy says, "no doubt because he was completely apolitical."[17] Neutrality was a logical outcome of Kinsey's belief that scientists were not necessarily equipped to make political evaluations, yet it was also a strategy to maintain his growing social legitimacy.

Kinsey's work was controversial enough and could be threatened by partisan stances. In the first pages of *SBHM*, Kinsey describes some of the difficulties he encountered:

> During the first year or two we were repeatedly warned of the dangers involved in the undertaking, and were threatened with specific trouble. There was some organized opposition, chiefly from a particular medical group. There were attempts by the medical association in one city to bring suit on the ground that we were practicing medicine without a license, police interference in two or three cities, investigation by a sheriff in one rural area, and attempts to persuade the University's Administration to stop the study, or to prevent the publication of the results, or to dismiss the senior author from his university connection, or to establish a censorship over all publications emanating from the study. Through all of this, the Administration of Indiana University stoutly defended *our right to do objectively scientific research, and to that defense much of the success of this project is due.* In one city, a school board, whose president was a physician, dismissed a high school teacher because he had cooperated in getting histories outside of the school but in the same city. There were other threats of legal action, threats of political investigation, and threats of censorship, and for some years there was criticism from scientific colleagues. It has been interesting to observe how far the ancient traditions and social custom influence even persons who are trained as scientists. (Emphasis added.) [18]

Kinsey's claim to objectivity and neutrality was in many ways a careful presentation of self. For his books make it clear that he had deep convictions regarding social and political mores. He was critical of the church, educational institutions, and homes for being "the chief sources of the sexual inhibitions, the distaste for all aspects of sex, the fears of the physical difficulties that may be involved in a sexual relationship, and the feelings of guilt which many females carry with them into their marriages." [19] And he railed against sex laws in the beginning of *Sexual Behavior in the Human Female* (*SBHF*):

> Our present information seems to make it clear that the current sex laws are unenforced and are unenforceable because they are too completely out of accord with the realities of human behavior, and because they attempt too

much in the way of social control. Such a high proportion of the females and males in our population is involved in sexual activities which are prohibited by the law of most of the states of the union, that it is inconceivable that the present laws could be administered in any fashion that even remotely approached systematic and complete enforcement. The consequently capricious enforcement which these laws now receive offers an opportunity for maladministration, for police and political graft, and for blackmail which is regularly imposed both by underworld groups and by the police themselves.[20]

Both *SBHM* and *SBHF* contain impassioned critiques of the "sexual psychopath" laws that originated in the 1930s and swept through many states and the District of Columbia. These laws were enacted in the wake of moral panics, often triggered by sexual crimes against children, but doing little, in fact, to protect their intended beneficiaries. Rather, they served to crystallize public sexual discourse around normality and deviance,[21] categories that Kinsey despised. Kinsey attempted to deconstruct the category of "sex offender" by pointing out that most people engaged in sexual behavior that was illegal.[22] To arrest and imprison some of them for relatively common activities was the height of hypocrisy. Kinsey also opposed the sodomy laws that, as a gay male writer noted in the 1950s, rendered "every homosexual in this country . . . a potential felon and traitor."[23] Yet despite the vehemence of his critique, Kinsey simultaneously believed that the only function of the Institute was to present factual data and their significance, not to lobby politically.[24]

This strategy has persisted at the Kinsey Institute for Research in Sex, Gender, and Reproduction, as the Institute is now known. Sex researchers there have refused, for example, to take public stands on pornography.[25] Kinsey's dilemma is inherent in the scientific study of sex. For both political and strategic reasons, many sexologists have attempted, like Kinsey, to ignore sexual politics and attend simply to the "facts." Since sex is so highly politicized in this culture, sexologists are continually sought out by special interest groups, legislators, lobbyists, and social activists who want them to act as advocates and give their expert opinions. The founders of the Sex Information and Education Council of the United States (SIECUS) realized this in 1965 when they were asked to sign a petition in support of Ralph Ginzburg, whose conviction for publishing *Eros* was being reviewed by the Supreme Court. In a letter to founder Mary Calderone, board member Lester Kirkendall wrote, "I think myself that we must take some stand in such matters. We can't deal with sex without getting into controversy."[26] Yet this realization of the inherently political implications of sexuality and sex research has throughout the century collided with many sexologists' aspirations to value-neutrality. Sexology has yet to resolve the tension between sexual politics and sexual science.

The Kinsey Method

K insey's commitment to the scientific method is palpable in both *SBHM* and *SBHF*. Both are replete with passages that reflect his passion for, even awe at, the potential of science to expand the boundaries and improve the lot of humankind. One can almost hear him persuading the average reader of the wonders of the emergent sexual science. Yet, subtextually, it is clear that Kinsey felt that the success of his research depended on scientific rigor and, perhaps more important, on his ability to convince the public of the stringency and objectivity of his approach. He went to great lengths at the beginning of *SBHM*, published in 1948, to satisfy would-be critics as to his precision. In painstaking detail he described the research team's objectives and methods. He reviewed the foundations of taxonomy, the nuances of interviewing, statistical analysis, sampling problems, and the validity of the data. Kinsey acknowledged that his subject called for a different procedural approach from those used in "less intimate and less complex" areas.[27] He even included a proviso, which has gotten lost over the years as researchers authoritatively quote the Kinsey findings, that the data presented throughout the volume should be recognized as "probably fair approximations, but only approximations of the fact."[28] Nevertheless, Kinsey boasted a proficiency of method and uniformity of data that, he claimed, many would have thought impossible for "as taboo a subject as sex."[29]

The style and content of his research, as well as his fundamental sexual ideology, were both profoundly affected by Kinsey's background in biology and taxonomy. He was a collector of the "natural" and an observer fascinated by the minutiae of variation. In his introduction to *SBHM*, Kinsey lists nineteen taxonomic studies of sexuality that preceded his. Yet the major early figures in the scientific study of sex (e.g., Krafft-Ebing, Ellis, Freud, Davis, and Bloch) had essentially based their work on case studies or small samples. Although Kinsey ostensibly defers to the contribution of these pioneers, one can often detect scorn in his references to their theories or findings. He questioned their methodology, dismissing certain field methods as "barbershop techniques":

> Some persons are appalled at the idea of having to undertake a large-scale coverage of thousands of individual cases before they are allowed to generalize about the whole. Contacts with the statistics of small samples have provided rationalizations for some of this inertia; but no statistical techniques can make a small sample represent any type of individual which was not present in the original body of data.[30]

Whether the subject was the gall wasp or sex, the key to valid research, for Kinsey, was identical: amass a vast sample. In this case, his nonrandom sample consisted of the sex histories of individuals as varied as college students, prisoners, mental patients, white- and blue-collar workers, ministers, and prostitutes. His technique was the interview. The average interview lasted from ninety minutes to two hours, and covered from 350 to 500 items, or more. Kinsey devoted considerable space in *SBHM* to describing this method and defending it against critics who objected that subjects might exaggerate, distort, or simply forget the specific details of their sexual pasts:

> The testing of the reliability and validity of our data is as yet insufficient, and we shall continue to make such tests as the research pi am allows; but it may be noted that this is the first time that tests of either reliability or validity have been made in any study of human sexual behavior, and that there are few other case history studies of any sort which have made as extensive tests as we have undertaken in the present study.[31]

The interview was one of the most controversial aspects of the Kinsey research; even today curiosity persists about what exactly went on. It is clear that Kinsey's interviewing format was highly idiosyncratic. He admitted that certain techniques worked better for some interviewers than others and that approaches to different informants might vary in language, style, and the definition and construction of questions. He believed that an experienced interviewer (one trained in the Kinsey method) would be alert and responsive to intangibles that called for a modification in technique. In a rare lapse of his usual aspirations to scientific objectivity, he acknowledged that effective interviewing could require empathy from the researcher: "The interviewer who senses what these things can mean, who at least momentarily shares something of the satisfaction, pain, or bewilderment which was the subject's, who shares something of the subject's hope that things will, somehow, work out right, is more effective, though he may not be altogether neutral." He went so far as to describe the interview as "a communion between two deeply human individuals, the subject and the interviewer."[32] This was a striking departure from the traditional stimulus–response approach to the interview.

Given his devotion to rigor and objectivity, however, it is not surprising that Kinsey attempted to standardize his subjective and even idiosyncratic interviewing behaviors. He described such "technical devices in interviewing" as "putting the subject at ease" (by letting him or her smoke; engaging in comfortable chatter, etc.) and "establishing rapport" (treating the subject as a friend, establishing eye contact, since "people understand each other when they look directly at each other"). The goal was to present a more universalized and objective interviewer–respondent interaction that was consistent with a positivist research tradition. Social scientists have traditionally attempted to standardize and neutralize the interview with the hope of reducing bias,[33] yet more than usual was at stake in Kinsey's quest for standard, objective research techniques: the viability of his project and, by extension, sex research as a whole.

Kinsey's studies are a pageant of counting and categorizing. *SBHM* is based on data from the sex histories of 5,300 men. Kinsey divided the population on the basis of twelve demographic factors: sex, race–cultural group, marital status, age, age of the subject at the onset of adolescence, educational level, occupational class of subject, occupational class of subject's parent, rural–urban background, religious group, religious adherence, and geographic origin. Kinsey believed that it was necessary to have at least three hundred cases from a particular subgroup for it to be adequately represented. His ultimate plan was to obtain a hundred thousand sex histories, but he died before achieving that goal.

Although his sample was unprecedented in its diversity, neither *SBHM* nor *SBHF*, published in 1953, includes data from non-whites. *SBHF*, based on 5,940 histories, fails even to mention race in its breakdown of population characteristics. This shortcoming is a result of Kinsey's obsession with numbers; he felt that he had not obtained enough sex histories from Black men and women to permit valid extrapolation. In *SBHM* he wrote: "The story for the Negro male cannot be told now, because the Negro sample, while of some size, is not yet sufficient for making analyses comparable to those made here for the white male."[34] Although Kinsey planned to make revisions when he had more histories from Black people, he never did so, and he thus unwittingly colluded in the racial exclusion so pervasive in sex research. The most comprehensive sex research ever published, which has been used for decades to generalize and form conclusions about people's sexual activity (and has drawn new attention with the advent of the AIDS epidemic), is based exclusively on whites. The invisibility of Black people in sexology as subjects or researchers has undermined our understanding of the sexuality of Black Americans and continues to be a major problem in modern sexology.

Kinsey's approach to hiring staff and interviewers reflected his basic assumptions and values. (It also influenced later research decisions and interpretations of data and was related to the exclusion of Blacks from his reports). His major criteria for interviewers were as follows:

1. They must be happily married, but able to travel at least half-time. This criterion allowed him to exclude women, since, he explained to a colleague, "it is much more difficult for a woman to stay happily married and travel away from home a good deal."[35]

2. They should have either a medical degree or a doctorate, yet be able to get along with individuals from lower socioeconomic levels.

3. They must have been born and raised in the United States, exposed to American customs and attitudes, yet be able to refrain from evaluating what others did sexually.[36]

In addition, Kinsey would never hire anyone with an odd or an ethnic name, since he thought it might interfere with establishing rapport with subjects. He particularly avoided Jewish names for fear of alienating Protestants.[37] He adamantly insisted that his staff composition did not interfere with research efficacy or interviewing. Although Kinsey confessed that it was "astounding," given the cultural taboo against revealing personal sexual activities, that anyone had agreed to be interviewed, he did not believe the process would be enhanced if subjects were approached by a member of their own community. Against the need for women or Black interviewers he argued that if one had to match interviewer and subject on the basis of sex or race, then one should also do so for other social groups, such as prostitutes—a practice that he considered unworkable. His staff, then, consisted of male, heterosexual, white Anglo-Saxon Protestants, since for Kinsey these characteristics represented the yardstick of normality. WASPs, he believed, would be able to interview anybody.

This decision reveals two related features of Kinsey's world view: his devotion to the scientific method, and the strength of his covert biases about gender, race, and sexual preference. His ideology was so based in numbers and frequencies that he inevitably viewed the characteristics of any numerical majority as "natural," normative, or good. Since male WASPs represent, if not the statistical, at least the cultural, norm in the United States, Kinsey considered them to be natural researchers. With enough scientific training in the fine points of interviewing, he believed they could be neutral, win the trust of their subjects, and elicit information from anyone. It apparently never occurred to him that there was anything political about representing the dominant social group as the norm and refusing to hire more diverse interviewers.

It is impossible to say whether, and how, a different research team might have influenced the studies. A group of women, homosexuals, Blacks, and prostitutes might perhaps have asked different questions, elicited more accurate information from the interviewees, or even provided new perspectives calling for a reconceptualization of the entire project. And it is important to note that, as with all scientific endeavors, values and biases would inhere in the research whatever the composition of the team. Kinsey's unwillingness to consider the potential impact of his interviewers' profiles, however, reveals his inability to acknowledge research itself as a social intervention.

Kinsey on the Origins of Sexuality

The question of sexuality and the origins of sexual behavior was far from esoteric for Kinsey. Rather, the answer was central both to the arguments he would propound and to his efforts to convince the public of the viability of sexual science. Yet his analysis of sexuality is sometimes vague and often contradictory. In contrast to earlier major sexual theorists, notably Freud, for whom sex represented a profoundly mysterious force, Kinsey viewed the sex drive as straightforward. Repeatedly he asserts that human sexual behavior is the outcome of the interplay of biological, psychological, and sociological influences. On the other hand, despite his own scientific background and the penchant of his major funding source for biologically oriented study, Kinsey frequently cites the enormous importance of psychological and social factors in sexual development. Depending on the point he wanted to make, Kinsey identified one of three factors as preeminent in the origin of sexual behavior: "our mammalian ancestry," anatomical and physiological capacity, and social conditioning.

Kinsey's manifest goal was to persuade skeptics that sex was a topic suitable and appropriate for scientific investigation. Thus, in his description of human sexual response, he frequently emphasized physiological processes, with psychological factors treated as mitigating effects: "Erotic arousal is a material phenomenon which involves an extended series of physical, physiologic, and psychologic changes. Many of these could be subjected to precise instrumental measurement if objectivity among scientists and public respect for scientific research allowed such laboratory investigation."[38] Describing sex as a "material phenomenon" meant, for Kinsey, that it had a basis in biology or the physical world. There was nothing magical for Kinsey about sex, and, indeed, he was committed to demystifying the aura of secrecy that surrounded it. By the time *SBHF* was published, he was determinedly addressing his critics:

> With the right of the scientist to investigate most aspects of the material universe, most persons will agree; but there are some who have questioned the applicability of scientific methods to an investigation of human sexual behavior. Some persons, recognizing the importance of the psychologic aspects of that behavior, and the relation of the individual's sexual activity to

the social organization as a whole, feel that this is an area which only psychologists or social philosophers should explore. In this insistence they seem to ignore the material origins of all behavior. It is as though the dietician and biochemist were denied the right to analyze foods and the process of nutrition because the cooking and proper serving of food may be rated a fine art, and because the eating of certain foods has been considered a matter for religious regulation.[39]

Moreover, emphasizing the primacy of biological and physiological factors enabled Kinsey to criticize societal proscriptions against behavior that he believed was rooted in nature:

> Whatever the moral interpretation, . . . there is no scientific reason for considering particular types of sexual activity as intrinsically, in their biological origins, normal or abnormal. . . . Present-day legal determinations of sexual acts which are acceptable, or "natural," and those which are "contrary to nature" are not based on data obtained from biologists, nor from nature herself.[40]

Kinsey was an essentialist for whom "natural" equaled good. He defended whatever behavior he saw as originating from biological impulses, distilled from the contaminating effects of psychological or sociological variables. Eschewing the judgments of earlier sex theorists, Freud in particular, based on perceived "normality," he adopted instead a yardstick based on "naturalness": "It is unwarranted to believe that particular types of sexual behavior are always expressions of psychoses or neuroses. In actuality, they are more often expressions of what is biologically basic in mammalian and anthropoid behavior, and of a deliberate disregard for social convention."[41]

An analysis that emphasized biology would render sexuality less amenable to societal restriction, Kinsey noted. In *SBHM* he pointed out that cultures with purely social or religious interpretations of sexuality tend to institute restrictions on behavior, whereas a view of sex as simply biological would afford greater freedom: "A third possible interpretation of sex as a normal biologic function, *acceptable in whatever form it is manifested,* has hardly figured in either general or scientific discussions" (emphasis added).[42]

In *SBHF* he intensified this argument, no doubt in response to criticism of the nature of sex research as well as public outrage at the range of sexual behavior he had documented.

SBHF emphasized his two essentialist themes: the mammalian ancestry of humans and the notion of sexual capacity. At the beginning of every section, Kinsey undertook a review of historical and anthropological data on whatever behavior was under discussion. This was an attempt to contextualize human behavior and, ultimately, to illuminate the repressiveness of Western customs. He painstakingly reported, for example, on the "phylogenetic origins" of petting in cattle, hogs, dogs, rats, ferrets, and other mammals. Similarly, he noted that anthropologists have documented extensive petting in "primitive, pre-literate cultures." Petting, he concluded, is not unique or outrageous: "the independent but parallel development of such similar patterns in these widely scattered races is, again, further evidence of their phylogenetic origins in anatomic and physiologic characteristics which must have been part of the heritage of the ancient ancestors of all mankind."[43]

Kinsey bravely carried these discussions to absurd lengths, as when he observed that distinguishing between premarital and marital activity among animals is problematic, "since there is no institution of marriage among the lower mammals." Yet he quickly recovered and pointed out the implications of this fact. Our fuss about pre- and extramarital affairs is specious because "while human custom and man-made law may make a sharp distinction between coitus which occurs before marriage and the identical physical acts when they occur within a marriage, it is important to realize that physically and physiologically they are one and the same thing in man, just as they are in the lower mammals."[44]

The presentation of information on "our mammalian origins," "infrahuman species," and "primitive human cultures" allowed Kinsey to challenge or support social customs. On the one hand, to shatter the assumed rationality and sanctity of what he considered cultural constraints, he pointed out that avoidance of nudity during coitus was "a perversion of what is, in a biological sense, normal sexuality."[45] On the other hand, he found it just as easy to defend the status quo as an artifact of mammalian history. He frequently justified the double standard as a biological imperative: "The human male's interest in maintaining his property rights in his female mate, his objections to his wife's extra-marital coitus, and her lesser objection to his extra-marital activity, are mammalian heritages."[46] And he surmised that extramarital affairs sprang from an ancient desire for multiple sex partners that would not be resolved "until man moves more completely away from his mammalian ancestry."[47]

Kinsey's reliance on an essentialist understanding of the sexual patterns of other mammals and "primitive" cultures as the yardstick for natural human behavior was a logical outcome of his empirical methods. The scope of his research was vast and unprecedented, and his use of interviews was intriguing; still, Kinsey was ultimately simply counting the incidence and frequency of orgasms. Focusing his lens on the most quantifiable unit of sexual behavior allowed him to talk about patterns of behavior but never about its significance. Kinsey saw culture simply as an obstacle to the realization of a potential level of sexual activity, rather than as a set of influences that affect and shape the meaning of sexuality. His romantic gaze back to mammalian ancestors reveals a view of sexuality as a seamless, transhistorical force that, but for the impediments of modern social relations, we could extend into the present. In his discussion of homosexuality, for example, he notes that if all persons with any trace of homosexual history were eliminated from the population, there is no reason to think that the incidence of homosexuality in the next generation would be diminished. "The homosexual has been a significant part of human sexual activity ever since the dawn of history, primarily because it is an expression of capacities that are basic in the human animal."[48] From the perspective of outlets and behavior patterns, this is no doubt true. But his unwillingness to consider homosexuality as more than a particular configuration of orgasms kept him from considering that homosexuality, as both an activity and an organizing principle for a community of people, would be constructed very differently at different moments in history. This narrow view of the development and expression of sexuality forecloses a more nuanced analysis of the ways in which sexual behavior and identity evolve and change in their purposes and meanings both for individuals and for a society. This lack of vision is endemic in sex research and modern sexology in general. It was not, as some of his critics have charged, that

Kinsey ignored the cultural constructs of sex. However, when he did acknowledge sex laws, social mores, ethnic or religious traditions, or other cultural infusions of meaning, it was to describe them as fetters on what would otherwise be an untroubled, "natural" expression of sexuality. These customs, he notes, "originate neither in accumulated experience nor in scientific examinations of objectively gathered data. The sociologist and anthropologist find the origins of such customs in ignorance and superstition, and in the attempt of each group to set itself apart from its neighbors."[49]

Sexual capacity, the second essentialist theme of *SBHF*, is a fundamental, if inchoate, part of Kinsey's sexual world view. Without ever operationally defining it, he seems to have used the term in place of "libido" to connote an inner wellspring of sexual energy. The concept makes its strongest appearance in *SBHF*, where it is linked to anatomy and physiology: "We now understand that this capacity to respond depends upon the existence of end organs of touch in the body surfaces, nerves connecting these organs with the spinal cord and brain, nerves which extend from the cord to various muscles in the body, and the autonomic nervous system through which still other parts of the body are brought into action."[50] Functionally the term is related, rather simplistically, to sexual frequency: those with a low sexual capacity had sex less often than those with higher capacities. Kinsey made several uses of the concept. One, as we shall see, was to justify differences in sexual behavior between men and women. Women, he thought, had less sex and fewer sexual variations because of their lower capacity. Second, he used it to criticize Freudian theories of sublimation. Kinsey thought it was a mistake to believe in a fixed amount of sexual energy, some of which can be channeled into "higher" things, "as nervous energy is shunted from one to another portion of a nervous system, or electricity short-circuited into new paths and channels."[51] Although he conceded that health and opportunity for sexual contact might affect sexual functioning, he believed that people typically manifested whatever variable amount of sexual energy they had. "Inactivity is no more sublimation of sex drive than blindness or deafness or other perceptive defects are sublimation of those capacities,"[52] he declared, his analogies making it clear that he considered those with less capacity to be less physically able. Kinsey hated sublimation theory because it resonated with traditional religious proscriptions against sex and implied that there were "higher levels of activity" in which one could engage rather than having sex. Sublimation theory, he believed, was merely moralism codified into scientific doctrine.

Finally, Kinsey wielded the concept of capacity to argue for the validity of every form of sexual expression. Although there might be differences in degree, all humans have the physiological equipment to respond to effective stimulation. He noted, for example, that daily orgasm is within the capacity of the average human male, and if humans were unrestricted by custom or culturally imposed inhibition, the more than daily rates observed in some primates could be matched by man. Similarly, all men and women have the capacity for homosexual behavior. It is simply the vagaries of experience that allow some people to engage in homosexual activities more readily than others. This concept of capacity enabled Kinsey to locate sexuality as a basic, intrinsic human drive and consequently to criticize cultural repression of such fundamental impulses.

A third element in Kinsey's sexual world view is the centrality of social conditioning. According to his learning-theory model of sexual behavior, humans' fundamental capacity for a wide range of expression is channeled in a particular direction by external influences, among them religion, the educational system, and the family. Sex laws, for Kinsey, were a prime example of custom and a metaphor for the destruction that cultural influences inflicted on sexual expression.

Analysts of Kinsey have alternately accused him of biological reductivism and cultural relativism. While such accusations would appear to be mutually exclusive, in fact both accounts are accurate. Kinsey simultaneously located himself on the far end of both sides of the argument over biological versus social influences on sexuality. He believed that sexual behavior was in some senses "predestined by its morphologic structure, its metabolic capacities, its hormones, and all of the other characters which it has inherited or which have been built into it by the physical environment in which it has developed."[53] And, as noted, he thought of sexual behavior in terms of outlets and orgasms, whose frequency might vary but whose meanings are consistent across history and culture. On the other hand, he professed that sexual conventions are normal only because culture deems them so.

Kinsey's sexual ideology is a complex weave of essentialist strands with social influences. His disdain for culture, which he saw as an inevitably restricting force on an otherwise robust sexual energy, was palpable. It is not surprising that his research aroused such ire, since he overturned traditional sexual morality. Freudian as well as religious tenets focus on the civilizing effects of culture and its ability to tame the potentially wild, uncontrollable libido. Kinsey, on the other hand, was arguing for the inherent health and naturalness of sexuality. His arguments were simplistic in many ways, ignoring, for example, the role of power relations in sociosexual hierarchies. But since he valorized *anything* he believed was rooted in nature, even when it challenged conventional morality, he subverted the traditionally oppressive use of essentialism to support the dominant ideology. In its historical context, Kinsey's essentialist impulse was basically a move to affirm sexual desire and all varieties of sexual expression in a culture where sexual attitudes and norms were intensely repressive.

Sex and Gender in the Kinsey Research

Kinsey's emphasis on the primacy of physiological response and his insistence on empiricism led him, as we have seen, to adopt orgasm as an accessible and quantifiable unit of measurement. He defined orgasm operationally, as "the moment of sudden release."[54] This formulation was less viable, however, in his research on women. He briefly mentioned in *SBHF* the difficulty of basing statistical calculations on orgasms, as had been done for the male, since he found that much female sexual activity did not result in orgasm. There is, he concluded, "no better unit for measuring the incidences and frequencies of sexual activity,"[55] but he attempted to supplement his information on women's sexuality by including in *SBHF* more qualitative data, such as diaries, letters, and other anecdotal material.

In the era in which Kinsey was writing, his use of orgasm as a measuring unit for women's sexuality was progressive. Given the aura of shame around female sexuality, and the lack of widespread support for women's pleasure, modifying the basic sexual yardstick for research on women could have underscored the popular impression that women's sexuality was more "diffuse" and orgasm less important for them. By retaining orgasm as the measure for both groups, he conveyed the legitimacy and importance of the female orgasm.

Armed with a unit of measurement, Kinsey turned to collecting data on the types of activities people engaged in and counting the number of times they engaged in them. A major construct of his research was "sexual outlet"—a taxonomy of the six major sources of orgasm (masturbation, nocturnal emissions, heterosexual petting, heterosexual intercourse, homosexual relations, and intercourse with animals). The sum of the orgasms attained from these varied sources was called the individual's total sexual outlet. The most significant ramification of this conceptualization was its elevation of typically marginalized behaviors (bestiality, nocturnal emissions) and stigmatized activities (homosexuality, masturbation) to an equivalent status with heterosexual behavior. Anticipating Masters and Johnson's conclusion that, physiologically, an orgasm is an orgasm is an orgasm, Kinsey accorded all equal dignity.

The sheer magnitude of the statistics Kinsey amassed was startling to many. With extreme care, he documented the minutiae of thousands of people's experiences with premarital sex, petting, intercourse, homosexuality, and sex with animals. Both volumes are thick with statistics that clearly document the gulf between mainstream morality and what people actually did. He noted, for example, that masturbation, common among women, was almost universally engaged in by men. Similarly, extramarital sex was widespread among men, and 26 percent of women had had affairs by the age of forty. Women were increasingly having orgasms during marital coitus. The rate of premarital intercourse among women reached 50 percent, and a large majority claimed to have no regrets. Even among children, sex play was reportedly extensive. With dispassion, Kinsey lifted the veil of privacy covering the scope and variety of white Americans' sexuality. He especially seemed to delight in reporting the ubiquity of culturally taboo sexual behavior. He stated, for example, that at least 37 percent of the male population had some homosexual experience: "more than one male in three of the persons that one may meet as he passes along a city street."[56] Since, for Kinsey, the very existence of a behavior was an indication of its naturalness, he hoped that societal sanctions against certain outlets would be modified if the public understood the frequency with which they occurred.

Another major construct was the homosexual–heterosexual continuum. Believing that sexual behavior was not discretely dichotomous, Kinsey utilized a seven-point scale on which he rated individuals after considering both physical response and psychological experiences:

0. Exclusively heterosexual with no homosexual
1. Predominantly heterosexual, only incidentally homosexual
2. Predominantly heterosexual, but more than incidentally homosexual
3. Equally heterosexual and homosexual
4. Predominantly homosexual, but more than incidentally heterosexual
5. Predominantly homosexual, but incidentally heterosexual
6. Exclusively homosexual

This scale has been criticized as having no advantages over the preexisting classifications of heterosexual–bisexual–homosexual. It was subsequently abandoned by later researchers at the Kinsey Institute because of its lack of empirical usefulness.[57] Yet for all its empirical shortcomings, the scale has been utilized through the 1980s to denote the variability of sexual behavior. In addition, its ideological significance for its own time should not be dismissed. The notion of the range and fluidity of sexual expression as embodied in the homosexual–heterosexual continuum represented a challenge to a more rigid nineteenth-century conceptualization that linked one's identity with a particular sexual behavior. Both Krafft-Ebing and Ellis wrote about homosexuality (or, more precisely, "inversion") as a congenital identity type. In contrast, Kinsey refused to talk about homosexuality as an identity or about homosexual persons. He believed everyone had the "capacity" for homosexuality, and so he spoke only of homosexual patterns of behavior: "There may be considerable fluctuation of patterns from time to time. . . . For instance, there are some who engage in both heterosexual and homosexual activities in the same year, or in the same month or week, or even in the same day. . . . The world is not to be divided into sheep and goats."[58] Again Kinsey was emphasizing that cultural norms are arbitrary, the sexual hierarchy hypocritical. If the scale was not extremely successful as a research tool, therefore, it still had pedagogical usefulness for gay people, who used it to question sexual labeling and assert the fluidity of sexual behavior and the existence of sexual oppression.

Kinsey's research on homosexuality came at the time when an urban gay subculture was forming in the United States. The massive mobilization for the war had entailed the temporary restructuring of family and gender roles, separated men and women with what some feared was "a barrier of indescribable experience," created opportunities for intense same-sex bonding,[59] and made it possible for thousands of men and women to discover their homosexuality and join in communities with others like themselves.[60] Kinsey's data on gay men and lesbians, published after the war, had contradictory effects. On the one hand, his figures reassured gay individuals, provided a statistical basis for the consolidation of the budding gay community, and exploded the myth that homosexuals could be easily identified. One lesbian wrote, "Probably the reams of material written in passionate defense of the homophile have done less to further the cause of tolerance than Kinsey's single, detached statement that 37 per cent of the men and 19 per cent of the women whom he interviewed admitted having had overt homosexual relationships."[61] On the other hand, the same information fueled the cultural panic of the early 1950s and paranoia about "sex perverts." Although Kinsey had hoped that his data would engender tolerance, they were in fact utilized to legitimate the McCarthy witchhunts against both communists and homosexuals.[62] Sexual perverts were considered by many to be as dangerous as communists, and this conflation of the red menace and the lavender menace was apparent in the popular culture of the day. Films like *I Was a Communist for the FBI* (1951), *The Red Menace* (1949), and *My Son John* (1952) portrayed communists as effeminate, seemingly invisible infiltrators who undermined family life and "seduce[d] 'impressionable' young men into joining the Party."[63] Paradoxically, Kinsey's work was utilized by vigilantes to fuel the postwar backlash and cited by gay activists, who rightly considered him an ally. The two-edged use of sexological research would become a familiar pattern.

Despite his background as a biologist, Kinsey's work is often considered to be sociological, since one of his major goals was to determine the factors (age, sex, class, etc.) that influenced choice and frequency of sexual outlet. Undoubtedly, his landmark finding was the significance of social class for male sexual behavior. He used three criteria to measure social stratification: educational level, occupational class of the interviewee, and occupational class of the interviewee's parents. Ultimately, however, he found classification by occupation too imprecise, and he came to rely on educational level as the most convenient criterion for statistical use. He rarely used the term "social class," preferring to describe findings for the "upper level" and "lower level." Journalists reporting on his work paid a good deal of attention to class distinctions in sexual behavior, but Kinsey's categories bear more definitional resemblance to the Weberian concept of status group than to a Marxist concept of class.

True to the descriptive nature of his work, Kinsey presented his findings and hinted at some of the social implications, but provided no broader analysis concerning the origins or function of the differences among social levels. "We do not yet understand, to the full, the origins of these diverse sexual philosophies," he concluded; "but it will be possible to record what the thinking of each group is in regard to each type of activity."[64] The data on males showed little variation among classes in frequency of sexual outlet, but major variances occurred in choice of sexual outlet and in sexual technique. Essentially, "upper-level" males masturbated more frequently and engaged in less premarital intercourse, homosexual behavior, or sex with prostitutes, but more petting; they experienced more nocturnal emissions. The "lower-level" males were found to be more genitally oriented and very sexually active, but to have little interest in foreplay or erotic activities other than intercourse.

In addition, a portrait of differing sexual world views emerged from Kinsey's descriptions. He noted that upper-level men tended to focus on issues of morality and rationalize their sexual activity according to notions of right and wrong. Lower-level males, by contrast, described their behavior in terms of what they considered to be natural or unnatural. Given Kinsey's own bias toward the "natural," it is not surprising that his sympathies fell squarely with the working class. When he discussed the wider implications of these social differences, he criticized the upper-level professionals—clinicians, lawyers, judges, teachers—who, he felt, judged all behavior by their own philosophy and imposed their sexual norms on the lower level. This practice, of which he gave examples, was anathema to him, given his idealization of nonjudgmental description and his implicit bias toward the working-class world view. His summary of the sexual conflict went as follows:

> In general, the upper level feels that "lower level morality" lacks the ideals and the righteousness of the upper level philosophy. The lower level, on the other hand, feels that educated and upper level society has an artificial and insincere pattern of sexual behavior which is all the more obnoxious because the upper level tries to force its patterns upon all other levels. Legends about the immorality of the lower level are matched by legends about the perversions of the upper level.[65]

Kinsey believed, however, in the healing power of scientific data. All polarities, he hoped, whether between social classes or between men and women, could be harmonized once people had the facts that facilitate understanding.

Kinsey's analysis of the role of social level in the sexual behavior of women contrasts sharply with his analysis in *SBHM*. The significance of class (or social level) was virtually dismissed in *SBHF*. Kinsey discounted a woman's occupation as a criterion for determining her social level, since her social status after marriage depended on the occupational class of her husband as well as upon her own social background (i.e., the occupational class of the parental home). His classifications are based on these latter factors. Using this derivative definition of class, Kinsey found that class (and other demographic variables) had little to do with women's sexual behavior. He concluded that males are more conditioned by the social groups in which they live than females are.[66] Since a major focus of *SBHF* is an attempt to delineate gender differences in sexual activity, it is at first surprising that Kinsey could not conceive of the category of "woman" as itself a social group in which women are taught historically and culturally bound expectations of sex and gender-appropriate behavior. Yet the male composition of the research team, the sociopolitical climate of the early 1950s, and Kinsey's own apolitical stance and biologistic emphasis were all more conducive to a generalization that carried psychophysiological implications than to an analysis of conditioning and socialization on the basis of gender.

In examining differences in sexual behavior between men and women, Kinsey focused on psychophysiological variables. Having devoted extensive sections to anatomy and physiology, he concluded that "in spite of the widespread and oft-repeated emphasis on the supposed differences between female and male sexuality, we fail to find any anatomic or physiologic basis for such differences."[67] And this knowledge should contribute to harmony between the sexes, since "males would be better prepared to understand females, and females to understand males, if they realized that they are alike in their basic anatomy and physiology."[68] This was a radical departure from the Victorian gender schema that mythologized and polarized differences between women and men.

Those sex differences that Kinsey found were attributed to the lesser "conditionability" of the female. The evidence came from what he interpreted as women's lower interest in pornography, voyeurism (described by Kinsey as vicarious sharing of sexual activity), writing graffiti in bathrooms, indulging in cross-dressing, and the like. Kinsey's interpretation of these findings was that although females are as capable of responding to tactile stimulation as males, they differ in their capacity to respond to psychological stimulation. Ostensibly this was a psychological difference, yet he struggled to reduce it to a biological one by, again, blurring the distinctions between physiology and psychology:

> Such specious distinctions between form and function have, unfortunately, lent encouragement to the opinion that the psychologic aspects of human sexual behavior are of a different order from, and perhaps more significant than, the anatomy or physiology of sexual response and orgasm. Such thinking easily becomes mystical, and quickly identifies any consideration of anatomic form and physiologic function as a scientific materialism which misses the "basic," the "human," and the "real" problems in behavior. . . .

Those aspects of behavior which we identify as psychologic can be nothing but certain aspects of that same basic anatomy and physiology.[69]

Kinsey continually and explicitly rejected a cultural analysis suggesting that women are sexually socialized differently from men. The disinclination of women to indulge in certain behaviors was not due to their adherence to moral or social conventions, he believed, but to their lack of erotic interest in them. And this, Kinsey thought, must depend on some internal mechanism that functions differently in men and women. Thus, he turned to neural and hormonal research in an attempt to explain these differences. After an extensive review of the research, Kinsey could state nothing conclusively, but, like many sexologists more than forty years later, he continued to believe that more research would reveal the origins of gender differences in sexual behavior in the physiological realm.

It was to these hypothesized variations in physiological structure that Kinsey attributed what he referred to as individual differences in sexual capacity. As we have seen, he believed in individual variations in sex drive almost as genetic givens, resembling differences in acuity of sight or hearing. In *SBHM* he referred to "fundamentally apathetic persons" who would go indefinitely without orgasm.[70] Not surprisingly, given that his concept of "capacity" was rooted in frequency of sexual activity, Kinsey believed that males had a greater sexual capacity than females. He stated that 30 percent of women were more or less sexually unresponsive.[71] This, for Kinsey, was merely a physiological fact that should be accepted graciously:

There is an inclination among psychiatrists to consider all unresponding individuals as inhibited, and there is a certain skepticism in the profession of the existence of people who are basically low in capacity to respond. This amounts to asserting that all people are more or less equal in their sexual endowments, and ignores the existence of individual variation. No one who knows how remarkably different individuals may be in morphology, in physiologic reactions, and in other psychologic capacities, could conceive of erotic capacities (of all things) that were basically uniform throughout a population. Considerable psychiatric therapy can be wasted on persons (especially females) who are misjudged to be cases of repression when, in actuality, at least *some of them never were equipped to respond erotically.* (Emphasis added.)[72]

Unfortunately, this biologically deterministic theory of sexual capacity supported the very stereotypes about female sexual indifference of which Kinsey was so critical. And it could be used to dismiss other reasons, such as power inequities or inadequate lovers, for female sexual dissatisfaction. In addition, Kinsey used it to explain the double standard as inevitable. Women, he noted, had been regulated more than men because their lower sexual capacity, and hence lower level of activity, made them more controllable.

An Ideological Precursor

K insey blazed a trail for the later sex researchers, Masters and Johnson. Secretly (for fear of losing funding), he observed and filmed sexual activity in the laboratory: twenty homosexual couples, ten heterosexual couples, and twenty-five men and women masturbating.[73] (The first step in this direction had been paying prostitutes to allow researchers to measure the length of their clitorises so that Kinsey could document anatomical differences.) Kinsey's associate Wardell Pomeroy notes that this quest for "original data" was a logical outcome for an empirical scientist.[74] Some of the physiological data presented in *SBHF* were derived from this work. In fact, much of the second half of the volume is devoted to the anatomy and physiology of human sexual response. Kinsey charted, in minute detail that foreshadowed the work of Masters and Johnson, changes in pulse, respiration, genital secretions, and body movement during sexual activity.

It was on the basis of this research that he planted a timebomb that would not explode until the work of Masters and Johnson—his challenge to the concept of the vaginal orgasm. He repeated continually that the walls of the vagina are devoid of nerve endings and so, for most women, insensitive.[75] Thus, he claimed that vaginal orgasm was a physiological impossibility and criticized Freud and other theorists for projecting male constructs of sexuality onto women. This led inevitably to questions about whether sexual intercourse could satisfy women sexually—an issue to be raised again by Masters and Johnson. Since Kinsey viewed the clitoris as the main center of sexual response and the vagina as relatively unimportant, he questioned the erotic merits of penetration. He noted that few women inserted fingers or objects into their vaginas when they masturbated and concluded that satisfaction from penile penetration was mainly psychological, or perhaps the result of referred sensation. This deemphasis of intercourse was consistent with Kinsey's schema of six sexual outlets. So although he accorded a certain primacy to intercourse, particularly marital coitus, he clearly challenged its sacredness in the arena of women's sexual pleasure.

Like Masters and Johnson, Kinsey emphasized the significance of masturbation. He found that it was the one sexual activity in which women most often reached orgasm and, like Masters and Johnson, he attributed this in part to effectiveness of technique and in part to the absence of distraction by or accommodation to a partner. Kinsey took exception to Freudian and psychoanalytic interpretations of masturbation as an immature activity, which he believed generated needless worry and conflict for individuals who masturbated. He justified his attempts to destigmatize masturbation by invoking the importance of improving both marriages and women's sociopsychological well-being. No other sexual activity was so worrisome to women, he claimed: "Whatever may affect the efficiency of some millions of individuals may be considered of social concern. Whether masturbation provides a satisfactory source of sexual outlet or becomes a source of psychologic disturbance is, therefore, a question of some social import."[76] In addition, his data showed that women made better sexual adjustments in marriage if they had been regularly attaining orgasm (by any means) before marriage. Masturbation was especially significant in this respect, since it provided women with the quickest and most reliable orgasms.

Kinsey's emphasis on the similarity of the genders, both anatomically and physiologically, also helped lay the groundwork for Masters and Johnson. There is a reason for this emphasis. Kinsey devoted considerable space to discussion of the family and frequently analyzed certain sexual behaviors in terms of their impact on marriage. In his chapter on marital coitus, he noted that it "is socially the most important of all sexual activities, because of its significance in the origin and maintenance of the home."[77] He then provided a brief description of the origin and history of the family, one of the few places in which he offered more than a cursory account of the social context of a sexual behavior.

Whereas Masters and Johnson and later sexologists have shown a romantic investment in marriage, however, Kinsey believed in its functional importance. His functionalism was all the more striking given the post–World War II idealization of home and the nuclear family. While critical of anachronistic customs, Kinsey believed that history had proved the viability of the family as the foundation of the social order. It provided an effective partnership for men and women, produced a stable environment for raising children, and served to control promiscuity by furnishing a regular sexual outlet. In his view no alternative structure with which communal groups or communist countries had experimented provided a satisfactory substitute for marriage.

Kinsey noted the increasing divorce rate with alarm, and he focused on women as a causal factor. Fundamental conceptualizations about marriage were changing because of "the emergence of the female as a significant force in the political, industrial, and intellectual life of our Western culture."[78] He believed marriages were evolving out of male domination into a more equal partnership between men and women. As a scientist, Kinsey believed that the present challenge to home and family life could be approached pragmatically:

> There is developing in this country, as well as in some other parts of the world, an increasing interest in understanding some of the factors which contribute to the effectiveness of a home, and an increasing emphasis on training modern youth and adults to be more effective marital partners. It is in these terms that the significance of sex education, of pre-marital sexual outlets, of non-marital sexual activities for adults, and of the techniques and frequencies of marital coitus are being evaluated today.[79]

He viewed his own research as a major contribution in this area, and believed that emphasizing the similarities between men and women would foster understanding, harmony between the sexes, and a conceptualization of marriage as a partnership.

Significantly, like Masters and Johnson, Kinsey focused on the importance of good sex for better marriages. While noting that a good sex life was not the primary variable in maintaining a marriage, he frequently warned that "the female's failure to respond to orgasm in her sexual relationship is, nonetheless, one of the most frequent sources of dissatisfaction in marriage, and it is not infrequently the source of other types of conflict which may lead to a dissolution of a marriage."[80] According to his data, sexual factors accounted for as many as three-quarters of the divorces in his sample. Kinsey believed that science was the answer to this social problem. He thought that freer discussion of sex, prompted by scientific sex research and marriage manuals, had led to the greater frequency of female orgasm during the early decades of the twentieth century. One of his rationales for conducting research was his concern that many marriage manuals of the day were inaccurate and his hope that an increase in scientific data would filter down, via clinicians and new marriage manuals, to improve the sex lives of the general public. He reassured skeptics who worried that sex research might undermine marriage:

> There are some who have feared that a scientific approach to the problems of sex might threaten the existence of the marital institution. There are some who advocate the perpetuation of our ignorance because they fear that science will undermine the mystical concepts that they have substituted for reality. But there appear to be more persons who believe that an extension of our knowledge may contribute to the establishment of better marriages.[81]

Kinsey's pragmatic, functional commitment to marriage was the filter through which he evaluated other sexual behavior. His advocacy of masturbation and premarital sex sprang from data that indicated their role in increased sexual responsiveness in marriage. Similarly, he was tolerant in his approach to extramarital coitus, since he believed that it was based on "our mammalian ancestry" and need not lead inevitably to marital conflict. This focus on solving the crisis of marriage and heterosexuality is not unique to Kinsey; rather, it is thematic in sexology. Yet Kinsey's commitment to marriage was considerably more tepid than that of Masters and Johnson, who began publishing at the height of the "sexual revolution" when, like all institutions, marriage was increasingly challenged.

Kinsey, American Society, and Sexology

K insey's work is of great importance for many reasons: his role in the development of modern American sexology; the scope of his work; the vast amount of data he accumulated; and his ideology. His research reflects the sociopolitical tenor of the time and helped consolidate sexology's right to intervene in gender relations and the crisis of the family.

The implications of Kinsey's research about women are complex. On the one hand, he channeled some of his findings toward promoting and maintaining conventional heterosexual relations. He consistently ignored the ways in which women as a social group may have been taught to avoid or dislike sex and sought biological explanations for their supposedly lower sexual capacity. However, Kinsey's relentless empiricism and sexual enthusiasm were generalized to his research on women in a fashion that was truly supportive of female sexuality. He was relatively dispassionate about marriage and assumed that equality in marriage was desirable and important. He challenged the primacy of the penis and sexual intercourse as a source of pleasure for women. In many ways he assessed women's sexuality on its own terms, and he afforded it a certain importance and validity through the seriousness with which he studied women's sexual behavior. In a sense his actual interpretations (for example, his emphasis on clitoral as opposed to vaginal orgasms) were less important than his reporting that women engaged in a wide variety of sexual activities with great frequency. Though *SBHF* was published in a repressive time for women, Kinsey discussed their sexual pleasure, separated the concept of sexual pleasure from reproduction, cited the pleasures of masturbation, and regarded women as sexual agents. These were all issues of sexual liberation that feminists would not discuss until well over a decade later.

Such groundbreaking challenges to received ideas about women's sexuality were not welcomed by Kinsey's contemporaries. Several years after the publication of *SBHF*, one journalist noted the lack of substantive response to it, compared with the reception of the volume on men: "My opinion is that the American public, both male and female, was afraid to read the report on female sexuality because it was afraid to confront what it knew it would find there—confirmation of the unsettling idea that in their sexual behavior women are just as good, or bad, as men."[82] This was a radical concept, cloaked in scientific neutrality, in an era that lacked a radical political movement to organize around these issues.

It has been suggested that Kinsey had more interest in male sexuality and so his work had little impact on attitudes toward female sexuality.[83] Yet his data on females were as extensive as his data on males. It seems likely that the lack of public attention to his findings about female sexuality had more to do with sociopolitical variables than with Kinsey's personal research interests. *SBHF* was, after all, published in 1953—the period of the Cold War and McCarthyism. In 1954 a conference of the American Medical Association passed a resolution publicly criticizing Kinsey for contributing to a "wave of sex hysteria,"[84] and he was attacked by many doctors who had concluded that the book's effects were not beneficial.[85] A *Newsweek* article entitled "Sex vs. America" reported the criticisms of Representative Louis Heller of Brooklyn, who had proposed a congressional investigation of Kinsey and asked the Post Office to bar *SBHF* from the mails. Kinsey was, Heller charged, "hurling the insult of the century" at American women and contributing "to the depravity of a whole generation, to the loss of faith in human dignity . . . to the spread of juvenile delinquency, and to the misunderstanding and confusion about sex."[86] Not surprisingly, in this atmosphere of repression and paranoia, many professionals ignored Kinsey's conceptual challenges to their work. And, more important, there was no feminist movement to publicize Kinsey's findings on women. Publishing in the late 1960s in the context of a reemerging women's movement, Masters and Johnson were credited with revolutionizing female sexuality when they presented findings that Kinsey had published over a decade before.

But if Kinsey's specific observations were ignored, his work was not. The predominant response was outrage. Social scientists objected to what they perceived as Kinsey's reductionism. They criticized him for draining sex of its social and emotional meaning and for concentrating on performance to the exclusion of relationships. Psychoanalysts in particular were incensed. In general, Kinsey had either ignored basic psychoanalytic tenets (developmental theories of sexuality) or refuted them (sublimation, vaginal orgasm), and the analysts in turn saw him as naive. Popular critics, such as Lionel Trilling, complained that Kinsey was materialistic and that his work was rife with unsubstantiated assumptions about sex.[87] Ironically, it is quite likely that it was Kinsey's commitment to science, and a particular scientific method, that generated this impassioned and vehement response to his work. Although the transition from reverence for philosophical/theological authority to a scientific, medical approach to knowledge was well under way, Kinsey differed from early sexologists such as Freud and Ellis both stylistically and methodologically. He was blunt, practical, and obsessed with numbers. His empiricism and derision of psychoanalysis left him with an atheoretical approach to sex. This lack of a psychodynamic theory would not be remedied by Masters and Johnson and would eventually, in the 1980s, result in a clinical crisis around disorders of sexual desire.

Whatever conservative politicians and professionals thought, the reading public was enthralled. Working at a time when sexology was focused on establishing itself as a science and was not searching for a clientele, Kinsey demonstrated that there was, in fact, a potential market. His research was popularized and sensationalized, and his books quickly became best sellers. In part, this success was due to the sophistication of the mass media and the growing awareness that sex sells, whether in magazines, movies, or other commodities. Yet beyond the surface clamor, Kinsey had clearly touched a cultural nerve. People had concerns, questions, and problems related to sex and wanted somewhere to turn. Scientific sexology was becoming a place to turn. The Kinsey reports provided people with basic information about sex. Best-selling books about sex throughout the century, from Radclyffe Hall's lesbian novel *The Well of Loneliness* to Masters and Johnson's physiological research, would evoke thousands of letters from readers around the country who wanted advice or information about a troubling sexual issue. The two volumes popularly referred to as the Kinsey reports were no exception. They were the first large-scale empirical studies and so served as standards by which people could evaluate their own sexual behavior. This could reassure, or it could engender anxiety. In later decades the work of sexologists would do both. When Kinsey—the taxonomist and quantifier—transferred his method of studying the gall wasp to the study of human sexuality, he helped open the door to a rapid intensification of sex research. By omitting questions about ethics, emotions, and the social context of sex, Kinsey played a powerful role in reinforcing the transition from religious to scientific hegemony over matters of sex and sexuality. The debates surrounding his research had as much to do with content and method as with the appropriateness and morality of the application of science to a hitherto profoundly personal and emotional arena. Ultimately, the Kinsey research advanced the ongoing shift of the discourse on sexual issues from the private to the public arena.

Though Kinsey had made the scientific study of sex more legitimate, it was still an enterprise profoundly influenced by politics. In 1954 the Rockefeller Foundation, headed by Dean Rusk, began to reconsider its funding commitment to Kinsey after learning that it was under congressional investigation for its support of his Institute. After hearings by the House Committee to Investigate Tax-Exempt Foundations, chaired by ultra-right-wing Representative B. Carroll Reece, the Rockefeller Foundation terminated the Kinsey Institute funds. As Wardell Pomeroy, one of the original Kinsey investigators, wrote: "The truth was that the Foundation had simply quit, under pressure and out of fear, in direct contradiction to its frequently reiterated principles. . . . Its staff wanted to continue support but the Foundation could not take the heat."[88] Kinsey died of a heart attack two years later, and the Institute foundered for some time after his death and the termination of funding.

Around this time a young gynecologist in St. Louis named William Masters, who wanted to embark on sex research, was warned by his mentors that such research could ruin his career if he did not establish himself within the medical profession first. Kinsey, as Masters later said, "opened the door."[89]

Chapter Two

Science, Medicine, and a Market

> Now sex can be discussed
> frankly and openly.
>
> WILLIAM MASTERS

The publication of *Human Sexual Response* (*HSR*) in 1966 was a landmark. It successfully consolidated the alignment of sexology with medicine. Moving the study of sex into the laboratory had involved risk: previous sexologists had conducted such research clandestinely, and even though Masters and Johnson themselves attempted to keep their work a secret, their laboratory was sabotaged in the early years. When Masters tried to publish some preliminary data in 1960, his work was rejected by a psychiatric journal for being pornographic, and he was banned for life from publishing in two journals of obstetrics and gynecology.[1] Yet when *HSR* was finally released, the *Journal of the American Medical Association* asked, "Why was this study so long in coming?" And out of seven hundred reviews of the text, only 10 percent were unfavorable.[2] The combination of changing cultural mores and the rigorous respectability of Masters and Johnson's research resulted in such widespread popular response that one journalist commented, "The world of our sexual perception before that time might be designated simply as pre-*HSR*."[3]

Masters and Johnson drew on the social and moral authority that medical science commands in this society. Their style and presentation facilitated their acceptance by the public. Magazines like *Time* and *Newsweek* continually ran staid portraits of them in white lab coats, and most articles emphasized the dignity and benevolence of their physical appearance (Virginia Johnson once commented, "People are surprised that we don't have two heads").[4] Masters and Johnson toured the country for eighteen months after *HSR* was released, discussing sex physiology in terms of heart rates and vasocongestion. They frequently invoked "medical authority" in the pages of *HSR*, and emphasized the dispassionate nature of the medical study of sex: "We would sit and stare for an hour at a four-inch-square patch of skin, trying to determine significant color changes."[5]

HSR represented a quantum leap in the public dissemination of knowledge about the human body and the physiological facts of sexual functioning. Masters and Johnson, and later sexologists, were able to draw on what they claimed was established "scientific fact" as the basis of their authority on sexual matters. In addition, their research provided a data base from which they could later establish the legitimacy of sex therapy. Locating sexual behavior within the medical model had two appealing consequences for sexologists. First, the "magic bullet" mythology was extended from cures for diseases to the healing of sexual problems. Second, like the physician, the sexologist could become a cultural hero. For many, Masters and Johnson achieved this status. One writer said of them:

> Heroism in any area, as depicted in the ancient epics, usually entails a prize to be attained, with attainment perceived as both difficult and dangerous; the hero must summon the courage to surmount the difficulties and risk the dangers. Masters and Johnson went after a prize of knowledge. They did research never before achieved, overcame enormous difficulties, performed labors it would not be preposterous to call Herculean, and ran the real dangers of ruining their careers, being sued, facing possible shame for themselves and

their families, even risking criminal prosecution. By any means, then, it seems to me that Masters and Johnson have earned their niche in the pantheon of scientific heroes.[6]

Masters and Johnson did not reach this status immediately upon publication of *HSR*. In the years of their early research in the 1950s, Alfred Kinsey had lost his funding and died frustrated and discouraged; Masters and Johnson had sent their children away to boarding schools because they had been teased so much about their parents' being "sex mongers"; and Masters worked in fear of being ostracized by the medical profession.[7] Even in 1964, when one popular writer had announced that sex—in life or literature—was no longer shocking, it was still not completely acceptable. The same *Time* writer concluded, "Perhaps it is time that modern Americans, who know a great deal about sex, once again start talking about love."[8]

The sex and gender mores of the period from the early 1950s until the publication of *HSR* in 1966 require a complex and contradictory portrait. A disparity between ideology and behavior, between public discourse and private expression, is a striking feature of that time. The 1950s are typically depicted as a period of conservatism and quiescence, when Americans were preoccupied with home and family. Many white, middle-class Americans moved to the suburbs. In a retrenchment from the wartime ideology of the 1940s that enabled women to replace men as military–industrial workers, the propaganda of the 1950s reshaped women's roles to make attractive the jobs of wife, mother, and consumer. Traditional gender-role images depicted the man as breadwinner toiling in the public sector, and the woman as homemaker tending to the nest. For the white middle class, the cultural ideal was the nuclear family and the notion of "togetherness," promoted by popular magazines.[9] Statistics showed that more people were marrying, and they were marrying younger. The birth rate was increasing, and the divorce rate rose more slowly than in the decades before or after.[10] Fear of communism, homosexuality, atomic destruction, and changing gender roles was the subtext of family life. Surrounded by the threat of subversion, the family was considered the cornerstone of social stability, the bulwark against communism.

A closer inspection of family life in the 1950s reveals a more tempestuous picture, including family fragmentation, men and women discontented with their roles, and a growing interest in sexual behavior. For women, in particular, there was a colossal disparity between roles and expectations. The proportion of wives and mothers who were part of the public workforce continued to increase during the 1950s.[11] Many women thus found themselves at odds with cultural stereotypes that saw them solely as wives and mothers. In fact, the 1950s proved to be a golden age of mother-bashing. Even women who stayed at home were characterized in the popular press as domineering and overprotective caretakers who fostered dependence and immaturity in their children, particularly their sons. Fear that the masculinity of boys was at risk was widespread in this postwar culture, as men struggled to reassert their competence and dominance at home and in the workplace. In *Generation of Vipers*, Philip Wylie coined the term "momism" to denote the allegedly pernicious influence of mothers.[12] And there is some evidence that mothers saw these attacks as just. In 1957 Mrs. L. R. Maxwell wrote a letter of advice to other mothers with gay sons in a gay journal, the *Mattachine Review*:

> You may find that you have protected him too much in your own expression of mother love. It so often becomes "smother love." (Read Philip Wylie on "Momism.") You have probably not cut the apron strings sufficiently to allow him his own initiative in daily activities. If this is true I assure you that it is not an easy thing to face. It means facing yourself as much as facing the situation. And it is a difficult thing to accomplish: it may take years of hard work. Does that dismay you? Does that scare you into doing nothing? Then I can only repeat that you do not really love your son![13]

In an era of intense cultural insecurity about masculinity, anxieties about changing female roles were channeled into a maternal imperative to produce hearty, rugged boys.

For white, middle-class men in the 1950s, the masculine imperative was to be the patriarchal provider of ranch house and station wagon. Yet Barbara Ehrenreich points out that there was resistance to and outright rebellion against this role. She notes that *Playboy* magazine, which began publishing in 1953, embodied the new ideology of male revolt against conformity, maturity, responsibility. It beckoned men to a lifestyle of freedom and casual sexuality and disdained married life as dull and stifling. She concludes, "*Playboy* loved women . . . and hated wives."[14] In 1954 *Life* magazine was referring to "The New American Domesticated Male," who was submitting to suburban life.[15] There were growing references in popular culture to the emasculation of men; a *Time* writer noted that "American women often still seem too strong and American men too weak."[16] Men in the 1950s had cultural models that ranged from John Wayne and Hugh Hefner to *Father Knows Best* and Dagwood Bumstead.

If roles and expectations were complicated for those in the mainstream, they could prove even more problematic for those outside. The fifties were a fiercely contradictory decade in which to be "deviant." Although the Kinsey data had eased the "coming out" process for many, the emphasis on virile men and frilly women rendered gay identification fraught with potential conflict. The furor over communists and sex perverts swept many gay people out of employment in the public sector and intimidated the rest. Vice squads routinely raided gay bars and viciously harassed the patrons. And many gay people exercised the option of "passing," just as sexually active single heterosexuals often hid their behavior. Yet, for the emerging community of lesbians and gay men, the postwar decade marked a period of identification, expansion, and political organizing. Exclusively gay bars, which had emerged in the 1940s, became community forums for the evolving gay consciousness. The founding of the Mattachine Society (1951) and Daughters of Bilitis (1955) reflected the growing gay political consciousness.

Confusion about the confining definitions of family and gender roles manifested itself in the bedroom. Many people found themselves caught between contradictory social messages about sex and sexuality. While overt sexual messages were patently conservative, the increasing sexualization of the burgeoning consumer culture projected growing openness and interest in sex. Within popular mythology, the most frequent references to sexual behavior in the 1950s emphasize what did *not* happen. As one comedian describes it, "The fifties was the most sexually frustrating decade ever—ten years of foreplay."[17] But despite this popular notion, evidence indicates a sexually engaged population. Kinsey had reported, for example, that 50 percent of women and 67 to 98 rpercent of men (depending on educational level) were not virgins when they married, and, furthermore, that most had no regrets. In addition, he found that 37 percent of men and 28 percent of women had had at least one homosexual experience sometime between adolescence and old age. These sexual patterns persisted through the decade, despite the surface insistence on chastity—at least for women. As Wini Breines puts it, hypocrisy was the theme of the fifties, when everybody was doing it but everybody was denying it.[18] Women were often trapped in the dichotomy that simultaneously required of them virginal innocence and seductive sensuality.

Options for individuals with sexual problems were limited. Some turned to clinics run by Planned Parenthood, where they received a modicum of sex information and advice.[19] Others turned to marriage manuals, which by the 1960s accounted for one million dollars a year in sales.[20] Along with the popular media, marriage manuals represented a major source of sexual information and provided assistance with sexual problems before the glut of sexological publications in the early seventies. The manuals served some of the same functions as the later sexological publications—sometimes reassuring, sometimes misleading their readers, but always setting normative standards of behavior. A reviewer of manuals in *Newsweek* in the mid-1960s explained their popularity among

> young men and women frightened by the prospect of sex relations, newlyweds embarrassed by their ignorance of anatomy, older couples fearful that their sex life falls short of some cultural ideal. "People want to measure their performance with that of others," said Dr. David Mace, executive director of the American Association of Marriage Counselors, explaining the continued virility of the how-to handbooks. "We have to measure up in cars and homes with our neighbors. We're anxious whether we're measuring up in sex too."[21]

Sex books of the 1950s, for both teenagers and adults, contain mixed messages of sexual conservatism and enthusiasm. This is not surprising, given the cultural ambivalence about sexuality. Books for teenagers generally provided little information and discouraged sexual activity as much as possible. One of the most popular books at that time discussed sexual intercourse only in a section on marriage near the book's end. The author tersely explains:

> Physically it is a relatively simple procedure. After an initial period of sexual excitation, the penis becomes erect and is thrust into the vagina. A series of in and out movements eventuates in the ejaculation of semen from the penis. The woman may or may not have a climax in which her sex tension is released. Following the sexual climax is a period of relaxation and usually sleep.[22]

Sexually inexperienced adolescents must have wondered at all the hoopla over such seemingly humdrum behavior.

Advice books for teenagers typically attempted to reinforce traditional concepts of marriage and gender roles. Although it was hard to ignore Kinsey's data, authors often reinterpreted them to fit their own agendas. With respect to homosexuality, for example, some books distinguished between "normal homosexuality (the kind most people experience) and abnormal homosexuality (the kind that results in perverts),"[23] although this distinction would have been anathema to Kinsey. Additionally, some authors warned that failure to conform to acceptable teenage behavior would lead to homosexuality. At risk were tomboys, sissies, those overly interested in sex, shy girls, aggressive boys, and "other creeps," which presumably includes anyone who may have escaped the foregoing categories. "Sex and self-consciousness is carried to perverted degrees by those who are 'physically unattractive or have grotesque disabilities. . . . Their twisted minds may lead them into all kinds of unnatural sexual relations with those of their own sex.'"[24]

Adults fared somewhat better. *Ideal Marriage*, published in 1926 by the Dutch gynecologist Theodore van de Velde, was the popular forerunner of the modern marriage manuals and included advice on improving marital sex. At least one manual of the 1950s broke with tradition and enthusiastically endorsed sexual experimentation: *The Art and Science of Love* by Albert Ellis.

Public dissatisfaction with marriage, gender roles, and sexuality grew. Life in the suburbs proved not to be the utopia promised by popular mythology. In the late 1950s Betty Friedan began to uncover women's frustration with what, in 1963, she would call "the feminine mystique" —the gender script pushing women back into the home and into traditional femininity. By 1960 the discontent of women had become a public issue. When *Redbook* magazine ran a contest offering a prize for the best essay on "Why Young Mothers Feel Trapped," more than twenty-four thousand women responded.[25] By the early part of the decade, the divorce rate had begun to climb more rapidly, age at marriage rose, and the birthrate dropped[26]—all developments that traditionally trigger anxiety about the demise of the family. A disdainful article on the sexual revolution in *Time* in 1964 played on these fears: "The dominant fact about sexual mores in the U.S. remains the fragility of American marriage. The institution has never been easily sustained."[27] In this "pre-*HSR*" world, the nuclear family was still the cultural ideal, but it was becoming harder to maintain, even for the white middle class.

Women's resistance to stultifying expectations was becoming more palpable. Women who were participants in the labor force or who had been highly educated sometimes found the dissonance impossible to sustain. An article in the lesbian journal *The Ladder* in the mid-1960s, entitled "I Hate Women: A Diatribe by an Unreconstructed Feminist," expressed the frustration of one woman with "the current model of American femininity, trussed into the Feminine Role of Wife and Mother, with a Good Housekeeping Seal of Approval stamped across her Maidenform-upholstered bosom."[28] The contradictions in women's gender roles were at the breaking point.

Sexual mores were in fact becoming less restrictive. In 1967 the Institute for Sex Research conducted a study on the sexual behavior of college students and found that patterns essentially matched those of the 1940s and 1950s with one exception—a much larger proportion of young women were having sexual intercourse.[29] Wider access to more effective, inexpensive forms of contraception was certainly a factor in this increase. But even without birth control, people felt free to have sex, as evidenced by the fact that the number of illegitimate children born to teenagers rose dramatically from 1940 to 1961.[30] The increase in sexual activity among college students, particularly women, was sensationalized by the media. One female student was quoted as saying: "Sex is so casual and taken for granted—I mean we go to dinner, we go home, get undressed like old married people, you know—and just go to bed. I mean I'm not saying I'd liked to be raped on the living room floor exactly. But I would love to just sit around on the sofa and neck."[31] Teenage sexual activity was a major cultural concern, and popular magazines encouraged parents to enforce rigid rules on dating and to provide no information on contraception.[32]

As in the 1950s, there were complex undercurrents in the sexual mores of the early to mid-1960s. Some greeted the "sexual revolution" with cheers, sighs of relief, and a sense of mission. The Sex Information and Education Council of the United States (SIECUS), created in 1964, devoted itself to sex education. For many, however, the loosening of sexual attitudes was "an orgy of openmindedness" that could only lead to depravity.[33] Scores of groups with names like MOMS (Mothers Organized for Moral Stability) and SOS (Sanity on Sex) arose to combat sex education in the schools.[34] Despite these contradictions, however, issues of sex, sexuality, and gender received growing public attention throughout the 1960s. A decade of increasing discontent among both men and women affected, and was beginning to be exposed in, popular culture. Sexually explicit advertising, television programming, and films promised sexual satisfaction and fulfillment. The director of SIECUS noted that in one week she received two letters from married couples with the plaint: "We've been married . . . nine months, we have great sex, she has an orgasm every time, but we think we might be missing something. . . . Isn't there a book on techniques we could be reading?"[35]

Such public discourse about sex facilitated sexologists' consolidation of a market for their services by making it easier for people to seek help for real or imagined sexual problems. Even before the publication of *HSR*, sexologists had begun to attack the credibility of marriage manuals, the major source of sexual information up to that time. Sexologists proclaimed their credentials as scientists and contrasted the rigor and accuracy of their data with the experiential folk wisdom of the marriage manual. In 1965 several blasted the manuals for being inaccurate and possibly dangerous. Calderone announced: "The day of the marriage manual is past. They served a useful purpose when we were trying to break the shackles of Victorianism. Now they do more harm than good."[36] Sex education (the mission of her own organization, SIECUS) could alleviate the sexual ignorance that had contributed to the success of the manuals. Similarly, Masters and Johnson predicted in 1965 that their forthcoming work would render marriage manuals obsolete. *Newsweek* explained:

> Dr. William H. Masters and his colleague Virginia E. Johnson at the Reproductive Biology Research Foundation in St. Louis believe that new research offers hope for effective books of sexual instruction. "Sex research has not been accepted in this country," says Masters. "And there has been little scientific information available." To fill this void, Masters and Johnson will publish next year a textbook on the physiology of sex (among its findings: despite what the manuals say, there is only one kind of female orgasm). "The manuals written five years from now will be presenting fact not fiction," says Masters. "Van de Velde, Stone and Chesser will either be overhauled to conform with modern findings or fall by the way."[37]

In 1970, describing the new liberal attitudes toward sexuality, *Newsweek* proclaimed, "In time, that could mean goodbye to the sex manuals, goodbye to one of the nation's most profitable cottage industries."[38] Although the seventies did not in fact see the disappearance of sex manuals, sexologists did tap into a vast market of people eager for a new kind of book on sexuality and sex techniques.

By the time of the publication of *HSR*, sexology had reached a major juncture in its professionalization. It was successfully consolidating a scientific data base and forming professional associations such as SIECUS (1964) and AASEC (1967). Yet internal developments alone do not account for successful professionalization. Relationships to the public, to dominant social institutions, and to cultural developments are crucial. A profession is most successful if it can reflect the dominant values of a society while simultaneously addressing public concerns. Sexology in the late sixties successfully navigated this narrow channel.

The key to its success was its resonance with the major cultural dilemmas of the 1950s and 1960s. Its alleged ability to solve complex problems threatening the social fabric enabled sexology to skirt resistance by conservatives and curry the favor of many groups seeking solutions. Widely known sexologists, including Kinsey, Calderone, and Masters and Johnson, located their work solidly within a similar framework, promising to untangle dilemmas about marriage, heterosexual dissatisfaction, and changing gender roles. By holding out scientific fact, as opposed to "phallic fallacy," the profession established legitimacy with other professions and with the public. The sexology of the 1960s continued the approach established by Kinsey in the 1940s: scientific solutions to social problems. (This approach was consistent with the Great Society's simultaneous efforts to diagnose and treat massive social problems, first with scientific studies, then with elaborate programs such as the War on Poverty.) The initial resistance from dominant professions whose turf sexology threatened—for example, medicine and psychiatry —faded. Some of these professionals jumped on sexology's bandwagon; others acquiesced to sexology's claim of greater effectiveness; others simply ignored the budding science.

In the same way in which sexologists denigrated marriage manuals, they also criticized (often correctly) the ability of other professions to practice sex therapy:

> The main burden of loosening Queen Victoria's lingering grip and treating sexual hangups falls to the large army of "service" professionals—clergymen, marriage counselors, doctors, psychologists, and even lawyers. And the most interesting thing about these advisers is that, traditionally, they have actually known less about sex—and been more frightened of it—than anybody on their block. . . . As some sexologists see it, the general state of prevailing ignorance was made worse by the fact that many well-meaning and comparatively well-educated advisers—ministers and marriage counselors as well as doctors—were leaning on rigid psychoanalytic theory that turned out to be wrong and damaging.[39]

With their appeal to greater scientific legitimacy, sexologists thus attempted to consolidate their authority, edge their competitors out of the market, and appeal to individuals with sexual problems to seek professional help.

These efforts met little public resistance, and no organized political opposition. The few books that challenged traditional gender roles and the myth of family togetherness, among them *Adam's Rib* by Ruth Herschberger (1947), *The Second Sex* by Simone de Beauvoir (1953), and Betty Friedan's *The Feminine Mystique* (1963), could not counteract the relentless wave of popular literature that depicted woman's role as nurturing wife and mother. Thus, when *HSR* was published, sexologists could anticipate limitless expansion of their authority.

Sex in the Laboratory

D espite their reputation as pioneers, most of Masters and Johnson's research was not innovative. They had many predecessors in physiological research on sexual behavior. The first known American observations of orgasm were conducted by Dr. Joseph Beck, whose findings were published in the *St. Louis Medical and Surgical Journal* in September 1872.[40] The marriage and the career of John B. Watson, a pioneer in behavioral psychology, ended in the early part of the century when it became publicly known that he had connected his body and that of his female partner to scientific instruments in order to measure physiological response during intercourse.[41] Other researchers who conducted empirical investigations of sexual activity were Ernst P. Boas, Ernst F. Goldschmidt, and Ernst Grafenberg (United States), Felix Roubard (France), Theodore van de Velde (Netherlands), and G. Klumbies and H. Kleinsorge (Germany).[42] The work of the American gynecologist Robert Latou Dickinson is particularly noteworthy. Working in the early decades of this century, Dickinson not only observed sexual response during intercourse and masturbation, but constructed a phallus-shaped glass tube through which he observed the physiological responses of orgasm inside the vagina. This unsung pioneer of sex therapy also introduced the electric vibrator to facilitate orgasmic response in women. By the mid-twentieth century, extensive research documented heart rates, blood pressure, electrocardiograph readings, metabolic rates, respiratory changes, and the like during the course of sexual activity.

In many ways the impact of Masters and Johnson was largely symbolic. For although the scope of *HSR* was unprecedented, much of its content was simply replication or speculation.[43] Masters and Johnson have admitted that their equipment was antiquated and even out of date. And they are often the first to concede the inadequacy of *HSR*. Masters told an interviewer, "No one really knows anything about sexual functioning. Really. This little thing that we put out is embarrassing in that it doesn't even scratch the surface."[44] The uniqueness of Masters and Johnson's work lay more in their timing than in anything else. Whereas most prior researchers had kept their physiological work secret, Masters and Johnson's initial research findings appeared at a time when cultural mores had loosened sufficiently to make the publication of their work less of a risk. The vast media coverage of Kinsey's research had paved the way for greater public acceptance of sex in the laboratory. And for most people, it was irrelevant that the studies were flawed. Masters and Johnson's fame derived from the courage or irreverence, depending on the perspective, of their application of the techniques of biomedical science to the study of sexuality.

Getting Started

M asters began his physiological sex research in 1954, just one year after the publication of Kinsey's *Sexual Behavior in the Human Female*. Trained as a gynecologist, he had worked in the laboratory of Dr. George Washington Corner of the Rockefeller Foundation and the Committee for Research in Problems of Sex. In part, it was his experience there with sex research on animals that inspired Masters' interest in the sexual physiology of humans. He was drawn to one of the few areas of medicine in which little work had been done.[45] As Corner had advised, Masters waited until he was thirty-eight and an established gynecologist before beginning his sex research at Washington University.[46]

Political expediency led him to ask Virginia Johnson to join the research project in 1957. Masters was told by one of the original subjects, a prostitute, that he should have a woman join him in the work. His criteria for an assistant were that she be in her late twenties or early thirties, able to work well with people, and that she be married or divorced, with at least one child. What was most essential, according to Masters, were not academic qualifications, but that the candidate "knew where babies came from" and did not have "a professional virgin psyche."[47] Virginia Johnson, who was thought to meet all of these requirements, seems to have been chosen not as an academic equal, but as a person able to understand and elicit the cooperation of female subjects and clients. The collaboration between the two led to the development of the now-famous "dual-sex team," a hallmark of the Masters and Johnson program. Although Masters and Johnson may have been the most renowned practitioners, the dual-sex team, or treatment of a couple by a couple (dubbed TCC by the popular press), enjoyed a flurry of popularity in the late sixties.[48] Two major premises underlie TCC: both partners are involved in a couple's sexual problem, whatever its nature, and women and men can best be understood by a therapist of their own gender. Since male experts typically have spoken about women's sexuality without considering (conceptually, at least) women's subjective experience, dual-sex therapy represented an ideological advance for women.

When they initiated their research, Masters and Johnson faced the professional obstacles, funding restrictions, and public obloquy common to sex researchers. In 1955, when the Reproductive Biology Research Foundation (RBRF) was established under the auspices of the Washington University School of Medicine in St. Louis, the word "sex" could not be used even at a medical meeting.[49] Masters was initially given a small grant by the Department of Public Health. Later the project was funded by the National Institute of Health, although it began rejecting his grant applications in 1960. Since then, Masters and Johnson have relied on funds from the Playboy Foundation, book sales, local corporations, workshop and clinic fees, and continuing donations from individuals, which are solicited in part by the Masters and Johnson Institute Fellows Program. In 1979, to commemorate the twenty-fifth anniversary of their research, the RBRF's name was changed to the Masters and Johnson Institute. The original name, chosen to sound nonthreatening, had proven too clumsy and difficult to remember.

Believing that early publicity could destroy their research program, Masters and Johnson asked for, and secured, the cooperation of the press in delaying coverage. Secrecy was facilitated by the board of the RBRF, whose members Masters had shrewdly handpicked. (They included the chancellor of Washington University, the police commissioner, and the publisher of the local newspaper.)[50] The strategy was successful to a point. In 1964, however, psychoanalyst Leslie Farber, who had read one of Masters and Johnson's early articles for a medical journal, penned a scathing attack entitled "I'm Sorry, Dear," which drew widespread attention to the St. Louis research.[51] Masters and Johnson began to feel pressure to publish their work so that it would be portrayed accurately. They published *HSR* in 1966.

Written in six weeks, *HSR* has been described as "an almost impenetrable thicket of Latinate medicalese."[52] The style reflected the sex researchers' expectation of public outrage. Masters explained:

> Every effort was made to make this book as pedantic and obtuse as possible and, may I say in all modesty, I think we succeeded admirably. Although we were specifically writing a textbook for the biological and behavioral professions, we were all aware that the text would be dissected paragraph by paragraph by others, and that if one line, or even a suggestion of "pornography" could be established in any context, we would have had to face a holocaust.[53]

Nonetheless, *HSR*'s reception was remarkably similar to that of the Kinsey reports years earlier. The first printing sold out within three days of publication, and *HSR* was soon number two on the *New York Times* nonfiction best-seller list.[54] Once again, it was obvious that there was a vast market for sexual information.

The Body Politic

Masters and Johnson continued to conduct laboratory observations until they completed their physiological research in 1970, at which point the laboratory was dismantled. For *HSR* they used data from over ten thousand orgasms from 694 individuals. As with Kinsey, critics frequently attacked their work on the basis of their research population. While some criticized the demographic representativeness of the participants, others took the position that anyone who would allow himself or herself to be filmed while having sex must be abnormal. Masters and Johnson have in fact always explicitly eschewed any claim that their population was representative. Still, a closer look at their subjects is instructive.

In the first nineteen or twenty months of the sex research program, Masters recruited prostitutes in the belief that they were the only women who would be willing to participate in such a project. He later eliminated those data from the final results, since he thought that the chronic pelvic congestion from which prostitutes suffered disqualified them as "normal" subjects. His work with prostitutes was invaluable to Masters in many ways, however. His early observations of them served as a trial run for the later project, and the prostitutes made numerous suggestions for refining the research. Not only did they help him develop recording techniques, but they "described many methods for elevating or controlling sexual tensions and demonstrated methods for innumerable variations in stimulative technique. Ultimately many of these techniques have been found to have direct application in therapy of male and female sexual inadequacy and have been integrated into the clinical research programs."[55] Finally, the prostitutes were instrumental in helping Masters secure his later sample of "respectable men and women" who were willing to participate in the research.[56]

From Masters' descriptions, it seems his relationship to the prostitutes was not that of researcher to subject, but essentially that of collaborator—an interesting departure from the tradition of early sexologists such as Iwan Bloch, who viewed prostitution as a social plague that would be eliminated by the new science of sex. The prostitutes who cooperated in Masters' early research can be considered sexologists in their own right. They knew much more about sexual technique and sexual functioning than the scientists who turned to them. Without their collaboration, it is doubtful that Masters and Johnson's research would have achieved the degree of sophistication it did, at least within such a short time frame.

The "respectable" volunteers who were eventually chosen for the laboratory research were selected for their ability to perform successfully under glaring lights and before rolling cameras. The volunteers had other things in common, however. Overwhelmingly, they were white, upper-middle-class, and highly educated. These qualities are largely related to the fact that most of them came from the surrounding metropolitan, academic community. Yet, while Masters and Johnson state in

HSR that the preponderance of white, upper-middle-class subjects "has not been offset by a statistically significant number of lower-range family units obtained from out-patient clinical sources," they later note that "the sample was *weighted purposely* toward higher than average intelligence levels and socioeconomic backgrounds" (emphasis added).[57] Masters and Johnson frequently explain that it was important that the volunteers be able to "vocalize effectively" and "communicate finite details of sexual reaction."[58] In addition, they eliminated anyone who exhibited "sociosexual aberrancy"—a euphemism they do not define. It seems that Masters and Johnson simply assembled a group of "respectable" volunteers who would be easy for them to work with and who would incur the least amount of public criticism. They defended their selection of subjects by claiming, "If you are going to find out what happens, obviously, you must work with those to whom it happens."[59]

These sampling problems are replicated in *Human Sexual Inadequacy* (*HSI*), published in 1970, which delineated their fundamental clinical principles. These were based on research with 510 married couples and 57 single people. Demographically, this population was similar to that in *HSR* in the predominance of white, middle- and upper-middle-class, highly educated individuals. The class and racial bias was accentuated in the clinical population, however, because Masters and Johnson did not accept patients into this group unless they were referred "by authority." They waived this rule for physicians and clinical psychologists, however, and consequently "these individuals, permitted the professional courtesy of self-referral, comprise a significant segment of the research population."[60]

Economic factors play an unacknowledged role, for Masters and Johnson used their physiological data, along with clinical data from a similarly narrow sample, in order to develop a therapeutic treatment program for sexual problems. They chose a sample that reflected the demographic profile of the population that would be most inclined financially and ideologically to seek the services of sex therapy professionals. It is likely that both the structure and the function of their psychological program were affected by this decision. In fact, two of the requirements for the "St. Louis" model of therapy—dual-sex therapists and a two-week treatment period in isolation—were dropped by later therapists who found that they rendered sex therapy inaccessible to lower-income couples.[61]

The intentional narrowness of the Masters and Johnson research population represents a significant departure from Kinsey's practice. It is especially noteworthy in view of Kinsey's striking demonstration of how demographic variables affect sexual behavior. Masters and Johnson defended the narrowness of their sample by emphasizing that their research was physiological, not psychological. This defense reflects their belief in the primacy and universality of the human body: "The higher-average educational level of the women volunteers is hardly likely to affect the acidity of their vaginal fluids."[62] But it would have been more congruent with Masters and Johnson's framework to test the truth of this assumption. Increasingly, feminist researchers and others are demonstrating that the social can indeed affect the biological. And, ironically, Masters and Johnson seem to have abandoned this belief when they replicated their research with a gay population in order to determine whether homosexuals have a different physiological sexual response than heterosexuals.

In addition to the public speculation over who would do such a thing, there were questions about what they had done. Masters and Johnson made every attempt, when they described the laboratory research, to make procedures sound, if not quite boring, at least mundane. Once inside the lab, the volunteers had the proceedings explained to them and were given time to acclimate to the surroundings. The basic sexual activities in which they engaged were:

1. Masturbation with the hand or fingers
2. Masturbation (rarely) with the mechanical vibrator
3. Sexual intercourse with the woman on her back
4. Sexual intercourse with the man on his back
5. "Artificial coition" with the transparent phallus, Ulysses
6. Stimulation of the breasts alone, without genital contact[63]

The more than ten thousand orgasms accumulated as a result of these activities led to the cornerstone of *HSR*: the sexual response cycle. Here again, Masters and Johnson were not innovators. Although his description was not empirically based, Havelock Ellis had earlier, very simply, divided the sexual process into "tumescence" and "detumescence," with orgasm as the boundary. What Masters and Johnson did was to expand this model into four stages rather than two. Each stage comprises a distinct set of physiological changes that the human body undergoes during sexual activity. The excitement phase is the body's first reaction to sexual stimulation. For the female these responses include nipple erection, vaginal lubrication, partial elevation of the uterus, swelling of the clitoris, and rises in heart rate and blood pressure. The male undergoes erection, partial elevation of the testes, flattening and elevation of the scrotal sac, and rises in heart rate and blood pressure. The plateau phase is essentially a heightening of these bodily responses. In females, the clitoris withdraws into the clitoral hood, and the uterus becomes fully elevated. Males secrete two or three drops of fluid containing active sperm (a finding that empirically demonstrated the ineffectiveness of coitus interruptus as a method of birth control). During the orgasmic phase, the vagina contracts at 0.8-second intervals; penile contractions occur at the same rate. In both women and men, the rectal sphincter muscles contract at 0.8-second intervals as well. The resolution phase is the rapid or gradual disappearance of the changes begun in stage one. Masters and Johnson concluded that the time necessary for complete resolution roughly equals the length of the excitement and plateau phases. They also note that, without orgasm, the body may take forty-eight hours to return to its normal state.

This schema was a stimulus for much modern sex research and therapy. At the sixth World Congress of Sexology in 1983, Dr. Shirley Zussman compared Masters and Johnson's work to the launching of the Soviet space capsule *Sputnik,* which brought a new urgency to the American pursuit of science. In this view, the delineation of the four phases of human sexual response was similarly effective in directing people toward sexual science.[64] Yet, as noted, Masters and Johnson's conception was not a new one, and many subsequent sexologists have modified or abandoned it, claiming that it is of limited usefulness in research and clinical intervention.

Taxonomies, typologies, and other schemata are the methods of scientists. Thus, Masters and Johnson's division of the gamut of bodily changes that occur during sex into stages was a logical step. Perhaps they were loath merely to replicate the two-stage model promulgated decades earlier by Ellis. Masters once stated, "I went into sex research with the full knowledge that I had to win. I had to come up with something or I would have been destroyed professionally."[65] In fact, however, by positing a response cycle with four distinct phases that entail specific physiological correlates, Masters and Johnson were stretching their data to support their construct. Their research does not clearly show physiological changes occurring in discrete stages rather than as progressive phenomena. Historian Paul Robinson points out that the entire notion of four stages is based on "groundless differentiation" that the researchers were unable to document scientifically. Robinson deconstructs the research as vague and unscientific, and concludes:

> Ironically, Havelock Ellis's doctrine of tumescence and detumescence, though more general, turns out to be a more appropriate and far less pretentious abstraction, since it allows for both those phenomena that are cumulative and those that are sudden and evanescent rather than imposing boxlike categories that correspond to neither.[66]

Nevertheless, despite its conceptual flimsiness, the four-phase human sexual response cycle helped to consolidate Masters and Johnson's professional reputations.

The Scientists as Ideologues

Like Kinsey, Masters and Johnson invoked the culture's idealization of science to legitimize their work, emphasizing at every turn their devotion to the scientific method and the pursuit of knowledge. Yet they differed from Kinsey in that they invoked the power of the medical profession as well. In their preface to *HSR*, they asserted "medicine's responsibility" to uncover and disseminate accurate information on sex.[67] Their books are peppered with references to themselves as "professionals" and "medical authorit[ies]"—for example, "The white coat of authority is quite sufficient to inspire confidence."[68] They assumed that those white coats of authority were the guarantors of objectivity and scientific neutrality, but in fact their work is laden with values and assumptions.

The concept of the human sexual response cycle, for example, provided the tools for Masters and Johnson to advance one of their major ideological tenets: the similarity between women and men. As already noted, this has been a major theme in twentieth-century sexology, as opposed to the sexual ideology of the Victorian era, which emphasized the differences between the sexes, the double standard, purity of women, and the mandate of the man as protector. The complementarity, rather than the similarity, of the sexes was seen as the foundation of heterosexual relationships. Kinsey and Masters and Johnson were aware that this edifice had been so seriously eroded by the mid-twentieth century that it could no longer support the crumbling institution of marriage. In light of changes they perceived in sex/gender relations, sexologists have focused on the similarities between men and women in an attempt to sustain heterosexual relationships.

It is clear that Masters and Johnson interpreted their data selectively in their delineation of the four-stage model, for they found so many physiological differences between men and women that their emphasis on similarities is overdetermined. There are, of course, similarities in the physical sexual responses of women and men: parallels in the timing of muscular contractions during orgasm, similar changes in muscle tension, heart rate, and blood pressure. A closer look at *HSR*, however, reveals many descriptions of discrepancies between male and female bodily responses sandwiched between Masters and Johnson's insistence on their similarities. A major difference is presented in the very first pages of *HSR*. Having explained the four-stage response model, Masters and Johnson write:

> Only one sexual response pattern has been diagrammed for the human male. . . . Comparably, three different sexual response patterns have been diagrammed for the human female. . . . There is a great variation in both the intensity and the duration of female orgasmic experience, while the male tends to follow standard patterns of ejaculatory reaction with less individual variation.[69]

Or, as they later say, "the male orgasm is more a-rose-is-a-rose-is-a-rose sort of thing. Now a thing of beauty is a joy forever, but it is still a rose. The female goes all the way from poppies to orchids."[70] They conclude decisively that women do not ejaculate,[71] and they describe other major differences between female and male orgasmic responses as well:

> First, the female is capable of rapid return to orgasm immediately following an orgasmic experience, if re-stimulated before tensions have dropped below plateau-phase response levels. Second, the female is capable of maintaining an orgasmic experience for a relatively long period of time.[72]

Masters and Johnson note this ability of females to maintain an orgasm most explicitly in their discussion of orgasmic patterns during masturbation, a sexual practice in which many women experience sequential orgasms, to the point that "usually physical exhaustion alone terminates such an active masturbatory session."[73] Masters and Johnson dubbed this occurrence "status orgasmus" and explained it as follows:

> This physiological stage of stress is created either by a series of rapidly recurrent orgasmic experiences between which no recordable plateau-phase intervals can be demonstrated, or by a single, long-continued orgasmic episode. Subjective report, together with visual impression of involuntary variation in peripheral myotonia, suggests that the woman actually is ranging with extreme rapidity between successive orgasmic peaks and a baseline of advanced plateau-phase tension. Status orgasmus may last from 20 to more than 60 seconds.[74]

This pattern differs from that of the male, who reaches orgasm and then moves into what Masters and Johnson term "the refractory period," during which he is unable to be stimulated further. This finding filtered down through the popular press as "multiple orgasms." Women could have them and men couldn't.

Other sexual differences between women and men are listed in *HSR*. Only women, for example, possess an organ that exists solely for sexual pleasure—the clitoris. In addition, Masters and Johnson describe women and their orgasms as much more influenced by psychological factors than are men and their orgasms. And, in a complete reversal of Kinsey's view, Masters and Johnson assert that the female's capacity to respond to sexual stimulation, unlike the male's, is virtually unlimited. Even in the last section of *HSR*, where they devote a chapter to "Similarities in Physiologic Response," one can find as many physiological differences as similarities. It is clear that their decision to focus on similarities represents ideology rather than science.

This insistence on the similarity between men and women reflects one of the quintessential dilemmas for women in modern sexological thought, and in feminist thought as well. In the nineteenth century, some feminists criticized the rigid, stereotypic sex differentiation prevalent in the culture as a method used to maintain distance between men and women, and to enforce the oppression of women. These women posited the "equivalence of the sexes," as a feminist strategy toward liberation. In the late 1960s, many radical feminists noted that ideologies that advance the notion of an inherent male or female essence or nature, whether based on biology or socialization, typically have the same oppressive result as the Victorian categories. They therefore echoed the efforts of nineteenth-century feminists by seeking an end to repressive categorizations of gender.[75]

Masters and Johnson's work would seem to provide scientific legitimation for the feminist strategy of equality and equivalency. Their findings, as popularized, were read as a blow to the sexual double standard. But their analysis is deceptive. Masters and Johnson advance their claim of male–female similarity in the absence of any broader analysis of male dominance and heterosexism. When they assert that men and women are similar, while ignoring the effects of sex and gender oppression, the result is an analysis that fails to account for the special circumstances women face in a male-dominated society. In fact, like many conservatives, Masters and Johnson have charged that a feminist analysis that would account for power and inequality is dangerous to social relations. When asked by an interviewer if they were feminists, Virginia Johnson once replied, "Not remotely. In a million years it wouldn't occur to me to do that because that is just as devastating as what we call the double-standard bit, you know."[76] It was clear from *HSI* and later *The Pleasure Bond* that, for Masters and Johnson, women's liberation in the bedroom was most important.

Their focus on "similarities" and lack of an analysis of power sometimes lead Masters and Johnson to draw inexact parallels, such as the one based on Masters' study of male victims of sexual assault. Although the entire study was based on eleven men seen in the 1960s and Masters acknowledged that "we haven't seen anything in the '70s," he concludes that the nature of sexual assault is "identical" for women and men.[77] The claim that victimization is gender-neutral conflates male and female experiences in an inaccurate and unhelpful way. While the researchers could find only a handful of men who had been sexually abused, women live with a daily threat of sexual violence. FBI statistics indicate that one out of three women will be raped during her lifetime, and by age eighteen, 25 percent of girls will have experienced sexual abuse, probably by a family member.[78] The extent of sexual violence creates a climate of terror that magnifies the actual experience of assault for women. The assertion that men suffer the same consequences ignores the substantial power differentials between men and women and differences in the meaning, the consequences, and the extent of sexual violence against women.

Particularly in their early work, Masters and Johnson are sexual essentialists to an extraordinary degree. They go one step beyond Kinsey, who based his notion of "naturalness" on what people did, in that they base their idea of "naturalness" on the physiological responses people exhibit. Their catch-phrase is that "sex is a natural function," and the basis of their therapy "consists of putting sex back into its natural context."[79] What they mean by "natural" is basically that the capacities for penile erection, vaginal lubrication, and orgasm are genetically programmed into the body. They maintain that since girls experience vaginal lubrication within twenty-four hours of birth, and boys have erections in the eighth month of fetal development, the opportunities for learning such behavior are minimal, and therefore sex is a natural bodily process like eating or sleeping. In 1983 Masters stated, "Our greatest failure is the failure to convince medicine first and the behavioral sciences second that sex is a natural function."[80] They combine this concept of a natural, unfettered sexual response with a reluctance to deal with cultural conditioning and power issues except in the most elliptical way, as when they refer to the oppressive sexual socialization of women with euphemisms such as "negatively based psychosocial influences."[81]

As was true of Kinsey, the intent of Masters and Johnson's essentialism was liberatory. Their assertion that sex is "natural" was meant to contravene thousands of years of punishment, prohibitions, and mysticism. There is no mystery, and, most important, we are all capable. By ignoring the social and political construction of sexuality, they could convey instead the image of an inherent, lusty sexuality hidden inside everyone, a sexuality that could be brought to the surface with a few practical suggestions for changes in technique and position. This understanding of sexuality was vital for the development of their clinical practice. One can establish a market only with the promise of simple and effective techniques and commodities that will ameliorate, if not solve, the presenting dilemma. To succeed as a business, sexology had to view sex as simple, natural, and responsive to technical intervention, not overgrown with thorny social relations.

As professionals and scientists, Masters and Johnson have an investment in the maintenance of the dominant ideology. They share with earlier sexologists a commitment to marriage and the family. Consistently, they have channeled research and practice into salvaging crumbling marriages as a way of legitimating their work. On the basis of their own clinical research and an examination of divorce records, Masters and Johnson have frequently stated that they believe at least half the married couples in the United States suffer from sexual problems.[82] In their preface to *HSR*, they warn that "the greatest single cause for family-unit destruction and divorce in this country is a fundamental sexual inadequacy within the marital unit."[83] In the wake of controversy over their research method, sex in the laboratory, "Dr. Masters defended the project on the grounds that human sexual maladjustment is the leading cause of marital disharmony and divorce."[84]

Masters and Johnson's commitment to the institution of marriage is reinforced by their terminology as well as their research practices. The sex partners copulating either in the lab or at home as part of their therapy are not called "couples," but rather "marital units" or "family units." And, as already noted, few unmarried persons were accepted as part of the laboratory population. Those who were, were allowed limited participation in sexual intercourse. In *HSR* the authors wrote:

The unrehearsed physiologic and anatomic response patterns of the unmarried were recorded and contrasted to the mutually conditioned and frequently stylized sexual response patterns of the marital units. *This technique*

for experimental control was abandoned as soon as it was established un-
equivocally that there is no basic difference in the anatomy and physiology of
human sexual response regardless of the marital status of responding units.
(Emphasis added.) [85]

Most unmarried volunteers participated in the less controversial "auto-
manipulation."

Masters and Johnson have been criticized for "intellectual ineptitude"
and a "chronic inability to be precise." [86] This failure, however, stems
less from their research capabilities than from their inability to resolve
the tension between their roles as scientists and as ideologues. As scientists, they have disseminated the data that they painstakingly gathered
in the laboratory. In their interpretations, however, they have often attempted to fit divergent information into pigeonholes consistent with
mainstream ideology about marriage. This results in a body of con-
fusing material. They present data that have radical implications, yet
they attempt to interpret and channel them to avoid undermining traditional ideas. One example is their position on masturbation. Like
Kinsey, they clearly indicate the greater potential for sexual pleasure for
women in masturbation as opposed to intercourse. Some women later
interpreted this as "scientific validation" for the potential irrelevance of
men.[87] This is clearly not an interpretation that Masters and Johnson
sanction, and one that they go to great lengths to mitigate in their own
interpretations of their data. For Masters and Johnson, masturbation is
primarily important for its contribution to marital intercourse. In their
therapy program, they advise couples to share with each other their masturbation techniques so that they can have better intercourse. Women
who do not have orgasms are taught to reach orgasm through masturbation as a first step; then they make a "bridge" to intercourse. Masters
and Johnson also recommend masturbation as a way of keeping in shape
for intercourse, and they predict dire physical effects from prolonged
abstinence from sex, particularly in the elderly. Some of their data have
been used by feminists—for example, to challenge the myth of the vaginal orgasm.[88] But while Masters and Johnson are sometimes credited as
the source of radical interpretations, essentially they organize their data
around their own conservative interpretations.

The implications of their data for women are in fact ideologically complicated. On the one hand, their disdain for feminism, their emphasis on marriage and family, and their inability to articulate power differences regarding sex and gender would suggest that they are not friends of feminists. On the other hand, their enthusiasm for more and better orgasms, and their development of the technical skills to achieve them, lend Masters and Johnson an air of progressivism. However, there is nothing inherently radical about the espousal of sexual fulfillment. In the absence of broader sociopolitical change, even the benefits of improved technique can be reduced by prevailing sexual norms and expectations. Some have charged that Masters and Johnson's research has been used to enforce new sexual standards for women, such as multiple orgasms. One critic reported cases in which men complained that their partners must be faking orgasms because they failed to develop the sex rash that Masters and Johnson described.[89]

Yet these stories can be matched by others told by women who credit Masters and Johnson with salvaging their sex lives and their self-esteem.[90] Masters and Johnson asserted a woman's right to sexual pleasure at a time when this idea was still faintly salacious. By introducing the dual-sex team, they insisted on the importance of a woman's voice in describing her own sexuality. Although it was the feminist movement that popularized the implications of the clitoral orgasm, Masters and Johnson faithfully insisted on the importance of the clitoris and masturbation in the expression of female sexuality. Their research has produced improvements in contraceptive methods, as well as new information on reproduction and infertility. Masters and Johnson are undeniably traditional, yet many women have benefited from the implications of their research, even if it merely amounts to the dissemination of the notion that many women like sex.

Any valid assessment of Masters and Johnson must account for these seeming contradictions within their work. What remains consistent is their self-presentation as solid, no-nonsense scientists. The First Couple of sex research has, over the years, remained staunchly conservative, although they would deny any ideological intent. It is likely that, especially in the early years, this conservatism helped legitimate their research in the public eye. To a great extent, Masters and Johnson saw themselves as responsible for a new field of sex research and therapy that they feared was unregulated and potentially destructive. The professionalization of sexology, in their view, could only succeed through a fierce dedication to the ideal of scientific rationality. Yet, as we will see, it was precisely this ideal that was challenged by so many in the late 1960s and 1970s.

Masters and Johnson could not know that *HSR* had appeared on the crest of a wave of sociopolitical change that would break at the end of the decade. At that point a number of groups would emerge to challenge the hegemony over sexual issues that scientific sexology was attempting to establish.

Part Two: Sexology at a Crossroad

Consolidation and Confusion

T he late 1960s and early 1970s were a time of expansion and divergence within sexology. While still risky and unconventional,
choosing a career in human sexology was no longer professional suicide.
Sexology's growth resonated with the cultural ambience of freer sexual
mores. The media heralded the arrival of the "sexual revolution," and
the catchwords of the time were freedom and experimentation. Heterosexual men of the counterculture and the radical left were frequently the
most enthusiastic proponents of "free love." Meanwhile, radical movements organized by heterosexual women, lesbians, and gay men profoundly challenged implicit assumptions about what was "normal" and
"natural" behavior. These challenges were bolstered by new technologies of birth control, women's increasing economic independence, the
consolidation of an urban gay culture, and the waves of antiwar protests

by the New Left and counterculture. The already shaky foundations of the American sex/gender system were being overhauled.

It was inevitable, then, that sexology would be touched by, and participate in, these landmark changes. As a struggling science in the late 1960s, sexology sought to demonstrate its ability to solve the very crises of sexuality and gender roles that its findings were helping to generate. Masters and Johnson crusaded to save marriages, for example, while simultaneously demonstrating the physiological potential for women's sexual autonomy from men. And, paradoxically, their agenda for a rigorous, scientific sexology was subverted, in part, by their own work, which served as a beacon for less scientifically inclined practitioners.

The publication in 1970 of Masters and Johnson's *Human Sexual Inadequacy* was a landmark for sexology. *HSI* was the first comprehensive textbook of sexual problems and treatment. It served as a guidebook for practitioners and became the cornerstone for the emerging specialty of sex therapy. Glowing with medical respectability, *HSI* provided scientific legitimation for the new field. Not only scientists were drawn to the new specialty, however. Sex therapy promised to be a very attractive commodity at a time when the marketing of sexual ideas, products, and services was beginning to flourish.

William Masters estimated that less than five years after the publication of *HSI*, between thirty-five hundred and five thousand clinics and treatment centers devoted to sex problems were established in the United States.[1] Many were reputable programs for therapy and education. Some were connected with major universities and hospitals. But the field was attracting a growing number of practitioners with esoteric, unconventional, or merely exploitative techniques. Capitalizing on the ambience of "free love," some of these new clinicians subscribed to "the therapeutic value of normally proscribed sexual activity."[2] For sexual problems or ailing marriages, they might well prescribe extramarital affairs, group sex, swinging, or patient–therapist sex. Determining the validity of these techniques often proved difficult in a field where sex therapy with surrogates had once been an established practice for even the most conservative sexologists.

The profession, however, was attempting to consolidate. Those entering the field of sexology in the early 1970s found many professional associations, publications, and conferences. Graduate training programs were developed, and eventually the University of Pennsylvania, New York University, and the Institute for Advanced Study of Human Sexuality in San Francisco began granting doctoral degrees in human sexuality. Several professional organizations founded in the 1950s and 1960s attempted to carve out separate territories. The organizational statement of the Society for the Scientific Study of Sex declared, "It is the focus on the scientific method that distinguishes the SSSS from other sexological organizations."[3]

The Sex Information and Education Council of the United States (SIECUS) took a slightly different direction. SIECUS described itself as a health organization, and Mary Calderone served as medical director of Planned Parenthood Federations of America for eleven years until she resigned to start SIECUS. While committed to the scientific method, SIECUS adopted a public health approach to sex, focusing on public awareness and education. "What can SIECUS do?" its newsletter asked. "SIECUS can contribute simply by existing. The existence of an organization that focuses clearly on sexuality as an area of health meriting study, understanding, and protection has therapeutic value in itself."[4] SIECUS took a leading role in the tempestuous campaign to introduce sex education programs in the schools. By the late 1960s, SIECUS was the target of virulent attacks by sex education opponents such as the John Birch Society and the Christian Crusade, and both SIECUS and the American Medical Association were accused of being tools of the Communist Party.[5] Nevertheless, numerous sex education programs were implemented in the early and mid-1970s.[6]

In 1967 the American Association of Sex Educators and Counselors was established. A decade later it changed its name to the American Association of Sex Educators, Counselors, and Therapists. The Society for Sex Therapy and Research (SSTAR) was formed in 1978. And after a dispute within AASECT over its code of ethics, The Association of Sexologists (TAOS) was founded in 1978 to accommodate practitioners who favored the options of sex with clients and nudity in their practices.

In the midst of sexology's heady expansion, however, there were also attempts to regulate the field. A primary motive was, in fact, the vast proliferation of sex experts and sex clinics. In 1973 *Time* magazine warned its readers that entrepreneurs had discovered the vast potential market of men and women who had sexual problems and were willing to pay to find solutions.[7] That same year journalist Linda Wolfe wrote about Norman C. King, a media consultant who had decided to become the "emperor of sex in New York by building a chain of clinics called 'Male Potency Centers of America.'"

> Anyone can call himself a sexologist, or expert in human sexuality. These days more and more unqualified men and women are doing just that. He has polled 1,500 Wall Street executives earning over $40,000 and 1,500 men earning around $12,000 to see how many of them were (a) sometimes impotent and (b) interested in doing something about it. "In the mail order business," King explains to me, "even a 5% return is considered fantastic. Imagine my astonishment when close to one-fourth of the men I wrote to actually phoned back to me and said they were sometimes impotent and wanted to know what to do about it. That's how Male Potency Centers of America got born." Actually, King's chain of clinics is still fetal. It exists in a detailed financial prospectus in King's office in the Seagram Building. But like a host of other new and privately run sex clinics, it will be born next year. Sex therapy, what a friend of mine in the field calls "America's greatest cultural contribution after jazz," is about to become big business.[8]

Wolfe's critique was timely and to the point. The field of sex therapy was (and, in fact, still is) completely unregulated. Although other professions, such as medicine and psychology, had established claims and boundaries through licensing and other regulatory mechanisms, sexology had not been granted control from the state over issues of human sexuality. Anyone could advertise as a "sex therapist," and the promise of fast and easy money beckoned. There is no licensing, no universally accepted standard of training or practice, no code of ethics with regulatory clout, and no legal definition of what constitutes legitimate sex therapy. In short, the field lacked the accoutrements of professionalization that would establish its territory, protect its market, and protect the public.

In response to allegations of exploitation, sexologists have decried the unsavory element in the field. Leading sex professionals publicly excoriated what they termed "sexual quackery."[9] William Masters was quoted frequently as saying, "The current field of sexual therapy is dominated by an astounding assortment of incompetents, cultists, mystics, well-meaning dabblers, and outright charlatans."[10] A banner headline warned: "Most Sex Therapy Clinics are Frauds! Dr. William H. Masters of Masters and Johnson says fewer than 1 in 700 can be considered legitimate—and tells how you can protect your patients against the 'charlatans' in the field."[11] Masters and Johnson in fact spearheaded the effort at professional regulation. For Masters, the central dilemma was that he and Virginia Johnson had pioneered a new area of medicine that held out hope to a "deluge of patients" who were now demanding help.[12] In his estimation, the field was so new that there were not enough competent professionals to meet the demand, and thus clients were prey to charlatans. This situation was also a concern for AASECT, which warned of two dangers inherent in the proliferation of sex practitioners whom it viewed as unorthodox. One was the potential harm to clients; the second was bad publicity for "legitimate therapists who tend to get blamed and restricted for some of the not too ethical practices of the poorly trained people."[13] In short, the quacks gave the legitimate professionals a bad reputation.

Subsequently, AASECT decided to become the regulatory arm of sexology. In 1972 the organization formed the Committee on Training and Standards, which issued guidelines detailing the contours of appropriate sex therapy and outlining the credentials of those qualified to practice. A year later, a committee was formed to certify sex professionals. In 1975 AASECT began certification procedures for the categories of sex educator, sex therapist, and sex counselor. In addition, a code of ethics was issued that attempted to specify professional standards of conduct. Along with Masters, AASECT was the most visible gatekeeper of the field. Its purveyed standards were set in the Masters and Johnson mold: sexology would aspire to rigorous scientific credibility, and practitioners would be appropriately credentialed. AASECT requirements for certification as a sex therapist, for example, included at least a master's degree, and preferably a medical degree or doctorate. Similarly, Masters noted that sex clinics must "offer treatment methods that have been developed with proper scientific care; have been subjected to long, conscientious testing and evaluation; and are administered by trained, fully competent personnel."[14]

The prime movers who were attempting to define sexology believed that, ideally, it should resemble medical science. Masters frequently compared the confusion within sexology to medicine's historical struggle over regulation and specialization:

> Back in 1910, most branches of medicine were in about the same state as sexual therapy is now. There was a chaotic lack of standards. It took a lot of time and a lot of struggle, but today most branches are fairly firmly regulated by both laws and self-imposed ethics. You are reasonably safe in assuming that a man who calls himself "M.D." really is one, and that the degree means he went through a specific amount of training. The same is true of specialist titles such as "gynecologist" or "ophthalmologist." One day, perhaps, it will also be true of "sex therapist."[15]

Medicine thus provided the model of how a profession could and should develop. Masters was concerned with more than the protection of patients from unethical or untrained practitioners. Grounded in scientific sexology, he was committed to the cultural mythology that idealized science and medicine. Attacking clinics that "offer unevaluated theories, mystical cant, pop-psychology remedies, and simplistic pseudoscience,"[16] he moved to discredit sex practitioners other than those from a strict scientific or medical discipline. Sexology was struggling to be a "real" science, since sex professionals had been afforded a certain legitimacy by the public acceptance of Masters and Johnson's research. Operating in a public field that clearly had a ready market for its services, many sexologists believed that they could maintain that legitimacy only by emphasizing a commitment to science and medicine.

The attempts at regulation and control, however, have raised controversy. Over the course of the decade, as we shall see, some sexologists challenged this agenda for professionalization. Despite increasing pressures for internal coherence, sexology is not a monolithic discipline. Sexual issues and concerns fall within the purview of many types of practitioners from very divergent backgrounds. The contemporary history of sexology reflects the tensions of a field trying to accommodate varied and sometimes antagonistic groups under a common banner.

In the midst of the professional chaos of the late 1960s and early 1970s, a cohort of sexologists with a distinct philosophy and technique can be identified. I have chosen to identify them as humanistic sexologists because of their clear methodological connection to the humanistic psychology movement. These practitioners provided a counterpoint to the scientific rationality embodied by the more prominent sex researchers. Their methods emerged from the social and political influences of the era, as well as in response to a rigid scientism that focused more on the mechanics of sexual functioning than on the possibilities of sexual pleasure. Throughout the decade, humanistic sexology challenged and acted as a vocal alternative to the hegemony of scientific methods within the field.

The emergence of feminism and the lesbian/gay liberation movement in the late 1960s brought new points of view to the major issues within the purview of sexology: sex, marriage, family, and gender roles. These movements politicized issues of sexuality and gender, sometimes appropriating the data of scientific sexologists to underscore a political position. Both posed a major challenge to both the market and the authority of sexologists. By presenting the options of an alternative world view and an alternative way of living, they represented resistance to expert control over sexual definitions and behavior.

By the end of the decade, scientific sexology faced attacks from within and without. This section will explore the emergence of humanistic sexologists, and will chart the rise of sociopolitical movements that questioned and sometimes opposed both schools of sexology.

Chapter Three

The Humanistic Theme in Sexology

> Perhaps the whole
> process of becoming
> emotionally open
> and intimate would
> be hastened and
> intensified by nudity.
>
> PAUL BINDRIM
> *humanistic therapist*

By the late 1960s, new sexological practitioners were radically departing from the scientific rationality of the Masters and Johnson model.
Their philosophy and methods, evolved from a different tradition, have
triggered some of the core conflicts within the field about the proper
constitution of sexology. These tensions usually coalesce around issues
of appropriate content and techniques, as well as the code of ethics for
the field. The designations "scientific" and "humanistic" sexology require the caveat that accompanies any delineation of ideal types, but they
are conceptually useful in understanding, and tracing the roots of, one
distinct source of tension within the profession. As with any typology,
when the extremes are in focus, the rest of the picture may be blurred.
While I draw out the distinctions between humanistic and scientific sex-

ology in this chapter, I also explore the ways in which the two cohorts compete as well as overlap with and accommodate each other.

To some extent, humanistic sexology was a logical reaction to the dry, empirical approach to sexuality. Humanistic sexologists focus on the promotion of sexual enhancement and fulfillment. In this cause, their techniques are as varied as individual and couple sex therapy, sexual enhancement and therapy groups, Sexual Attitude Re-assessment workshops (SARs), massage and bioenergetic bodywork, and marathon sessions (nude and otherwise). Since their emphasis is on feelings, various experiential exercises are utilized to assist individuals in discovering and exploring their emotional responses to sexual activities. Humanistic sexologists draw on the research and techniques of the orthodox sexologists but frequently modify them to downplay their quantification or their more mechanistic aspects. In contrast to the scientific sexologists such as Masters and Johnson, who lionize data, graphs, and statistics, humanistic sexologists are often suspicious of an emphasis on facts and view it as a defense against "getting in touch" with one's "visceral clutch" about sex.

The humanistic branch of sexology is represented in part by the National Sex Forum, established in California in 1968. The founders coined what could be the slogan of humanistic sexology as a whole: "We believe that it is time to say 'yes' to sex."[1] Ideologically, humanistic sexologists tend to be strongly liberal, espousing a do-your-own-thing sexuality. In the NSF's words:

> Sexuality is the most individualistic part of a person's life. It is up to each individual to determine and then to assume responsibility for her or his own sexuality. All of the varying modes of expression are available to everyone. As long as people know what they are doing, feel good about it, and don't harm others, anything goes.[2]

At the AASECT conference in 1978, when Virginia Johnson complained that "up until now there has been an underlying orgy atmosphere at these kinds of meetings,"[3] she was referring to the sexually free style of the humanistic sexologists. Particularly in the 1970s and early 1980s, this caused tension whenever sexologists convened. The "anything goes" philosophy of humanistic sexologists is often experienced by the orthodox as unscientific and a danger to the profession. Johnson criticized a conference in Montreal where "many of those who attended insisted on demonstrating their own lifestyles and invited the media to observe orgies. It made everyone in the field aware of how vulnerable we are."[4] If, in fact, orgies occurred at these conferences, they were a logical outcome of the individualistic pursuit of sexual pleasure espoused by this branch of sexology.

Humanistic sexology must be understood, however, not merely as a reaction to the dominant scientific tenor of the field, but as a methodology with its own history. It is no coincidence that these practitioners emerged in the countercultural moment of the late 1960s. The ideologies and techniques apparent in humanistic sexology were achieving cultural prominence in other contexts as well. Rebellion was not simply the province of youth; certain professions were marked by disruption and internal dissent. Both psychology and medicine, from which sexology draws heavily, were experiencing challenges to dominant theory and clinical practice. An impulse toward wellness and wholeness rather than an emphasis on sickness and dysfunction characterized the movements of humanistic psychology and holistic healing. The group that I am calling humanistic sexologists were simply practitioners who adopted the philosophies and therapeutic innovations that were emerging from an amalgam of alternative traditions within the American counterculture.

From Reich to Esalen: The Roots of Humanistic Sexology

H istorically, this group of sex professionals is rooted in humanistic psychology and, more specifically, in the human potential movement, which emerged in the 1960s. Yet it is important to distinguish between the two. The occasional silliness and excess of the human potential movement, while not unrelated to the theory and methods of humanistic psychology, must be understood within the broader context of experimentation and therapeutic adventurism of the counterculture.

From its earliest days, the concept of humanistic psychology involved rebellion on two fronts. First, humanism was a challenge to the dominant traditions within psychology. Called the "Third Force," humanistic psychology was posed as an alternative to both Freudianism and behaviorism, the preeminent traditions within the field, which, along with structuralism and functionalism, dominated psychology through the middle of the twentieth century. Behaviorism, which was epistemologically grounded in logical positivism, claimed that empiricism and the physical sciences were the only valid models for the pursuit of knowledge about individuals and society. Some of the earliest humanistic psychologists, such as Abraham Maslow, Carl Rogers, and Gordon Allport, rejected positivism and attempted to insert a more holistic model of the individual as a conscious agent. A person's actions, they believed, were not simple responses to stimuli, but a composite of physical, psychological, and social factors. Humanistic psychology did not reject science, but envisioned a more humane science that focused on wellness, wholeness, self-actualization, and the integrity of the individual. The movement sought to introduce into psychology certain philosophical traditions, such as existentialism, as a counter to mechanistic theories of the mind that emerged from a reliance on models from the physical sciences.[5]

The founders of the Association of Humanistic Psychology in 1962 sought to articulate the vision of this new orientation. The charter statement called for:

> a focus on experience as the primary phenomenon in the study of man. Both theoretical explanations and overt behavior are considered secondary to experience itself and to its meaning to the person . . . an emphasis on such distinctively human qualities as choice, creativity, valuation, and self-realization, as opposed to thinking about human beings in mechanistic and reductionistic terms . . . and an opposition to a primary emphasis on objectivity at the expense of significance.[6]

In its celebration of hope, creativity, and transcendence in the human experience, humanistic psychology was more than a reaction against a stultifying social science. The movement marked a growing undercurrent of rebellion in American society, characterized by disillusionment triggered by two world wars, fear of nuclear destruction, a critique of suburban life and the "organization man," and anxiety over poverty and racial strife.[7] Humanistic psychology inhabited the same cultural landscape as "the Beats," the ban-the-bomb movement, and civil rights protests.

The exponential increase in social unrest in the 1960s, sparked largely by the anti–Vietnam War and civil rights movements, spawned a counterculture receptive to the vision of humanistic psychology. The quest to expand human potentialities and change cultural consciousness was pursued most zealously by proponents of what was dubbed the "human potential movement." Drawing on the philosophy of humanistic psychology, the human potential movement was an amalgam of theoretical and methodological avenues for individual expansion and self-awareness. It was axiomatic in the early days of the movement that the average person generally functions at less than 10 percent of capacity.[8] The task at hand was to explore and achieve one's full potential. This was to be achieved through such techniques as encounter groups, sensory awareness enhancement, meditation, bioenergetics, and bodywork massage. These methods drew on the work of practitioners such as Fritz Perls, J. L. Moreno, Alexander Lowen, Ida Rolf, and Charlotte Selver, many of whom were German and Viennese immigrants. In terms of the integration of the body, emotions, and sexuality, the theoretical and clinical work of the sexologist Wilhelm Reich had a particularly profound influence on the movement, and on many practitioners of humanistic sexology as well.

Reich formulated his theory of orgastic potency, which he differentiated from simple sexual climax, in the early 1920s. In orgastic potency, the sexual experience results in both voluntary and involuntary contractions of the entire body musculature. Sexual gratification comes from "a flowing back of the excitation from the genital to the body. This flowing back is experienced as a sudden decrease of the tension. . . . The excitation tapers off and is immediately replaced by a pleasant bodily and psychic relaxation. . . . What continues is a grateful, tender attitude toward the partner."[9] Reich believed the attainment of orgastic potency was rare, yet, significantly, he linked its achievement with broader sociopolitical changes. While other sex reformers recommended privacy for improving their clients' sex lives, Reich realized that this was pointless unless public policy was changed to ensure adequate housing for all. In the late 1920s he took his sex information and his political opinions to the streets, driving his van to mostly working-class sections of Vienna, where he and some colleagues did counseling and dispensed contraceptives. His "sex-pol" movement aimed to help the public with their sex problems and simultaneously to locate issues of sex and love within the framework of a larger revolutionary movement.[10]

In the 1940s Reich, now a political refugee, was working at his Orgone Institute in Maine. His writings about the dangers of sexual repression and the healing power of the orgasm struck a responsive chord in Big Sur, California, which was already developing a reputation as a haven for bohemians and those exploring alternative lifestyles. The Esalen Institute at Big Sur would at one time or another attract most of the luminaries of the human potential movement. In 1947 "The New Cult of Sex and Anarchy" described for readers of *Harper's* the religious mysticism with a focus on sexuality that characterized the philosophy of many of the Big Sur bohemians. Its author, Mildred Edie Brady, also reported on the influence that Reich exerted on this group. Since his psychological theory and sexual philosophy were vital to the emerging philosophy, his works were standard reading. In addition, many of the leading figures in what would be known in the 1960s as the human potential movement, were students of Reich's. Many were immigrants like him.

Reich's critiques of key aspects of contemporary society made him mentor and kindred spirit to those in the emerging human potential movement. During the country's love affair with science and medicine in the 1940s and 1950s, Reich had warned of the danger of relying on pills, chemicals, and technology. He was a critic of what he considered economic and political collusion among the medical establishment, pharmaceutical companies, and federal regulatory agencies. Yet it was his innovations in psychotherapy that most attracted countercultural followers. His notion of a universal life energy that was blocked by a repressive society was consonant with the new humanistic psychological theory. Reichian therapy emphasized that feelings must be experienced and released from the body rather than merely discussed and analyzed in the traditional therapeutic setting. Massage of the deep musculature was essential to letting go of old blocks and achieving cure. Reichian bodywork techniques became a key element of human potential therapies. As we shall see, his theories on sexuality were also integral to later techniques of humanistic sexology.

Ironically, Reich's influence on the Big Sur community played a role in his eventual imprisonment. Mildred Brady, who had explored Reich's influence in her earlier *Harper's* piece, wrote another article entitled "The Strange Case of Wilhelm Reich." Published in the *New Republic* in 1947, the subheading read: "The man who blames both neuroses and cancer on unsatisfactory sexual activities has been repudiated by only one scientific journal." In an article rife with errors and distortions, Brady implied that Reich was a charlatan, and she called on the profession of psychoanalysis to police itself and curb "the growing Reich cult" before it was "disciplined by the state."[11] Brady's article alerted the Food and Drug Administration. Reich, given the radical and iconoclastic nature of his work, was vulnerable to attack. The federal government eventually destroyed his inventions, burned his books, and imprisoned him. Yet Reichian theory continued to be a common thread binding the early experiments in alternative lifestyles at Big Sur in the 1940s, the Beat Generation in the 1950s, and the hippies and counterculture of the 1960s. The Esalen branch in San Francisco acknowledged the debt to Reich by sponsoring a conference on him and his work in 1974.[12]

In the early 1960s, Esalen's extensive program combined mysticism, philosophy, and therapy.[13] Three "personal-development commodities" identified with the institute (though now scattered through the American landscape) are encounter groups, gestalt therapy, and bodywork. Typically regarded as phenomena of the 1960s, all of these techniques have origins in Europe in the 1920s. Many of the therapists and practitioners who came to Esalen to teach were immigrants who had fled from the Nazis. Los Angeles in the 1960s was dubbed "the Vienna of group therapies." Fritz Perls, one of the luminaries of the Esalen era, was a patient and student of Reich's who immigrated from Germany and later founded gestalt therapy: an integration of existentialism, gestalt psychology, holistic philosophy, Reichian armor theory, and Eastern religion. The basic philosophy of gestalt therapy posited that "a human being can be understood only as a whole and within his or her actual environment; neurosis consists in being out of touch with one's own feelings and sensory experience; and therapy is the recovery of awareness."[14]

Bodywork and sensory awareness exercises were also highlights of Esalen. Charlotte Selver, an immigrant who pioneered in sensory awareness work, practiced at Big Sur. She taught her techniques to a number of psychiatrists and other students, including Fritz Perls, Erich Fromm, and Perls's student Bernard Gunther, who also studied yoga and massage. Gunther eventually became a leading practitioner of sensory and body awareness exercises, and wrote several books on these techniques, including *Sense Relaxation: Below Your Mind* and *What to Do Till the Messiah Comes*.

It was perhaps encounter groups that made Esalen notorious. Pioneered by a social psychologist, William Schutz, encounter groups integrated such techniques as psychodrama, group therapy, and bioenergetics, which was a body-focused therapy developed by another student of Reich's, Alexander Lowen. Encounter groups were not so much a form of therapy as a way to promote "personal growth." The leader, or "facilitator," introduced various "exercises" designed to elicit certain emotional responses. These included trust exercises, massage and body-oriented interventions, and verbal confrontations. Schutz believed that encounter groups would facilitate "openness and honesty, a willingness to take personal risks and accept responsibility for one's acts, a deeper capacity for feeling and expressing emotions, greater freedom from false morality, an enhanced sense of the body."[15] For the human potential movement's amalgam of gestalt therapists, Jungians, Adlerians, and neo-Freudians, the goal was expanded consciousness, and the vehicle was "experiential" exercises. The focus was on knowing-by-doing, a rebellion against the positivist rationality embodied in scientific and academic thought.

This dichotomy between intellect and emotion was fundamental to the movement and surfaces later in humanistic sexology. At Esalen, the intellect was downplayed. Walter Truett Anderson writes: "It was becoming unacceptable to think or analyze without having experienced. It was all right, however, to experience without thinking or analyzing; frequently you would be asked to do precisely that."[16] Anti-intellectualism was widespread in encounter groups, as participants were encouraged to connect with "gut-level feelings." Abstraction and thinking were denigrated as distractions from—or, worse, denials of—emotions.

Implicit at Esalen was the "permission" to experiment and experience. There was a focus on the Self—one's mind and body—and all

enterprises that aided self-exploration and enhancement were encouraged. As an Esalen participant noted, "This attitude converted rather
easily into an operational assumption that you could do whatever you
could get away with."[17] The norm of permissiveness would evolve
into the encouragement to take risks, and, ultimately, into "the smiling
tyranny"—pressure to participate and take risks in the experiential exercises.

Esalen became a symbol of a countercultural vision—a revolution
in consciousness. An individualistic bias was central to the movement.
Abraham Maslow, who in 1954 helped lay the intellectual foundations
for the human potential movement with his book *Motivation and Person-*
ality, redefined the ideal of psychological health from the individual who
was "well-adjusted" to one who was "self-actualized."[18] The promise of
transformation and self-actualization was a challenge to the model of
social conformity so characteristic of the 1950s. There was much that was
liberating about this emphasis on the autonomous individual. A similar emphasis is, for example, a philosophical basis for feminist demands
for self-determination.[19] In terms of change and vision, humanistic psychology and the human potential movement represented a liberating
alternative to the stultifying tradition of early psychoanalysis, and from
the one-dimensionality of behaviorism. It offered the hope of health,
wholeness, and the integrity of the individual.

The very concepts of humanistic psychology and the human potential movement were radical gestures in the historical context of the 1950s
and 1960s. The will to individual transformation was congruent with
the demands for social change asserted by the civil rights and antiwar movements. Yet despite its early goal of broadening psychological
theory, the ultimate shortcoming of the human potential movement was
its almost obsessive focus on the individual to the exclusion of the social
environment. Maslow, for example, failed to locate his self-actualizing
person within the family, educational system, or workplace. He created, as Robert Sipe notes, "an abstract individual in an equally abstract
society, both void of race, class, and sex considerations."[20] Without a
political analysis, the potentially radical gesture of self-actualization and
individualism could readily devolve into myopic indulgence and the
exploitation of those with less power.

Criticized for its apolitical orientation, Esalen sporadically attempted to sponsor programs with more of a political focus, but these attempts were largely unsuccessful. Anderson writes that, moving into the 1970s, "the personal-growth therapies flourished, the political activists went their own way, learning to speak with disdain of 'growth trips,' and the press began to talk of narcissism and the Me decade—putting Esalen at the forefront of what was taken to be the 1970s' retreat from political commitment into sterile self-love."[21] By the early 1970s the Esalen-style growth centers, and a larger cultural ethos extolling therapeutic liberation, had spread throughout the country. New and revised therapy trends flourished, such as EST, Arica, primal scream, transactional analysis, and transpersonal integration—all designed to effect individual transformation. Esalen's emphasis on experiential techniques and the celebration of feeling over intellect was maintained.

No Esalen program focused explicitly on sexuality, but Esalen techniques developed to enhance growth and closeness in relationships frequently involved physical touching and sexual experiences.[22] As the Esalen philosophy and methods permeated the culture, they influenced professionals who were working in the field of sexology. In addition, some Esalen-style practitioners shifted their therapeutic focus to issues of sexuality. The influence of the human potential movement became evident within the field of sexology. In its quest for sexual fulfillment, its emphasis on feeling above intellect, and its use of experiential techniques such as encounter groups, massage, bodywork and sensory awareness, humanistic sexology is the Esalen of the profession of sex.

The Practice of Humanistic Sexology

The demarcation between the medical, scientific sexologists and the humanistic sexologists is not absolute—there is overlap and sharing of goals and techniques. Both espouse a very positive philosophy about sex and hold the enhancement of sexual functioning as a major therapeutic enterprise. Both groups occupy considerable space within sexology. Having emerged from different theoretical traditions, however, their emphases are different, and so are their judgments about what appropriately defines the field.

On one end of the continuum are scientific sexologists, who focus on rigorous empirical research, quantification, and experimentation. Their clinical techniques evolve from voluminous physiological and psychological data. The trappings of medicine and science abound and are manifest in dense, complex textbooks, replete with charts, graphs, and anatomical drawings. It seems almost accidental that the topic of their research concerns one of the most volatile and intimate issues of daily life—sex. There is an unswerving focus on the primacy of studying sex as a science. The application of the intellect and the tools of science and medicine to the area of sexuality is seen as the ultimate route to designing effective sexuality enhancement programs. These sexologists rely heavily on the validity of rigorous, empirical scientific investigation to legitimate the study of sex.

Conversely, the branch of sexology with its roots in the human potential movement and Esalen-like techniques is characterized by its emphasis on the experiential. Humanistic sexologists rely on human experience as the foundation of their practices. Information and the intellect are secondary to the goal of getting in touch with one's feelings. In groups, marathons, and couple treatment, experiential exercises are designed to confront people with their sexual feelings, fears, and desires. As at Esalen, it is a damning criticism to call a program or a person's therapy participation "too heady." When humanistic sexologists want to impart information, they attempt to embed it in an experiential exercise, since they believe that people will more readily grasp and integrate it. They justify their work not by statistics, but by whether people report feeling better. Their publications are written in an easy, accessible style, and drawings tend to be visually aesthetic rather than anatomically accurate. When they use a clinical technique developed by scientific sexologists, they attempt to mitigate what they consider to be its mechanistic aspects.

The goal of humanistic sexology is less an empirical understanding of sexuality than the enhancement of sexual functioning. The route to sexual enhancement is primarily allowing oneself to feel good about sex, both emotionally and physically. Their sex therapy or sexual enhancement programs include the use of experiential exercises, neo-Reichian techniques, bioenergetics, and massage. Nudity during group therapy sessions, a therapeutic innovation heralded by Abraham Maslow, is often accepted or encouraged. Some exercises have clear roots in Esalen programs, but with an explicit sexual emphasis. Guided fantasies are often used, but with a sexual theme. Bodywork exercises in the Selver, Gunther, and Lowen tradition are employed, but with an emphasis on the genitalia and improved sexual response. Sensory awareness exercises are used, with a focus on sexual feelings. Erotic films are shown, and then participants discuss their emotional responses in small encounter-like groups.

Humanistic sexology combines complex and paradoxical tendencies. The diffusion of humanistic techniques throughout sexology brought some advances. Like humanistic psychology, humanistic sexology posed a challenge to rigid empiricism in theories and clinical practice related to human functioning. Its deemphasis of science was a much needed corrective to the field's narrow focus on the biomechanics of sexuality. Information and texts were much more accessible. Experiential techniques could be a refreshing and useful addition. The humanistic sexologists introduced the simple notion of sexual pleasure, which was often so obfuscated by the scientists.

Humanistic sexology, then, represents an impulse toward openness, flexibility, and experimentation in the understanding of human sexual behavior. Drawing as it does on the methods developed by practitioners in the "growth centers" of the counterculture, however, it is also vulnerable to the excesses of that practice. And, at its extreme, humanistic sexology can exemplify some of the worst aspects of the human potential movement. Esoteric and symbolic technique can mask superficiality and incompetence. The focus on experience and risk taking can be used to coerce participation in nudity, group sex, or sexual relations with the therapist. The balms, massages, and symbols employed in the individualistic pursuit of fulfillment can substitute for a more cogent analysis of structural or material barriers to sexual pleasure. At its most innocuous, the liberal tolerance embodied by humanistic sexology implies merely the freedom to have more orgasms. At its most insidious, it represents a tolerance of sexism and heterosexist imperatives in the pursuit of those orgasms.

The Institute for Advanced Study of Human Sexuality has played a vital role in the development of humanistic sexology and represents some of these conflicts within the movement. Directed by Ted McIlvenna, a minister of the United Methodist Church, the Institute evolved from the National Sex Forum, which was begun in 1968 as a service of San Francisco's Methodist-oriented Glide Foundation. The staff of the Glide Foundation, originally committed to work in the gay community, realized that their work was complicated by the general lack of understanding of human sexuality among religious and social service professionals. Glide, and later the NSF, developed training programs on sexuality and expanded into the Institute for Advanced Study of Human Sexuality, which was formally incorporated as a graduate program in 1976. Since its inception, it has provided academic training in sexology and serves as a clearinghouse for sexual information. The Institute produces educational materials, such as sexually explicit films and sourcebooks on acquired immune deficiency syndrome (AIDS), and it houses a vast collection of archival material. In true humanistic fashion, training at the Institute comprises formal, academic-style lectures, videotapes, and a program of ten different bodywork techniques.[23] Its students are extensively trained in a range of sexual information, and they are active participants in some of the professional sexology associations, such as the SSSS.

It is the bodywork training, some of which occurs in hot tubs, that has given the Institute its somewhat controversial reputation. Critics have sarcastically dubbed it "Hot Tub University," or "Fuck U."[24] Nudity is encouraged, and the bodywork consists of various types of erotic massage, self-examinations both individually and in groups, and self-stimulation.[25] In trust exercises conducted in the hot tub, a group of individuals will support one another in floating. And, in a body image exercise, students are expected to disrobe in class, stand in front of a mirror, and discuss their feelings about their bodies.[26] Instructors insist that no one is forced to participate in activities with which they are uncomfortable.[27] There is a free-wheeling atmosphere at the Institute. No rules prohibit sexual interaction among program participants, as long as they do not have sex in the building.[28] As McIlvenna notes, "We have only one rule here—that you couldn't solicit in front of the building to raise your tuition."[29]

Reichian therapy is another strand in humanistic sexology. Humanistic sexologists who employ Reichian techniques resonate most with his theory of libidinal life energy. Reich posited a deep, universal sexual energy, which, when blocked, results in sickness, emotional problems, and a repressive society. This notion is congruent with humanistic thought, which seeks to liberate a repressed human potential. Some sex therapists have integrated Reich's concepts about sexuality, orgasm, and the "genital character" into their practices.[30] This practice falls outside the parameters of traditional, biomedically based sex therapy. Its goal is not simply more and better orgasms, but the achievement of what Reich termed "orgastic potency" and the genital character—the quality of being emotionally unblocked. Sex therapists working in the Reichian tradition question the uncritical pursuit of orgasms, when such climaxes are defined solely as the ejaculation and contraction of physiological release. Orgastic potency, according to Reich, was not simply release, but an emotional state that was connected to the individual's mental health and the quality of the relationship. Emotional health in the Reichian sense results from a full discharge of sexual excitation at orgasm, which "provides the sensation of 'satisfaction' and prevents neurosis by withdrawing all sources of energy for neurotic fixations."[31] Reichian sex therapists have adopted the theory and clinical techniques of the early sexologist, but they have ignored his insistence that sexual freedom is integrally connected with social change. There is no attempt by these practitioners to organize, as Reich did, a movement for broader sexual and political liberation.

Other major figures representative of humanistic sexology are William Hartman and Marilyn Fithian, often called "Masters and Johnson West." Now semiretired, Hartman and Fithian are the founders of the Center for Marital and Sexual Studies in Long Beach, California. Both taught at California State University, where Hartman was a professor of sociology, and Fithian an instructor in comparative literature. Their book, *Treatment of Sexual Dysfunction*, was self-published in 1972. Practicing together since 1964, Hartman and Fithian had two major research projects: social nudism and nonorgasmic women. During their work with nonorgasmic women, they began observations of intercourse. Although they do not describe the research, they report having made 1,264 observations of intercourse. In contrast to the minutiae supplied by Masters and Johnson, Hartman and Fithian provide no demographic information about the research population, no description of their methodology, and no evaluation of their program. The "Results" section of their book consists of one paragraph, which reads, in part:

> We are loath to report statistical "success rates." We are not interested in developing a numbers game where centers such as ours will enter into a kind of spurious competition based on numbers. . . . We can report, and we can honestly assure candidates for therapy, that at the time of follow-up, couples who have completed our two-week program describe the benefits achieved in approximately the same proportions as are reported by Masters and Johnson.[32]

The dismissal of attempts at scientific verification in favor of earnest hope for a cure permits the reconstruction of therapy programs to suit the therapists' predilections. Hartman and Fithian's two-week sex therapy program borrows from the work of Masters and Johnson, with some important differences. Hartman and Fithian also employ psychological screening tests and conduct a sex history, for example, but their screening procedure includes the pop Luscher Color Test along with the traditional Minnesota Multiphasic Personality Inventory. Their sex history covers many of the basic topics explored by Masters and Johnson, as well as areas such as astrological sign, pleasant and unpleasant odors, and attitude toward music, motorcycles, and airplanes.[33]

Most of the two-week program consists of experiential exercises such as guided fantasies, body imagery exercises, massage, and viewing erotic films. In a major divergence from Masters and Johnson's practice, most of the sexual exercises are done in the presence of the therapists. In sessions, clients are taught how to perform certain sexual techniques and caresses, and then they practice them with the therapists. Hartman and Fithian write:

> An important aspect of our work during the caressing activities is in giving permission to experiment by suggesting quietly that the giver try nibbling on the partner's ear, big toe or whatever seems to be indicated at the moment, suggesting that the giver may want to try some things in our presence where

we can ask for feedback. . . . The last phase of sexual caress is for the male to use his index finger and the emollient oil to massage the female vagina. . . . Conclusion of the sexual caress of the male involves the female putting lotion on her breasts and caressing the male from his collarbone down to and including his genitalia using only her breasts. This gives the therapists definite clues as to how the female moves in the female superior control position.[34]

In addition to observing the sexual activities of their clients, Hartman and Fithian themselves engage in touch with clients. This, in fact, is a major rationale for their use of a dual-sex team:

Touch between clients and therapists can take place much more readily and comfortably in such a situation [when both sexes are present]. Touch is the most effective method we have found to get feelings flowing. Superficial touch from one or both professionals in a responsible professional situation is often necessary to get therapeutic clients comfortable with touching.[35]

Hartman and Fithian routinely touch clients in bodywork, massage exercises, and group hugs. They also sexually stimulate women clients in that stage of their therapy program that they call the sexological examination, "checking for sexual response."[36] Both therapists stimulate the woman's clitoris and vagina to see if she lubricates or has nipple erections and other physical signs of sexual excitement. In their text, Hartman and Fithian are less specific about the male sexological examination, which appears to consist mainly of visual examination of the penis and a brief physical inspection. They later implemented an examination of the elevation of the testicles and the responsiveness of the penis, which was accomplished by the therapist's running a fingernail down the patient's inner thigh and applying a wet swab to areas such as the abdomen and the head of the penis to check for reflex changes. On occasion, this would result in erection of the penis.[37]

In the 1970s, Hartman and Fithian implemented a weekend marathon counseling session for sexually dysfunctional couples. In this "desert retreat," a couple traveled with Hartman and Fithian to a trailer park in the desert of Southern California and underwent a treatment program consisting of massage, hypnosis, soaks in hot tubs, and instruction in sexual techniques. The program was rife with symbolism and mysticism:

En route to the desert a carefully arranged stop was made at Hadley's Fruit Ranch and Orchard in Cabazon. . . . Symbolically speaking, the wide variety of dates, nuts and figs were reminiscent of early sexual symbols, and with a background of one of the counselors in mythology, sex can be openly and freely discussed in the context of the situation. At the store each individual is asked to choose a package of fresh nuts or fruits which they regarded as their favorite and from which they received the greatest enjoyment. We found that these favorites eaten at a later time brought back a recurring and positive feeling about the desert experience as well as enhancing the enjoyment of the marathon itself. . . . Some of the couples were taken up the world's largest tramway in aerial cars. The experience of up and over symbolically suggested to the non-orgasmic female that with increased warmth of body and emotional feeling in an environment of complete relaxation she would be closer to "shooting the moon" than had ever previously been true. This was reinforced through post-hypnotic suggestion.[38]

The Hartman and Fithian program is not a Southern California anomaly. The therapists have been training dual-sex therapy teams in an eight-hour program since 1972. And although they see few clients now, they still conduct professional training. No sexological certifications carry the legitimacy of state licensing, but Hartman and Fithian confer diplomas that certify the recipient's status as a sex therapist on psychologists, doctors, ministers, and other professionals.[39] The Hartman and Fithian sex therapy techniques have spread throughout the country, although access to the world's largest tramway remains limited to Southern California.

Hartman and Fithian's program is based on a rather loose approximation of scientific research that they attempt to legitimate by credential dropping. They report throughout their book that professionals from various disciplines have either requested training from them or served as research associates:

> Along with our clinical program, we have on-going laboratory research which contributes to more effective methods of treating sexual dysfunction. In several of these projects, we have worked in cooperation with other professionals coming from the disciplines of psychology and medicine with specialties in neurology, obstetrics and gynecology, physiology, neuro-endocrinology, biochemistry, and sociology.[40]

Undoubtedly these therapists have worked with other scientists and practitioners. Hartman and Fithian have practiced and trained professionals for years and occupy an established niche within sexology. Yet the invocation of cooperative ventures with a myriad of scientists does little to mitigate the fundamental lack of published detail on their research methodology and outcome criteria. Hartman and Fithian represent a common tendency in the practice of humanistic sexology, an amalgam of quasi science, experiential and experimental technique, and mysticism.

Some aspects of humanistic sexology are anathema to the scientific sexologists. Since they believe that empirical, quantitative research undermines public hostility or mistrust, orthodox sexologists are unswerving in their commitment to the scientific method. They allude to sex professionals without adequate professional credentials as "charlatans" and "mystics." William Masters complained that in 1974, out of the plethora of existing sex therapy clinics, "only 50 out of a possible 5,000 offer treatment methods that have been developed with proper scientific care; have been subjected to long, conscientious testing and evaluation; and are administered by trained, fully competent personnel."[41] Although, again, the opposition of humanistic and scientific sexologists should not be understood as a mutually exclusive schema, some of the major conflicts within the profession can be understood through this conceptual lens.

Internal Conflicts Within Sexology: Lab Coats or Nudity?

Humanistic sexologists' emphasis on "touchy-feely" techniques is a threat to the scientific image constructed by medical sexologists. Equally threatening to the public perception of the field, however, are the use of nudity, surrogates, sex films, and touch between client and therapist. The field of sexology faces a dilemma that, to this date, remains unresolved. As a new field, it is in a stage of expansion and exploration. There is the challenge of developing new techniques and experimenting with different methods. The flip side, however, is that sexologists deal with a topic of intense taboo and cultural charge. Exploration on the boundaries of the hard sciences is fundamentally less suspect and prone to controversy than experimentation within the area of human sexuality. Orthodox sexologists adopt conservative techniques and eschew whatever may smack of immorality, such as nudity or the use of surrogates. A 1975 article in *Physician's World* in which Masters and Johnson attempted to educate doctors about incompetent sex therapists warned: "In the twilight zone of sex therapy there are organizations that offer programs of a nature that qualified therapists criticize and, in some instances, totally condemn. These range from nude encounter groups to demonstration sessions of actual intercourse to the use of so-called surrogate partners."[42]

Nudity, surrogates, and touch between therapist and client are areas of conflict between scientific and humanistic sexologists. Although ostensibly related to effectiveness, the struggle often reflects attempts by scientific sexologists to protect the field and avoid charges of exploitation. Masters and Johnson stopped using surrogates, not because of questions of effectiveness, but because of a lawsuit brought against them by a husband who claimed that his wife was working as a surrogate. After an interview with Masters and Johnson, Linda Wolfe stated that "they have never fully abandoned their support of the surrogate as a therapy approach that, when carefully utilized, is dramatically effective."[43] Issues of respectability take precedence over possible therapeutic efficiency, however, and most orthodox sex therapists do not use surrogates. One therapist commented, "I began to feel like a procurer, so I gave it up," while another said, "Even if we were using them, we wouldn't admit to it."[44] Surrogates are still in use, however, and some have organized a national surrogates' association.[45]

Even more than surrogacy, issues of nudity and touch between therapist and client have resulted in a major professional rift. Clients of helping professionals in general are vulnerable to exploitation because of power differentials. The issue of sex between therapist and client has been explosive within psychology, and such contact has been forbidden by both the American Psychiatric Association and the American Psychological Association. The problem is exacerbated, however, in sexology. In a field where the emphasis is on sex and on learning better sexual functioning, and where the observation of couples having sex has become a legitimate scientific method, a vast grey area surrounds acceptable therapy. From the perspective of many, the distinctions among observing sex, sex with a surrogate partner, and sex between therapist and client are abstract or spurious. Orthodox scientific sexology has attempted to draw lines by explicitly eschewing any nudity or sex in a therapeutic context, and by avoiding the use of surrogates. It is the white-lab-coat approach to sex therapy.

The philosophy of humanistic sexology, with its "anything goes" ambience, its emphasis on bigger and better sex, and its focus on feelings, opens the door to much greater confusion concerning ethics and the appropriateness of professional conduct. In a treatment group where nudity and touch are condoned, and risk taking is encouraged, sexual interaction among group members and/or between therapist and client certainly presents itself as a possibility. The Hartman and Fithian sexological examination, where the woman is sexually stimulated by the therapists, may fall short of intercourse, but it is certainly a sexual encounter between therapist and client. Peer pressure in groups or vulnerability to expert authority in individual therapy can coerce a patient to comply with the sexual demands of the situation. The techniques of humanistic sexology, such as nude groups, experiential exercises designed to engender sexual feelings, the use of bodywork and massage, and the viewing of explicit sex films, can evolve into sexually coercive situations—the "underlying orgy atmosphere" of which Virginia Johnson complained.

In a culture characterized by male dominance, it is women who are more vulnerable to sexual exploitation in these situations. In organizations where sex is the focus and the boundaries and limitations are not always clear, sexism and exploitation can masquerade as sexual liberation. In training programs, in particular, a subtle coercion can operate on two fronts: women students' wish to gain access to male power and expertise, and pressure on these students to demonstrate sexual ease and competence by participating in sexual activity within the program. Two examples illustrate this potential for exploitation.

The Institute for Advanced Study of Human Sexuality is probably no more sexist than any other institution. Yet the routinized nudity and explicit sexuality may well put greater pressure on women to engage in sexual activities in which they might otherwise be uninterested. Ted

McIlvenna acknowledges that some men have enrolled in the Institute primarily for sexual interactions:

> The "rub-a-dub-dubbers" caused us a lot of grief over the years, although we don't have that problem any more. Someone would come in and say, "Now I'm going to that sex school. Maybe I can get laid." Or get involved in genital massage and they wouldn't know what they were doing. . . . What we got was a lot of people coming in trying to work out their own sexual difficulties.[46]

Sex therapist and author Gina Ogden, who was a student at the Institute in the late 1970s, notes the dual nature of its liberal approach. She cites the creative use of video, the visiting faculty, and the experiential nature of the teaching: "There were enormous resources available in San Francisco at that time. There was a lightheartedness to it all—remember this was before the age of AIDS. The Institute was on the cutting edge of what was happening in human sexuality." But she also remembers the highly sexualized ambience of the training program and the exploitation of women: "There was a sexist bias in the preponderance of attention paid to male sex researchers. And there was the mating dance between classes: invitations for sex from students and male faculty members— under the guise of learning more about the subject, first hand."[47]

There was potential for exploitation even in a more controlled and traditional university setting. In the late 1970s, at the University of Massachusetts at Boston, several women were sexually abused at the Human Sexuality Center, which was run in the style of humanistic sexology. The Center employed work-study students to serve as peer-counselors and educators on sexuality to the university community. The students were trained by a sex therapist who had studied at both Esalen and the New York University Human Sexuality Program. His training techniques consisted largely of experiential exercises and massage. In 1979 fifteen of his women students filed formal complaints with both the university and the AASECT grievance committee alleging malpractice. The students complained that the sexologist abused his power both as their professor and as a male by coercing them into participating in sexual activities under the guise of sex education training. The complaints cited

seminude massages, group soaks in his home bathtub, sexually explicit
and harassing comments, and a phone call made to one woman by the
sexologist while he masturbated. Students who complained were told
that they would never succeed as sex educators if they could not open up
to him.[48] The complaint was dropped by the university when the therapist resigned, and the women filed a malpractice suit against him, which
was ultimately settled out of court. For several years afterward, however, the sexologist retained a position as a sex therapist at a prominent
sexological clinic in New England.

Divisions within the profession were highlighted by the case. While
it was pending, both the women students and the male sexologist obtained expert witnesses from within the field of sexology to testify on
their behalf. Ted McIlvenna of the Institute for Advanced Study of
Human Sexuality agreed to testify that the sexologist's techniques constituted acceptable sex education. Others believed, and were prepared
to testify, that the techniques were unethical. It is important to understand these professional differences not simply as conflicting opinions,
but as emblematic of the variances in belief systems and techniques of
humanistic and scientific sexologists.

Both cases illustrate the potential of training programs based on
humanistic sexological principles for crossing the line between liberation and exploitation, between creativity and coercion. Moreover, these
programs function in a larger context of sexual violence; the sexual
harassment of women, for example, is endemic at workplaces and in
universities throughout the country.[49] As we have seen, beyond the individual sexism of certain practitioners, features of the institutionalized
practice of humanistic sexology are conducive to sexual exploitation.
The fact that the content of the training itself comprises sexual issues
can blur the boundaries between professional goals and personal desires. When sex is the daily currency of instruction, the classroom can
appear limitless. The premium on sexual liberation inherent in the training philosophy, and trainees' desire to appear sexually uninhibited and
"hip" help foster a highly charged sexual atmosphere. This relaxed ambience can function as a welcome corrective to more mainstream sexual
repression. Yet often sexual liberation is unambivalently heralded as
the highest good, with little attention to gender differences and power

issues. The greater power that men and faculty exercise in charting the terms of sexual encounters is never discussed. Refusal of a sexual invitation is interpreted as rigidity or sexual meanspiritedness, charges of which no one wants to be guilty. An atmosphere of either subtle or explicit coercion is inevitable when sexuality is celebrated in the absence of a broader and more nuanced critique that acknowledges differences in sexual meaning and negotiation based on social factors such as gender, race, and sexual preference.

In part because of such complex and potentially explosive incidents, by the mid-1970s it was clear to many within the field that it was essential to establish some regulatory mechanisms to convince the public that sexology could police itself. AASECT began a certification procedure for three categories: sex educator, sex counselor, and sex therapist. For AASECT certification, one had to achieve a certain level of training and experience in the area of human sexuality. In addition, AASECT developed a code of ethics that forbids nudity (except in same-sex groups), sexological examinations, and any sexual contact between patient and therapist.

The AASECT attempts at regulation were controversial. No doubt because of their status as pioneers, Masters and Johnson were initially resistant to the idea that they needed certification (they eventually accepted AASECT's offer to certify them). Others, particularly humanistic sexologists from California, were opposed to what they perceived as the rigidity of the code of ethics. Disagreeing with the prohibitions on nudity and touch, they created both a new organization, The Association of Sexologists (TAOS), and a new certifying and accrediting body, the American College of Sexologists. Both resided at the address of the Institute for Advanced Study of Human Sexuality (TAOS no longer exists). McIlvenna and other instructors at the Institute expressed disdain for AASECT's regulatory efforts. "My feeling about AASECT is that they play this little game. . . . Most of them, we've found, don't know what they're doing. They know nothing really about sex."[50]

Despite such turf struggles, at times scientific and humanistic sexologists coexist tolerantly if uneasily. This is true in part because of the newness of the field and, hence, its lack of clarity and definition. In addition, these groups will form alliances when "sex experts" are attacked by the right wing, which does not discriminate between the various philosophies. This uneasy alliance is most glaringly evident at conferences, which are a curious melding of philosophies, content, and style. At the annual conference of the SSSS in 1981, a presentation entitled "Psychophysiological Methods in Sex Research" detailed new trends in physiological sex research and described the newest medical technology, such as devices that measure penile enlargement. In another room, a sex therapist presented a sample of her own clinical practice, which incorporated techniques from Reich, Lowen, and bioenergetics. She led the participants through a guided sex fantasy, then had them stand, rotate their hips, then snap their hips from back to front, aggressively saying "yes" with each frontward snap.[51] The patchwork of programs and lifestyles at sex conferences reflects the dilemma of contemporary sexology: how to consolidate and establish legitimacy as a profession, yet retain diversity and flexibility.

Another area of tenuous cooperation but implicit controversy is the use of explicit erotic films in the practice of sex education and therapy. The most ritualized structure for this practice is the SAR Workshop. The SAR process was developed in 1968 by the National Sex Forum, which wanted to develop a technique, grounded in humanistic sexology, that got people away from abstract analysis, confronted them with their feelings about sexuality, and gave them "permission to recognize and feel their own sexuality."[52] Thus, the SAR process, also called "Fuckarama" or "Sexarama," was invented.

The SAR format is a marathon. Participants gather in a room for twelve or more hours (some marathons last for two days) and watch explicit sex films. They usually sit on the floor on large, fluffy pillows, in the stereotypic marathon fashion, and are surrounded by screens. Often several films run simultaneously. Film topics include heterosexual intercourse, male and female masturbation, lesbian and gay male sex, and occasionally "paraphilia" (bestiality or sadomasochism). There are also short humorous films. After seeing films in a subject area (e.g., heterosexuality or masturbation), participants break into smaller groups to explore and compare their emotional responses. As in earlier encounter groups, participants at SARs are encouraged not to intellectualize by analyzing the film, but instead to find out which aspects of sexual behavior give them a "visceral clutch."

SAR workshops have spread across the country. They are implemented in medical schools and universities, and for various social service professionals. The summer training program at the Kinsey Institute contained a weekend SAR component, thus integrating scientific and humanistic sexology. For several years the Institute sponsored a two-week program wherein many of the leading figures in scientific sexology lectured throughout the day. The SAR was sandwiched between the two weeks of panels and lectures, and participants spent the weekend watching sex films and discussing their sexuality in small groups. In these discussions, participants were encouraged to be open and vulnerable, and there was an implicit mandate to take risks and be self-revealing.

Emerging as they do out of humanistic philosophy, the SAR workshops' acceptance is somewhat surprising. The holdouts are the pathbreakers of scientific sexology, Masters and Johnson. The *Boston Globe* reported their reaction to the SAR format: " 'We've never used a movie in our lives,' said Masters, with an edge of disdain in his voice. 'We don't use crutches of any kind,' says Johnson. 'We don't think they are necessary and we don't like to develop dependency.' " [53]

Other scientific sexologists, such as sex therapist Helen Singer Kaplan, think sex films have an appropriate function within sex therapy. Michael Carrera and Charon Lieberman, sexologists and health educators, state that part of the internal controversy surrounding the use of SAR centers on the context within which films are shown and the expertise of the group leader.[54] Perhaps SAR workshops have become acceptable to more orthodox sexologists because they have been able to restructure the format, deemphasize some of the more humanistic components, and "intellectualize" the process. A survey of eleven SARs in 1978 revealed that the original format had in fact been altered in many instances. Six SAR directors reported that body contact among participants occurred "seldom" or "sometimes," while five reported that it took place "often" or "very often." In nine programs nudity occurred "seldom" or "never," while in two programs it "sometimes" occurred.[55] Less than half emphasized attitude change as part of the program. In addition, the SAR format is sometimes altered by the directors so that, instead of a marathon time frame, the film presentations are shortened or shown in classes throughout a semester.[56] With such an overhaul, the SAR method can approximate the simple use of audiovisual aids—a technique that most scientists can appreciate. The major difference, of course, lies in the nature and content of these films, which are highly explicit.

The films used in SARs come from two major sources: "hard-core pornographic films from New York's 42nd Street, and specially designed explicit sexual films produced by the National Sex Forum . . . and EDCOA, an affiliate of Ormont Pharmaceuticals."[57] The demand for professional sex films created a new market for the drug companies and resulted in a surfeit of films with titles like *Sun Brushed* and *In Winter Light*, where sex is inevitably accompanied by chirping birds and running through the meadow. The SAR rationale is that there is a difference between explicitly erotic professional films and pornographic ones. According to Robert Francoeur, the professional films "convey a quite different view; instead of the leering, 'dirty sex,' exploitative, depersonalized, and mechanical clanking of genitals in 'Ping-Pong Orgy,' 'Western Lust,' and 'Helpful Handiman,' real persons relate in a warm, human way."[58] But the line between acceptable professional sex films and exploitative pornographic ones is often tenuous. The titles of some professional sex films available for SARs (e.g., *Flesh Flows, Boobs, Fast Ball*, and *Naughty Nurse*)[59] are indistinguishable from those Francoeur denigrates. Instead of being a radical departure from the pornography genre, the professional sex films also feature mechanistic sex between disembodied genitals.

Professional sex films generally reflect the market that sexology taps and the ideological agenda of sexology as a whole. The actors are typically young, white, heterosexual, middle-class, relationally stable, and sexually athletic. The sexual mythology constructed by the films mirrors the cultural ideal, not necessarily the cultural norm or the range of experience. "Sex" generally means heterosexual sex; anything else is separated into a distinct category. Traditional gender relations are reconstructed: males dominate by being more active, setting the pace, and initiating more of the action. Women are sexually responsive and eager, but essentially conform to male demands.[60] The film shown most frequently to depict sex and aging features an affluent white couple in their sixties, with firm bodies and attractive faces, having enthusiastic sex and frequent orgasms on their futon mattress and at other locations throughout the house.

While use of professional sex films is widespread in sexology, some criticism persists. One sex therapist, Bernie Apfelbaum, claims that these films represent a denial of the sexual reality most people know.[61] They do not reassure clients in therapy, he states, since people in sex films rarely have problems or have problems that are easily resolved. In particular, Apfelbaum criticizes a Hartman and Fithian production entitled *Ideal Sexual Functioning*, where the woman has eighteen orgasms during a twenty minute film. Apfelbaum has found that clients who watch the film get angry; one noted that the only aspect of a professional sex film with which he could identify was the pimples on the actor's back. At a conference in 1988, sex therapist Joe LoPiccolo issued perhaps the most damning criticism—SARs, he contended, were boring: "It's 'dog bites man,' the oldest of old news."[62]

Despite controversy over the SAR format and the content of the films, however, it seems likely that the use of explicit sex films will continue. Medical sexologists can continue to choose those they consider to be more benign, and show them in a more formal context, while humanistic sexologists can continue with the original marathon format. And the curious ambience typical of sex conferences will persist, with a technical, scientific presentation proceeding in one room while sex films run continuously next door.

The tenuous coexistence of humanistic and scientific sexology extends to the issues of gender and sexual preferences. This harmony has essentially come about through default. Humanistic sexology focuses less on these issues because of its emphasis on clinical practice as opposed to research, the involvement of some early and major figures in education and advocacy in the gay community, and its do-your-own-thing sexual enthusiasm, which results in a more consistently liberal stance toward varying sexual activities than is found within scientific sexology. Moreover, humanistic sexologists have been less concerned with building a research tradition by addressing the questions that dominate scientific sexology: how to understand maleness and femaleness; how to explain and possibly prevent homosexuality; and how to develop methods to regularize sexuality and gender. They do not gear their research (or their market) to problems associated with maintenance of gender roles, homosexuality, and bisexuality.

While there is no explicit conflict between these two branches of sexology over research and clinical intervention in gender and sexual preference issues, it is useful to consider similarities and differences in their ideologies. On the surface, both scientific and humanistic sexology espouse liberal acceptance of gender differences and alternative sexual lifestyles. As we shall see in Part Three, a closer examination of the research trajectories of scientific sexology reveals strict gender stereotypes, homophobia, and a commitment to traditional and conservative mores. Humanistic sexology appears strikingly more progressive, yet scratching the surface of its liberalism reveals a tolerance and individualism that can be disappointingly narrow. Humanistic sexologists typically conflate "sexual liberation" and "women's liberation," which leads them to the assumption that sexual freedom is always in women's best interests. This allows for the possible coercion or exploitation of women in training or therapy situations. Similarly, humanistic sexologists are individually accepting of sexual diversity but too often ignore or minimize structural obstacles such as institutionalized sexism or homophobia. The thrust of most humanist programming and education about lesbian and gay issues focuses narrowly on sex and is aimed at the education of heterosexuals. Anti-intellectualism and the emphasis on feelings facilitate simple tolerance rather than deeper analysis of social structures. Humanistic sexology may foster some personal growth and education, but it fails to achieve widespread social change.

Conflict and consensus continue to evolve within sexology. Divisions were most volatile during the 1970s and early 1980s, as was consistent with widespread changes in American society and therapeutic practice. By the mid-1980s, the spirit of the 1960s and the counterculture had virtually disappeared. The philosophy and methods of humanistic psychology and the human potential movement had been integrated into mainstream clinical theory and practice. The sharp edges of humanistic and scientific sexology have blunted somewhat. Sexology has been affected by the growing sexual anxiety occasioned by the AIDS epidemic. The freedom and experimentation of the 1970s have been tempered by social conservatism and sexual caution. The respectability and rationality of the late 1980s permeate the field. Many sexologists seem to assume that in the 1980s, as Helen Singer Kaplan remarked, "Everything's settling down to a nice, scientific, rational tone."[63] Yet this complacency is belied by ongoing tension and dissent. Significantly, competition over sexual theory, expertise, and the sexual market is not confined to the humanistic challenge within sexology, but, as we shall see, has emerged from radical movements for social change.

Chapter Four

Sexual Science and Sexual Politics

> For a woman to arrive
> at the point where she
> can enjoy her pleasure
> as a woman, a long
> detour by the analysis
> of the various sys-
> tems that oppress her
> is certainly necessary.
>
> LUCE IRIGARAY

The emergence in the late 1960s of radical movements for women's and lesbian/gay liberation proved to have myriad effects on sexology. Like sexology, feminism and lesbian/gay liberation speak directly to issues of sexuality, gender, marriage, and the family. Yet these movements speak with a different voice. They challenge the intellectual power of sexology to define the normative parameters of sex and gender and, offering a different analysis, are competitors in the marketplace of ideas and interventions regarding sexuality. This chapter will briefly sketch the contours of feminism and lesbian/gay liberation that are particularly salient to the issues of sex and gender. Further, it will explore the influence of radical scholarship on the profession of sexology and weigh the impact of sexual politics on the field of sexual science. The next chapter will consider several arenas of theory and practice where scientific sexology, humanistic sexology, feminism, and lesbian/gay liberation collide.

The Feminist Movement and Sexuality

T he 1960s saw the emergence of a modern women's liberation movement in the United States. With political roots in the civil rights movement and the New Left, feminism problematized and politicized gender. Feminists questioned the assumption of a binary gender system and challenged traditional concepts of masculinity and femininity. The "naturalness" of gender, an idea inherent in patriarchal culture, was undermined by feminist analysis that sought to identify how "woman" is, in fact, constructed by cultural practices. A major ideological contribution of feminism was the analysis of women's lives and experiences within the context of broader sociopolitical dynamics. The slogan "the personal is political" expressed the belief that the power inequities within society are replicated within women's individual daily experiences. This analysis opened the entirety of personal life to a political analysis, so that, logically, major emphases within feminism were issues of sexuality and intimate relationships. The practice of consciousness-raising (CR) grew logically from an analysis that privileged personal experience and observation as serious modes of inquiry.

Far from being a seamless whole, feminist discourse on sex and gender is multifaceted and covers several diverse sites of activism. Internally, varying political ideologies and agendas for social change coexist. Three major areas of feminist critique are particularly relevant to sexology: sexuality, gender roles, and marriage and the family. This critique represented a challenge to traditional notions of masculinity and femininity, to male-defined sexuality and the heterosexual norm, and to the acceptability of the nuclear family.

Early feminism developed in a context of rapidly changing sexual mores, influenced in part by a growing cultural openness, the accessibility of inexpensive methods of birth control, the emphasis on frequent and casual sex within the countercultural movement, and the increased availability of sexological information on physiology and technique. Fundamental to feminism has been the issue of control over and understanding of the female body. The goal of reproductive freedom is autonomy and self-determination with regard to sexuality, abortion, and contraception. In CR groups, political meetings, speak-outs, books, and articles, feminists discussed and organized around issues as varied as lesbianism, abortion and birth control, sexual violence, and heterosexual satisfactions and complaints.

Of major importance, however, is that feminism *politicized* sexuality. The analysis of sexual concerns and problems was situated within the political realities of power inequalities between men and women. The critique of male domination extended both inside and outside the bedroom. The 1971 edition of *Our Bodies, Ourselves*, the quintessential feminist text on health and sexuality, told women:

> We are simultaneously bombarded with two conflicting messages: one from our parents, churches and schools—that sex is dirty and therefore we must keep ourselves pure for the one love of our lives; and the other from *Playboy*, *Newsweek*, etc., almost all women's magazines, and especially television commercials—that we should be free, groovy chicks.
>
> We're learning to resist this double message and realize that neither set of images fits us. What really has to be confronted is the deep, persistent assumption of sexual inequality between men and women in our society. "Frigidity" in bed is not divorced from the social realities we experience all the time. When we feel powerless and inferior in a relationship, it is not surprising that we feel humiliated and unsatisfied in bed. Similarly, a man must feel some contempt for a woman he believes not to be his equal. This male-dominated culture imbues us with a sense of second-best status, and there is no reason to expect this sense of inferiority and inadequacy to go away between the sheets.[1]

Although the feminism of the 1960s envisioned new strategies for organizing around sexual issues, this analysis reaffirmed that of the feminists of the early 1900s: achieving sexual liberation for women was indistinguishable from changing wider sociopolitical power structures. The politicization of sex distinguished feminism from the general trend in the 1960s of more flexible sexual mores and the "do your own thing" sexuality so characteristic of the "sexual revolution" and of sexology itself.

The centrality of gender in an analysis that focused on the "private sphere" led feminism to a powerful critique of marriage and the family. In distinction to sexologists' unquestioning embrace of and support for the family, feminists have sought to expose the family as an institution that enforces the subordination of women and re-encodes oppressive social relations on the individual level. Again, ideological emphases within the movement vary, a more moderate approach seeking changes within marriage, a more radical position asserting the inevitable oppressiveness of marriage and monogamy. All, however, challenge the traditional assumption that "any specific family arrangement is natural or biological."[2] And eschewing deterministic analyses of the family allowed for a vision of change. "Instead of separate but equal roles," Susan Harding notes, "the revision eschews roles altogether, recommending equal rights and obligations of the spouses as sexual partners, household workers, parents, and wage workers."[3] As feminists point out, only a minority in the United States live in the stereotypic nuclear family consisting of father as breadwinner, a full-time mother as housewife, and at least one child.[4] Yet the tenacious ideology of *the family* both perpetuates oppressive gender expectations and renders invisible the experience of those living outside this monolithic ideal. Thus, feminists encourage alternatives to the stereotypic nuclear family, such as communal households, single parenting, gay and lesbian relationships, and celibacy. In effect, marriage can be viewed as merely one choice among many.

These challenges by feminism in the 1960s and 1970s not only advocated reforms within the marital institution, but loudly proclaimed alternatives. This was a broad threat to an institution that was already popularly perceived as eroding; as one critic noted, "The 'home is in peril' became a fact of sociological literature as early as 1904."[5] The conservative "pro-family" movement has exerted considerable pressure to bolster traditional family arrangements. Opposition to reproductive freedom for women, sex education, pornography, and homosexuality forms the cornerstone of such aggressive attempts to legislate social policy as the Family Protection Act, which was introduced in Congress in 1979. Pro-family advocates identify feminism as a key enemy of the family.

It was on the basis of these critiques of sexuality, gender, and the family that sexology and feminism entered into a problematic and complex relationship. Both sought to negotiate these volatile and crucially important aspects of social and personal experience. Yet the incompatibility of their concerns—science and market, on the one hand, versus movement, on the other—have led, as we shall see, to a contentious and emotionally charged history.

Out and Outraged: The Lesbian and Gay Liberation Movement

The modern lesbian/gay movement, which historians date to the immediate post–World War II era, mobilized with striking rapidity.[6] Grass-roots organizations of the 1950s, such as the Mattachine Society, Daughters of Bilitis, Veterans Benevolent Association, and Knights of the Clock, were the foundation for the contemporary gay liberation movement, which is dated from the Stonewall riots of June 1969 in New York City. For three days, gay people fought back against a police raid at the Stonewall Bar. Many of the rioters were drag queens, people of color, and street people, among the most socially marginalized of homosexuals, yet they ignited in protest against the routine police harassment. The Stonewall rebellion tapped the rage of a characteristically isolated community, and by the mid-1970s over a thousand gay organizations had been formed, with a kaleidoscopic social agenda.[7]

The visibility and effectiveness of sexual minorities as social and political actors served as a profound challenge to the most basic cultural assumptions. The movement sought to undermine the "naturalness" and inevitability of traditional gender stereotypes and the monolithic nuclear family. And whereas feminism had affirmed nonreproductive sexuality, gay sexuality involved an explicit separation of sex and reproduction, which foregrounded the option of sex solely for pleasure. By their very existence, gay people challenge the "principle of consistency," which links sex, gender, and sexual preference in a socially normative ideal. Similarly, the movement's embrace of drag queens, sissy boys, radical faeries, transpeople, transvestites, and others who have chosen unorthodox sex/gender configurations is a provocative statement of rebellion against traditional notions of what it means to be a man and what it means to be a woman.

Throughout the 1970s, gay activists flexed their political muscle and made substantial progress in changing both attitudes and policy. Sodomy laws were repealed in many states, while antidiscrimination legislation was enacted in cities around the country. A volatile three-year confrontation with the American Psychiatric Association successfully ended with the elimination of homosexuality from the diagnostic classification of mental illness.[8] But the radical lesbian/gay liberation movement sought much more than equal rights or reforms. A lesbian activist described its vision:

> The early gay movement demanded nothing less than a major transformation of society—personal, social, political and sexual. At its very least, gay/lesbian liberation, like women's liberation, raised a challenge to sex role stereotyping and the concepts of masculinity and femininity—of what it meant to be a man or a woman. We challenged the notion that women had to behave one way, dress one way and talk one way, and that men had to do it all differently. . . . We believed that our very existence was a challenge to sex roles, the traditional nuclear family, and therefore capitalism. . . . Gay/lesbian liberation would end gay/lesbian oppression, an oppression that served to keep everyone in line—not just gays and lesbians. We had as our goal not only freeing up our own sexuality but everyone's.[9]

Many of the sociopolitical goals of the women's movement and lesbian/gay liberation converged into a threat to the most fundamental underpinnings of the culture. They questioned not only the power differentials between men and women, but the very concepts of maleness and femaleness, masculinity and femininity. Combined, these movements touched thousands of people nationwide. They represented resistance against oppressive institutions and held out the possibility of success. Significantly, these movements presented alternatives to tradition and to experts. Therein lay their threat to American sexology.

Sexology and the Impact of Radical Theory

P olitical groups arose to challenge both the professional authority and the potential market of sexology at precisely the time when scientific sexology was expanding its services by offering therapy and surgery for sex-related issues. The feminist and gay movements had achieved early success in their encounters with many professions and disciplines. In some cases, as in the above-mentioned dispute with the American Psychiatric Association, outright confrontation was required. In other cases, most notably that of anthropology, feminist theory was incorporated into a discipline and effected a far-reaching paradigmatic shift.[10] In addition to seeking internal conceptual transformations in social institutions, feminism and gay liberation created alternative services and businesses. The women's health movement, for example, was a major force in undermining medical hegemony, particularly in the areas of gynecology and reproduction. Not only did the movement criticize the gender, race, and class myopia inherent in the medical profession, but it provided other health care options. Self-help groups, feminist health publications, women's health clinics, and women's health and sexuality groups were alternatives to traditional medicine. Self-help groups, begun in 1971, particularly facilitated the autonomy and empowerment of women. Sheryl Ruzek states:

> Self-examination and self-help gynecology (developing in its wake) were revolutionary concepts. For self-help provided women with the opportunity to reclaim parts of themselves controlled by male professionals. What seemed an "accident of anatomy" no longer prevented women from becoming acquainted with parts of their anatomy usually reserved for male observation.[11]

By formulating a political analysis of sex, gender, and marriage, moreover, the feminist and gay movements underscored the hollowness of solutions based on technique. By refusing to accept institutional authority, these movements raised a critique of professionalism and the "expert." And by their very existence they represented the option of collective organizing instead of individualistic solutions. Although, as we have seen, they organized successfully in other professions, feminists made no inroads into sexology in the late 1960s and through the 1970s. The two groups were like oil and water, in large part because of their strikingly different agendas regarding sexuality and gender.

The *modus operandi* of scientific sexologists has always been to defend themselves against challengers to their cultural authority by stressing their connection to medical science, impugning the credentials and methods of rivals, and focusing their practices in areas of major concern to mainstream culture: the clarification and regularization of gender, and the refinement of sex therapy techniques for the purpose of, as *Time* magazine phrased it in 1970, "repairing the conjugal bed."[12]

These were all strategies designed not simply to maintain their status and their clientele, but to locate themselves in opposition to feminist ideology and practice. The advice of Masters and Johnson, for example, sought to reinforce expert authority and undermine women's own informal networks of support and education as well as the more structured self-help groups. They consistently stressed the importance of seeking help only from medical professionals. They warned women that talking to each other might only exacerbate their problems. In *Human Sexual Inadequacy*, they wrote, "Husbands are gravely concerned that wives will discuss the sexual inadequacy at the bridge table or the coffee klatch and, sadly enough, some wives do just that."[13] Instead, they advised, "Seek professional help if trying together has reached an apparent stalemate. Your best friend or your partner may be your worst therapist."[14] By reducing women's informal connections to the stereotypic gossiping of the "coffee klatch," Masters and Johnson trivialized a traditional source of support for women.

The work of Masters and Johnson is merely emblematic of scientific sexology's intense discomfort with feminism. The uneasiness has assumed different forms. Some sexologists assume an oppositional stance, proclaiming outright that they are not feminists. This is not a typical position and is best illustrated by Masters and Johnson in the early years of their work. More frequently the oppositional posture is exemplified by work that implicitly supports a conservative ideology and the double standard.[15] *The Pleasure Bond*, for example, was an unabashed celebration of monogamy and marriage. The authors emphasize sex as the cement of a marriage ("Mutual pleasure sets a seal on emotional commitment"), and they condemn nonmonogamous relationships for threatening marriages. ("Beyond all rationalization, extramarital affairs would demonstrate two things: first, that they were incapable of meeting each other's most basic physical and emotional needs, and second, that they did not consider each other unique, and therefore irreplaceable, sources of satisfaction and pleasure.")[16] The lack of critical analysis of the institution of marriage, while congruent with sexology's history, was all the more striking in an era when the feminist movement was so demonstrably challenging marriage, the nuclear family, and heterosexism. As we shall see, childhood gender programs, which employ behavior modification strategies to teach young boys and girls stereotypic gender behavior, are another example of this oppositional posture.

A second response to feminism is conflation. Historically, sexologists have conflated sex and gender and hence logically assumed that sexual liberation implies women's liberation. Equality in the bedroom is their primary concern. Feminism, when considered at all, is considered for its contribution to this end. This stance allows sexologists to gauge the social status of women by changes in sexual mores. It fosters glib proclamations that women have gone from "sexual servant to sexual equal, all in the last ten to twenty years." [17] It assumes that that which benefits men sexually will be good for women. It is the logical outcome of the refusal to acknowledge sex and gender as highly politicized arenas of human activity.

Sexologists adopting an accommodationist stance toward feminism display some knowledge of, and agreement with, feminist principles. Thus, for example, Masters and Johnson urge an end to the double standard without really shifting from their conservatism. While for many sexologists the accommodationist strategy represents mere lip service to feminist ideology, for others it is a more heartfelt attempt at integration. The preorgasmic women's groups that emerged within sexology in the mid-1970s were distinguished from feminist sexuality groups by having professional leaders identified as sexologists. Some techniques of feminist groups were borrowed, and these groups, consisting solely of women, emphasized the sharing of women's experiences and focused on women's independent attainment of orgasm.

The prototype of the preorgasmic women's group was developed by Lonnie Barbach, a psychologist and sex therapist from California. Drawing on the work of Masters and Johnson and other sexologists, Barbach established a program based on techniques, exercises, lectures, and group discussions. In 1975 she published the details of this program in *For Yourself: The Fulfillment of Female Sexuality*.[18] Barbach's emphasis was on women's learning to have orgasms. She believed that becoming orgasmic would improve the rest of a woman's life: "Consistently orgasmic women tend to describe themselves as contented, good-natured, insightful, self-confident, independent, realistic, strong, capable, and understanding, while non-orgasmic women tend to describe themselves as bitter, despondent, dissatisfied, distrustful, fussy, immature, inhibited, prejudicial, and sulky."[19]

Clearly this approach borders on the conflationary view that good sex equals liberation. And Barbach is far from radical in her insistence that "without question it is possible to change your orgasmic response without changing your whole value system."[20] Yet she does deal with power differences and sexual scripting in these groups. And, not surprisingly, the Barbach-style groups have received some criticism from within sexology because of the impact of women's empowerment on marriages. In a conference presentation entitled "The Negative Influence of Group Sex Therapy on Marital Relationships," a male sexologist criticized the exclusion of men from these groups. His two major criticisms were that sometimes women leave their husbands after participating in the groups, and that the groups precipitate a sharp increase in male sexual performance anxiety. He read a case study of one group graduate who had divorced her husband and explained: "Feeling powerful in my own right and good about myself as a sexual being has given me a sense of wholeness, health and strength that made me feel distant from Harry."[21] In 1983, whether in response to this criticism or to the growing profamily backlash, Barbach published another book entitled *For Each Other: Sharing Sexual Intimacy*.[22]

Finally, scientific sexology responds to feminism by minimizing it. The "ignore it and it'll go away" approach characterizes an enormous cross-section of American sexology. This tactic, perhaps the most dangerous, is reflected in the virtual absence of feminist analysis and scholarship within sexual science. Professional meetings, sexological journals, and human sexuality texts evidence little feminist influence. After a review of professional literature, sociologist Carol Pollis concluded:

> While a large body of feminist scholarship has begun to recover women's experience of sexuality in history and document their efforts to promote social change in relation to sexual and reproductive concerns, this scholarship, and

the theoretical and methodological issues raised by it, has received uneven and inadequate attention within sexology. Thus, recent discussions of theoretical issues, research advances, and methodological issues in sexology have not acknowledged much less addressed challenges raised by feminist voices, at least in any direct way. Similarly, an examination of introductory human sexuality textbooks and specialized sex research journals, indicates a general lack of attention to and concern with feminist analytic perspectives or feminist scholarship on sexuality.[23]

Structural aspects of sexology perpetuate male dominance and inhibit feminist intervention. As an interdisciplinary profession that draws on both the natural and the social sciences, sexology is typically a secondary affiliation for most people in the field. Many feminists working in the area of sexuality maintain their primary professional identification in disciplines such as psychology or biology, and have little energy to invest in organizing within sexology. Thus, there are fewer feminists in the organizations, and those who are there have less time and are divided in their interests.

Moreover, sexology's internal pressure toward a rigorous scientific rationality is an obstacle to feminists, who have historically been less successful in influencing the natural sciences than the social sciences. The push for scientific hegemony escalated in the mid-1980s, reinforced infrastructurally through selective funding of increasingly medicalized and scientific projects. Women in the field, who fill the less prestigious and less powerful ranks of educators, health care workers, and therapists, face the structural dynamics of oppression inherent in such hierarchical ranking. The upper echelons of scientific sexology are dominated by male-defined physicians and scientists.

The professional hegemony of "well-trained scientists" resulted in the eruption of conflict between members of the Feminist Perspectives on Sexual Science interest group and the leadership of SSSS in May 1987. The occasion was the appointment of the new editor of the *Journal of Sex Research*. When Paul Abramson of the University of California at Los Angeles was appointed editor, he was given "absolute carte blanche."[24] What Abramson chose to do, according to FPSS members, was sweep the editorial board, not reappointing thirty-one of the original forty-one consulting editors, including eight women. The editorial staff became all-male, and the number of women serving as consulting editors was reduced from nine to six.[25] And Abramson's choice of one of these women, Rosalind Rosenberg, was criticized by FPSS because of her controversial testimony on behalf of the defendant, Sears, in a highly publicized sex discrimination case.

SSSS president David McWhirter aggressively defended Abramson against feminist criticism: "They're just wrong. Paul Abramson is not antifeminist. He just couldn't find enough women that had a high enough quality like the other people he appointed to the board. . . . We're not about to just appoint anyone to the board."[26] Since FPSS members had compiled extensive lists of qualified women, McWhirter's justification speaks more to the issue of who is considered "qualified." Abramson later claimed that his strategy was to increase the prestige and legitimacy of the *Journal of Sex Research* by appointing highly credentialed academics from prestigious universities to achieve a "halo effect and ensure that the journal would pass a quick, superficial test of its substance." If that meant not including women and minorities on the board, he believed it was a necessary sacrifice in the "rigorous pursuit of high scientific standards."[27] He eventually invited a well-respected feminist anthropologist to sit on the board, but ultimately the issue was less about numbers and more about the direction and emphasis of the field. Placing the issue in a political context, an FPSS member decried Abramson's move as indicative of the increasing medicalization of sexology:

> In general, the composition of the new board of consulting editors reflects a more medically-oriented, experimental, positivist, and hegemonic selection of individuals. Perhaps this reflects the Reaganomic influence on our field, and I would guess that this is not even a conscious process. There is little representation of women, lesbian/gay researchers, and social scientists who represent a feminist perspective.[28]

Feminist concern highlights both narrowing opportunities for women and the inherent male bias of rigidly scientific endeavors.

Finally, the subject area of sexology contributes to an inhospitable environment for feminist influence. The fringe nature and embattled status of sexology foster a clannishness that views internal dissent as divisive and overt political organizing as threatening. Psychologist Leonore Tiefer notes, "Women don't want to cause trouble within the profession because sexologists view themselves as an oppressed group already." Further, the sexualized nature of the field makes it harder to emphasize gender politics within it. Particularly throughout the 1970s, sexology conferences were characterized by cruising and flirting—the "underlying orgy atmosphere" commented on by Virginia Johnson. "Whenever sexuality is a big issue, the politics of gender are devalued," Tiefer adds, "if you want to sleep with someone you don't want to be yelling all day about women and how they're going to get their rights."[29] Complaints about gender oppression are often viewed as signs of (f)rigidity. In addition, liberal men in sexology who conflate sexuality and gender and who support reproductive freedom and the Equal Rights Amendment automatically think of themselves as feminists. Thus, they often greet criticisms of their sexism with incredulity and defensiveness.

These structural obstacles within sexology aside, the women's movement can hardly be said to have operated aggressively to influence the field. Internal feminist sexual politics have contributed to mutual antagonisms. Feminists such as Alice Echols and Ann Snitow have incisively documented the internal shifts within feminism regarding issues of sexual politics from the late 1960s through the 1980s.[30] The focus on consciousness-raising about sex, the impetus to know our bodies, the emphasis on sexual autonomy and sexual fulfillment that marked the early years of feminism later gave way to a discourse on violence and sexual victimization as the essential features of female sexuality. Years of tedious and sometimes demoralizing work against battering and sexual assault contributed to this shift. Ann Snitow wrote:

> Visibility created new consciousness, but also new fear—and new forms of old sexual terrors; sexual harassment was suddenly *everywhere;* rape was an *epidemic;* pornography was a violent polemic against women. It was almost as if, by naming the sexual crimes, by ending female denial, we frightened ourselves more than anyone else.[31] (Emphasis in original.)

For the group of women Echols calls "cultural feminists," sex has increasingly been viewed as an arena of violence and exploitation.[32] This ideology is clearest in the work of Andrea Dworkin and Sheila Jeffreys, who posit that all sex, particularly heterosexual sex and penetration, is inevitably oppressive.[33] In order to avoid being the "spitoons" of hetero-patriarchy, women need to avoid sexual relations. This strategy was encouraged by the small and rather short-lived group Women Against Sex, which urged women to become sex resisters, claiming: "If it doesn't subordinate women, it's not sex."[34] A similar strain can be seen in the antipornography movement, a central organizing strategy of cultural feminists.

The loci of conflict between cultural feminists and sexologists are obvious. The cultural feminist critique of sex and pornography strikes at the heart of the professional interests of sexology, and the recipro-cally supportive relationship between sexology and pornographic pub-lications. Sexologists publish frequently in magazines like *Playboy* and *Forum*. And sexologists are often supportive of pornography as a vehicle for sex education.[35] In return, the Playboy Foundation has funded the work of Masters and Johnson and Richard Green's "sissy boy" research (see Chapter Seven).[36] This mutuality merely confirms cultural feminists' suspicion of and disdain for sexology. In its coverage of the sixth World Congress of Sexology, the feminist newspaper *Off Our Backs* criticized the general tone of the conference as "whatever turns you on," and noted that "the sexologists themselves epitomized a disturbingly laid back attitude toward all sexuality."[37] D.C. Feminists Against Pornog-raphy passed out leaflets criticizing "a mechanistic approach to human sexuality which ignores the political, economic, and cultural factors that so deeply condition sexual behavior." The leaflet added:

> Sexology cannot develop as a science without addressing sexism and the real conditions of women's lives. We expect the sexologists participating in this congress to acknowledge their responsibility to women, revise their research agenda to examine the context of sexual behavior (not merely the mechan-ics), and to integrate a feminist analysis into their research and practice, so that we can work together in a joint effort to eliminate sexism in sex.[38]

Although women attending the congress quickly called a "Women's Concerns" meeting, there was little other response.

As this chapter makes clear, the women's movement as a whole offers a widespread and coherent critique of sexuality in this culture. Feminists both within and outside sexology who do not identify themselves as cultural feminists have also raised pointed criticisms of the field. But the antisex tenor of much cultural feminist analysis has enabled many sexologists to summarily dismiss valid feminist concerns about sexual assault, male-dominated sexuality, exploitation, and sexist pornography. Many male sexologists refuse to acknowledge the diversity of feminist sexual politics and instead reduce the movement to its cultural feminist wing and attack it accordingly.[39] The antisex tendency within part of the women's movement has enabled sexology to target feminism as an opponent in the same league as the New Right. In 1984 then SSSS president Joe LoPiccolo warned members of the threat posed by "the Neo-Conservative anti-sexual tone of the current administration, the Catholic Church's recent pronouncements on sexuality, and the odd confederation of the moral majority, the right-to-lifers, and the feminists against pornography."[40] For some sexologists, feminism represents a nascent enemy to be contained and marginalized. The lesbian/gay liberation movement has fared similarly with scientific sexology (Chapter Seven will demonstrate how sexological research on homosexuality resists the integration of gay research and theory), but, as we have seen, rather better with humanistic sexology.

Within academia, the gay and women's movements have had an effect on another front—the recognition of subjectivity. Defying the expectation that they will serve as mute objects of research, women and sexual minorities have spoken up as political agents with the prerogative and the ability to define and direct areas of inquiry. Feminism has facilitated the emergence of women's studies and women scholars, while lesbian/gay liberation enabled many gay researchers and academics to come out openly in their professions. Epistemologically, this has meant reframing central questions and shifting perspectives. Gay activists and researchers have been instrumental, for example, in insisting that in research on homosexuality, the medical gaze shift from issues of etiology and cure to social attitudes and homophobia. Research methodology has undergone scrutiny as well, with the development of an increasingly sophisticated feminist critique of science.

Both inside and outside the academy, feminist and gay scholarship has expanded research parameters and contributed some of the most innovative work on sex and gender. Yet there are several aspects of feminist and gay theory to which sexual science has been impermeable. This refusal to be informed by the scholarship of radical movements has weakened the conceptual underpinnings of sexology and impaired its credibility. Several theoretical categories are of special relevance to sexology.

1. *A theoretical framework for sex and gender.* Although feminism embodies diverse perspectives, there exists a cogent body of innovative theory on sexuality and gender. Analyses of male power and domination rest on a theoretical stance that contends that differences between men and women are produced by systems of gender that construct and differentiate activities and identities in accord with, although they are not determined by, biological sex. Even though these distinctions masquerade as universal, feminist anthropologists, among others, have demonstrated that gender systems are not immutable, but both respond and contribute to changing social and political contexts. The compelling question of similarities and differences with respect to gender and sexuality has sparked lively debate among feminists and has led to increasingly complex analyses.

Social construction theory, which acknowledges the roles of historical, cultural, economic, and political influences on the shaping of sexuality, is a widely accepted paradigm within feminist and gay scholarship, as well as other social science disciplines. Yet, with some notable exceptions, sexology remains essentialist in its theory about sex and gender. Sexologists tend to posit sexuality as a transhistorical and transcultural entity that they can discover and, if not liberate, either enhance or channel. If we can somehow peel off the layers of distracting and distorting cultural influence, they would have us believe, we would locate a healthy sex drive. An essentialist paradigm informs many of the major research and clinical programs within sexology.

Disregard for culture and politics has led gender sexologists to search for the "essence" of maleness, femaleness, heterosexuality, and homosexuality, and to develop programs that deny the malleability of gender and instead reinforce cultural stereotypes. Finally, they have ignored the gay movement's rebellious and playful inversion of traditional gender signifiers, embodied in the concept of "genderfuck." Rather, sexologists consistently fail to attend to the meaning inherent in varying configurations of sexuality and gender; instead, unorthodox presentations of sex/gender have been pathologized.

2. *An analysis of power.* An analysis of sexual and gender politics is the cornerstone of feminism. Feminist activism and research have sought to identify male dominance and eliminate gender inequities in all social institutions, from religion, work, and electoral politics, to marriage, the family, and heterosexuality. Feminist therapy, including feminist sex therapy, proceeds on the assumption that, as feminist sex therapist Margie Nichols writes:

> For women in general and lesbians specifically, our sexuality is political: It has always been used against us to oppress us. Think of the major issues that feminists have fought over in the last several decades, and it becomes obvious that many of them, such as abortion, birth control, rape, incest, lesbianism itself, and clitoral versus vaginal orgasms, have involved our sexuality. Thus it is essential that we be mindful of the political implications when we talk about sexuality.[41]

And feminist therapy is rooted in the knowledge that politics can, and always do, inform psychotherapy.

There is very little evidence of these feminist insights in sexological theories, research, and treatment. A cursory nod is given to culture and politics, while the emphasis remains on the mechanics of reaching orgasm, or a drug or sensory exercise that might spark desire. Sexologists continue to valorize heterosexuality and marriage, despite feminist critiques of dominance and exploitation in both. And there has been little integration of the feminist suggestion that sexual liberation cannot and will not occur in the bedroom alone. In the absence of an analysis of power, sexologists often simplistically conflate the sociosexual experiences of men and women, a serious conceptual weakness.

3. *The critiques of science and "expertise."* Like other professions, sexology could benefit from serious consideration of the myths of professional

neutrality and scientific "objectivity." Critiques of these myths have been major epistemological contributions by feminism to the philosophy of science.[42] Studying the social and political circumstances in which knowledge is created and received, feminists have specifically questioned the influence of the gender of the researcher, the audience, or those studied or written about. They emphasize that knowledge is always ideological, despite the seeming invisibility of the dominant ideology. For this reason, professionals cannot hide behind the smokescreen of "objectivity." Yet sexologists, who work with intensely volatile issues of sex and gender, routinely avoid taking stands on political issues so as not to compromise their status as "scientists." Moreover, feminist critiques of professional distancing and the cult of the expert have been ignored by sexologists intent on expanding the market for their services.

Conclusion

Like humanistic sexologists, radical movements have been disruptive of scientific sexology's strategy for professionalization, undermining control over the market while threatening the internal self-definition of sexology. As we have seen, sexologists responded to the challenge in varying ways. But the emergence of radical movements organized by the very objects of their research, at the moment when scientific sexology was attempting professional consolidation, would mean that the field's attempt at hegemony over issues of sexuality and gender was lost. Instead of technical, scientific solutions, these movements offered analyses about sex and gender that arose out of people's own experiences within a broader sociopolitical context. They traded client status for political community. A chorus of voices would make up the sex/gender discourse, with tension and overt conflict becoming the rule, not the exception.

Chapter Five

Conflict and Accommodation:
Who Defines Sexuality?

The sexual revolution is over.

DR. THERESA CRENSHAW
*sex therapist, 1987 AASECT
president*

Sexology's recent history reflects the complexity of consolidating professional identity and securing a market. Various constituencies have skirmished in many arenas, over issues of sex and gender. Conflicts between humanistic and scientific sexologists typically embody the field's internal concerns over professional identity and market competition. The feminist and gay movements, on the other hand, challenge the very underpinnings of sexual science. Some issues of contention represent little more than a turf war over intellectual territory. Others, however, constitute a struggle over concepts and definitions that directly influence educational strategies, therapeutic interventions, and public policy.

Three areas of controversy in the last decade—the research of Shere Hite, the G-spot, and AIDS—reveal some of the dimensions of these disagreements. They also underscore the essential point that the constituent groups are far from monolithic. Feminists, for example, were divided in their response to Shere Hite's work. So were scientific sexologists. The identification of competing groups does not imply absolute internal cohesion within those groups, and it should not obscure the sense of historical dynamism.

Finally, each of these groups occupies a different theoretical and political terrain, and commands a different level of power. Although sexology does not wield enormous cultural authority over issues of sexuality and gender, it has achieved a modicum of validity as a scientific field, and it can appeal more directly to groups in power. The strength of feminism and gay liberation is in their resistance.

Mixed Reviews of *The Hite Report*

The work of Shere Hite is emblematic of struggles over the nature of research and the value of the scientific study of sex. The response to Hite and her work revealed not simply the conflicts between the profession of sex and the feminist movement, but deep ambivalences within each. From the mid-1970s to the late 1980s, Hite published the results of research that spanned the issues of male and female sexuality and women's relationship to relationships. Each book of the trilogy, *The Hite Report: A Nationwide Study on Female Sexuality* (1976), *The Hite Report on Male Sexuality* (1978), and *Women and Love: A Cultural Revolution in Progress* (1987), was a massive, enormously commercial text. Each hit a sensitive cultural nerve about sexual fulfillment and relationships between men and women. And after the publication of each, battles raged over her methodology, her findings, her politics, and the health and welfare of American heterosexuality.

As a graduate student at Columbia University, Shere Hite wrote a critique of the use of the scientific method in the realm of human behavior. In particular, she focused on the cultural biases of science and termed herself a "cultural historian." Her later research on female sexuality was a challenge to male "expertise." It was launched, essentially, by allowing women to speak for themselves. Hite was explicitly critical of sex researchers who "all too often wound up *telling* women how they should feel rather than *asking* them how they do feel" (emphasis in original).[1] Unlike sexological survey research, Hite's work focused not just on the types and frequency of sexual acts, but on the feelings of the respondents and the meanings they attributed to sex. Her research was in the style of the interpretive strategies developed by feminists to place women and women's experiences at the center of inquiry. Eighty percent of *The Hite Report* consists of quotations from women who answered Hite's extensive questionnaires, which she had distributed since 1972 through the National Organization for Women, abortion rights groups, women's centers, and women's magazines. Hite's hypotheses and conclusions are supported by women's own words, unfiltered by "scientific" interpretation. Norma Swenson of the Boston Women's Health Book Collective described it as "like being in an enormous women's group for a prolonged discussion intensely re-connecting you with other women and with yourself as a sexual being."[2]

In many respects, *The Hite Report* contained little new information. The finding that received the most attention—that most women did not have orgasms through sexual intercourse—had been detailed long before by sexologists such as Kinsey, Albert Ellis, and Masters and Johnson. The difference, however, was the evidence, in the form of countless pages of quotations from women who reported that they were emotionally brutalized either by men or by social pressure to conform to the ideal of vaginal orgasm. For example, some women wrote: "Sometimes I get 'numb' if the activity is too heavy, and I feel unhappy. . . . I feel too much like a receptacle instead of a participant," and "It becomes no more stimulating than someone shoving a hand on my arm," and "I usually find intercourse with men a struggle; it doesn't usually flow, so usually the longer it goes, the less interested I become. I get too physically tired."[3] These women's words became for Hite a vehicle to challenge male dominance. She criticized sexologists such as Masters and Johnson, who she believed still identified intercourse as the normative form of sexual interaction. And she called for the redefinition of cultural values and ideals concerning sexuality.

Less widely heralded, Hite's research on male sexuality documented provocative and disturbing findings. Cast in the same self-reporting style, *Male Sexuality* reported that most men were no longer "in love" with their wives. Of men married more than two years, 72 percent had secret affairs. Particularly discouraging, in view of the widespread publicity Hite's earlier findings had received, was the news that most men in the study believed that women should have orgasms from thrusting during intercourse. Intercourse was widely described by men as the most satisfying sexual activity. One reported: "I get the most indescribable joy squirting a dozen jets of cum into the woman I'm with and feeling immense relief and satisfaction, especially when I know that I've pleased her as much as I've pleased me." Another wrote: "Naturally intercourse is most appealing on a physical basis. It's a relief of the pent-up sexual drive. One is relieved of the 'load' of sperm and semen."[4] Consistent with Hite's emphasis on the cultural construction of sexuality, however, the book sought to dispel the stereotype of an overpowering, biological male sex drive. Rather, Hite focused on the myriad factors in male sexual socialization that pressure men to live up to a mythic cultural ideal.

Hite's third tome, *Women and Love*, prompted protracted and occasionally vicious and voyeuristic media coverage.[5] Her findings on love in the eighties were blunt, some would say brutal, and amounted to an unrelenting critique of modern marriages. Women reported emotional harassment from their male partners (95 percent) and wanted more intimacy in the form of verbal communication (98 percent). Of the women who were married five years or longer, 70 percent reported having extramarital affairs, and most were guiltless about it. Although social scientists fought over the numbers, the portrait of troubled relationships was supported by other surveys and studies.[6] It was documentation of one of the century's most compelling terrors: the collapse of marriage and the nuclear family. And it was documentation with a vengeance. Women respondents pulled out the stops, and, to many, their anger was threatening. *Time* magazine reported: "Hardest to swallow is the unrelieved bitterness and rage against men expressed throughout the report's pages. *Women and Love* so resonates with angry voices that the volume fairly vibrates in one's hand."[7]

As social science, the three Hite reports undeniably raise questions. The most widespread criticism, concerning Hite's methodology, has some validity. For *Women and Love*, for example, Hite distributed 100,000 questionnaires to women's organizations such as church and feminist groups and garden clubs, prompting critics to claim that only unhappy women or joiners would be the respondents. After receiving 1,500 responses, she made a demographic comparison of her respondents to the rest of the U.S. population and then attempted to secure a more balanced sample. The final return rate was a fairly low 4.5 percent, giving her 4,500 respondents. The hostility of the methodological disagreements, however, barely masked the reviewers' covert political agenda. Some reviewers simply noted the research flaws without dismissing the findings in their entirety.[8] Others countered that weak methodology leads to weak generalizations and a potentially dangerous book. One critic claimed that Hite's sample was skewed toward women who were angry and wanted to complain. The book, therefore, "comes out with a tone of blame likely to discourage some men."[9] Hite herself offered little substantive response to the methodological criticisms, contending that the sample of 4,500 was adequate or disavowing the field altogether. "I don't like 'social scientist' as a term. It's so pretentious and silly," she said in a *New York Times* interview.[10]

Ironically, Hite, who describes herself as both a feminist and a sex researcher, has been valorized and criticized by both groups. Some feminists objected to her focus on technique and what they saw as the isolation of sexuality from broader political issues such as class.[11] "Designed and promoted as 'sex research,'" argued one critic, "*The Hite Report: A Nationwide Study of Female Sexuality* immediately raises the mistrust that feminists feel for this genre."[12] After the publication of Hite's first book, historian Linda Gordon called Hite's failure to place sexuality within social and political relations "implicitly antifeminist."[13] Others objected to her strategy. Hite, according to Barbara Melosh, did address power issues in women's lives, but she "offers only individual survival strategies . . . solidly in the American tradition of self-improvement strategies."[14] Some charged Hite with promulgating a mainstream feminism that ignored the complexity of unequal power and would ultimately prove unable to spark social change. Yet many feminists disagreed, and the book received an enthusiastic reception around the world.[15] Many women applauded Hite's emphasis on women's sexual autonomy and the importance of female sexuality. Her critique of male expertise won her acclaim:

> What Shere Hite and *The Hite Report* represent in this struggle is the first direct and contradictory challenge, popularly available, to that brand of expertise, not only by demonstrating how far from "value-free" is the research which has already been done in the name of the scientific study of sex, but also by insisting that it not be anyone's expertise, including hers, that is allowed to establish what female sexuality really is. Rather, the "truth" is what women themselves experience, think and feel.[16]

Hite received mixed reviews from the sexual scientists of whom, collectively, she was so critical. The most frequent public criticism focused on her methodology. Wardell Pomeroy, co-author of the Kinsey studies, criticized her use of different questionnaires for different groups, her sample, and her allegedly incorrect use of statistics.[17] Early attempts within the profession to disavow Hite culminated at the 1978 AASECT conference. In explaining her absence from Hite's keynote address, Virginia Johnson said:

> I just couldn't bear to listen to a thing like that. This is my first public critique of Shere Hite, but I am so incensed at her pseudo-science. This is the era of pop science and she is doing a great disservice to the field. What she's doing is political showmanship and you cannot make a science of political opinion. They aren't the same. Hers are kindergarten ideas. . . . What hurts is that people who are doing this kind of writing are perpetuating myths of their own personal experience. And by inviting Shere Hite here, it just gives her credibility.[18]

The *Boston Globe* reported that "many of the participants felt that Hite, not being a professional therapist, did not have the required credentials, and her presence tended to erode the credibility of the organization."[19] In part, these reservations reflected a concern with scientific rigor within the field as a method of legitimation. Hite's questionable methodology and her vast commercial success were seen as having the potential to bring the field into disrepute.

Yet, even on these grounds, not everyone within the orthodox scientific branch of sexology agreed. Hite was given the AASECT Award for Distinguished Service. After publication of *The Hite Report*, Pat Schiller, the founder and executive director of AASECT, said:

> She [Hite] hasn't trained to be a researcher nor was she trained to be a sex expert. . . . But I think she has been able, through this book, to really get a good handle on how a specific number of people in our population think and feel about sexuality. There are very few of us, including Virginia Johnson, I might add, who've had the kind of training and education that Bill Masters has. In an emerging field we've all been groping, scratching, trying to develop results. . . . Orthodox training isn't really available to anybody. I think she's a big plus. I would not be judgmental.[20]

Others believed that the messages in *The Hite Report* should supersede the "quibbling" over methodology. Psychotherapist Leah Schaefer, who wrote that Hite's insights would encourage sex therapists to teach women how to masturbate and teach couples to communicate, added:

> There are those who will quibble about many points in this remarkable book —about the methodology, or the sample, or the biases, or other points. But that kind of quibbling—which goes on a great deal in research—will cause us to deprive ourselves of a huge hunk of knowledge. . . . It might appear that what researcher Hite is pointing out is radical—but in reality it is natural![21]

Schaefer's use of the term "radical" is instructive, since it is likely that at least some of the expressed concern about Hite's methodology concealed disapproval of her explicit political views. Scientific sexologists eschew politics as a threat to "pure" science. In his criticism of the "several flaws" in *The Hite Report*, Pomeroy said:

> First, it is written with a decided women's lib slant. The author is director of the Feminist Sexuality Project and she was formerly connected with the National Organization for Women. Although I am very much in favor of women's lib in all its aspects, I do not favor biases or politics when they enter the portals of science.[22]

Pomeroy reflected the view, endemic within sexology, that science can and should be objective and value-neutral. By claiming the mantle of "sex researcher" and publishing work with an explicit ideology, Shere

Hite was a threat to sexologists who insisted that sex and politics could be separated. Again, however, not all sexologists agreed. After the publication of the volume on male sexuality, humanistic sexologist Ted McIlvenna, president of the Institute for Advanced Study of Human Sexuality, noted:

> Underlying the so-called "scientific criticism" of Hite's new book is an unwillingness to listen to the important things men are saying in the book. Few women have criticized Hite's methodology or research; most of the criticism comes from males who feel threatened. Men are attacking the methodology because the book is saying things about men that most men do not want to hear.[23]

The furor over Hite's work reflected deep ideological and methodological differences about how to define the "real" science of sexology, about the meaning of "science," about the possibility of studying sex scientifically, and about the nature of sexuality and relationships. Perhaps the most interesting aspect is the extent of the disagreement among sexologists and among feminists regarding Hite and her sex research. Yet the conflict was predictable. As an outspoken feminist and a highly commercial sex researcher, Shere Hite had provided grounds for both groups to love and hate her.

Hite was playing the game but she was not playing by the rules. She adopted the trappings of science but was unwilling to disavow politics. Some sexologists could respect her work as a valid inquiry into sex and gender issues, and could appreciate the widespread attention she attracted to the field of sex research. Others found her science a sham, her methodology shoddy, and her politics too explicitly radical. And, on a deeper level, Hite's findings were a threat to a profession committed to rehabilitating marriages through better sex. She demonstrated that the chasm between men and women might not be bridged so easily.

There was a parallel division among feminists. In the area of sex research, Hite gave women a voice and proved herself an advocate against sexism and male indifference. Yet many feminists were critical of Hite's liberal individualism and skeptical of the viability of any sex research. In that view, Hite's sexual cosmology was little different from that of Kinsey or Masters and Johnson, which quantified and disembodied sex.

Perhaps Hite's aspiration to science ultimately subverted her agenda of giving voice to women. The feminist critic Jane Gallop wrote:

> Inasmuch as Hite's science fantasy compels her to organize those voices into a "new theory," which is to say, inasmuch as she wishes to overthrow the old theories and usurp the place of the male sexologist, she necessarily comes to occupy that male place. Hite, the white-coated impartial theoretician, who interprets the confessions, can no longer hear the contradictory cries of the very women she has begged to speak.[24]

The volatile and often bitter division over Shere Hite's work speaks to the depth of feeling over who is entitled to address issues of sexuality, the appropriateness of scientific inquiry into sex, and the nature of that science. That Hite, an eccentric figure who was, at least initially, critical of sex experts, was capable of arousing such ire was not surprising. Yet controversy is not confined to mavericks, as was revealed in the early 1980s when research was published on a new version of the female orgasm by professionals who explicitly located themselves within the tradition of scientific sex research.

Sexology on "the Spot"

As with Shere Hite's work, the 1982 publication of *The G-Spot* by Alice Ladas, Beverly Whipple, and John Perry generated widespread and sensationalized popular response. This was a volatile addition to the ongoing debate on female orgasm. Since stories on this topic sell magazines, the discovery of "the spot" became an international media event. Proponents of the new erogenous zone gleefully welcomed the arrival of yet another sexual possibility; critics arose to decry the research methods, media sensationalism, and potential for profiteering involved, as well as the latest exercise of the tyranny of expert authority on the part of sexologists. The existence of the spot was debatable, some said, and if it did exist, the last thing women needed was yet another sexual imperative. Unlike *The Hite Report*, however, news of the G-spot was largely ignored by the women's movement, despite the political implications of the research.[25] Instead, shock waves from the publication of *The G-Spot* were confined largely within the field of sexology.

Like the disagreements over Hite's research, conflict over the G-spot and female ejaculation must be evaluated on several levels. The standard discourse prompted by this controversial research tends to emphasize methodological issues. And it is useful to assess methodology and to question the existence of the spot. Yet scrutiny of research techniques and questions about the chemical composition of the fluid emitted during some female orgasms should not obscure an analysis of the conflicts generated within sexology. It is important to understand what responses were made by the various players within the profession and why the controversy was so deeply felt both by individuals and within the field itself. Underlying the pragmatic question "Does the G-spot exist?" is the intriguing problematic, "Why does it matter so much to so many?" The G-spot and female ejaculation must be understood in the context of the evolution of scientific research,[26] conflicts within sexology over both female sexuality and the nature of scientific rigor, and broader cultural support for specific beliefs about sex.

The clitoral orgasm has been the reigning model in sexological research on female sexuality for decades. Initially posited by both Kinsey and Ellis in the 1950s, this concept was firmly consolidated by Masters and Johnson in the 1960s. This was a departure from the traditional tenets of psychoanalysis and Freudianism, which asserted the greater maturity of the vaginal orgasm. Sexology's belief that it had scientifically established "the myth of the vaginal orgasm" was one of the issues that separated psychiatry and sexology in the mid-1960s. At that time proponents of the clitoral orgasm were departing from the conventional cultural and psychoanalytic wisdom that posited clitoral–vaginal transfer. With their success, the clitoral model was quickly established as "normal science," and much sex research, education, and therapy has been predicated on its truth.

In scientific research, such shifts are facilitated both by needs and tensions within the discipline and by ideological dimensions of the culture. In the 1950s and 1960s, both of these factors functioned to the advantage of a model of female orgasm that centered on clitoral stimulation. Continued belief in the validity of the vaginal orgasm would have supported patriarchal conceptions of sex, and heterosexual intercourse could maintain its privileged status as the ultimate sex act. The growing area of sex research, however, and the increasing public dialogue about sexuality both indicated that this ideal was largely a myth; many women were not having orgasms and were dissatisfied with sex. Since women's right to sexual satisfaction was not only achieving legitimacy but on its way to becoming a mandate, Kinsey and other sex researchers noted that women who were unhappy with sex were a threat to the marital institution. With this looming social crisis, it was no longer viable for sexologists to attempt to perpetuate the vaginal model. It was more important, and ultimately would be less disruptive of dominant sexual and familial norms, if women began to enjoy sex more.

The women's movement provided a further impetus for a shift to emphasis on the clitoral orgasm. This model was more compatible with the political analyses of feminism, which were exposing and criticizing male dominance in sexual relations as well as in society at large. Critiques of sexism and heterosexism both emerged from and facilitated the establishment of the model of clitoral orgasm. It was a sexual world view that abetted women's autonomy and that was consistent with most women's experiences of sex.

Several factors within sexology facilitated the adoption of this model: the cultural imperatives of the field, its need to establish legitimacy, and its research methodology. Eager to establish its legitimacy by rescuing marriage, the family, and heterosexuality, sexology found a direct route to this goal in learning how women could have better sex and then teaching them how to do it. Kinsey and Masters and Johnson had determined that the clitoris seemed to be the locus of the most intense sexual pleasure, and that most women could masturbate quickly to orgasm by focusing on the clitoris. Shifting the sexual emphasis to the clitoris became a strategy for salvaging heterosexual relations. Sex therapy techniques that focused on the clitoris were more amenable to short-term therapy, which was another hallmark of sexology. The slide from status of vaginal intercourse could be justified on the basis of scientific fact and physiological necessity, as opposed to power issues between men and women or the ineptitude of male lovers.

Methodologically, the emphasis on the clitoris made sense because the organ itself was more empirically accessible. It could be seen, measured, and otherwise quantified more easily than the inner vagina. As the homologue to the penis, it resonated neatly with the Masters and Johnson bias toward establishing the similarities between women and men. Finally, the demographics of Masters and Johnson's subject population may have facilitated their focus on clitoral orgasms. Kinsey's research had established significant class differences in sexual styles. Working-class heterosexuals tended to proceed quickly to intercourse, while middle- and upper-class heterosexuals had more "foreplay" involving breast and clitoral stimulation. Since Masters and Johnson's population was almost exclusively middle- and upper-class, it was a group that already had a clitoral emphasis. As clinical sexology began to emerge, it made business sense to focus on the mores of the group from which they would recruit their clients. For approximately twenty-five years, the research and treatment practices of sexology have therefore revolved around an ideological model that posits the clitoris as the focus of female sexual pleasure and orgasm.

In the early 1980s, this phase of "normal science" within sexology was challenged by the publication of data by two researchers who posited a return to the concept of a vaginal orgasm. John Perry, a psychologist, and Beverly Whipple, a registered nurse, made two major claims. The first was the existence of a small spot on the anterior wall of the vagina that, when stimulated, expands and brings intense sexual pleasure to the woman.[27] They named this sensitive vaginal area the Grafenberg Spot, in honor of Ernst Grafenberg, a sex researcher who described the spot in the 1950s. Whipple and Perry claimed that the orgasm that occurred through this type of stimulation was of a different type than the vaginal–uterine "tenting effect" described by Masters and Johnson. They described the physiological appearance of the aroused vagina and uterus as resembling an "A-frame" instead. Whipple and Perry further claimed that there was a relationship between this type of orgasm and female ejaculation. Sexologists had denied the existence of female ejaculation for decades. Masters and Johnson had concluded emphatically that it was not possible. Yet Whipple and Perry claimed that 10 to 40 percent of women in the United States ejaculate (the percentage in California, they noted, is 79 percent), and that they do so as a result of an orgasm induced by G-spot stimulation.[28]

Whipple and Perry's findings were immediately sensationalized in scores of periodicals from *Omni* to *Hustler* and *Playboy*. Their research was described as "the most important since the work of Masters and Johnson in the 1960s."[29] But Whipple and Perry were not to become the new First Family of sexology. The roar of excitement in the popular media was certainly not echoed within sexology. Whipple and Perry had challenged the dominance of the clitoral model and had directly contradicted the icons of sex research and therapy, Masters and Johnson. The first reaction of the establishment was defensiveness. At a 1981 AASECT conference, William Masters reasserted his conviction that "all orgasms involve direct or indirect stimulation of the clitoris."[30] Other sexologists either ignored the findings or denied their validity. Some took up the challenge and began their own research.[31]

Not surprisingly, the major emphasis in the profession was less on the implications of the G-spot for female sexuality, and more on the spot's existence. Subsequent research attempted to verify the spot anatomically, and a substantial amount of ink was spilled debating the chemical composition of the urethral emission, or female ejaculate. Research on vaginal sensitivity has a history of inconclusiveness. Despite Grafenberg's work in 1950, and Kinsey's later acknowledgment of it, sexologists such as Kinsey and Masters and Johnson have asserted that the vagina has little or no erotic sensitivity. Before the publication of *The G-Spot*, some researchers were beginning, with little fanfare, to raise the issue of vaginal eroticism.[32] When the insistence by *The G-Spot's* authors on the existence of a specific physiological entity forced the issue, some were irritated at what they saw as a premature and irresponsible release of findings. Research done since the publication of *The G-Spot* is ambivalent: some researchers assume the spot's existence; many insist that although there is a diffuse area of vaginal sensitivity, there is no evidence of a discrete anatomical structure such as the G-spot.[33]

Attempts to verify female ejaculation have led to similar results. Theories that women ejaculate reach back at least as far as Aristotle, and more recent adherents include Ernst Grafenberg in the 1950s and J. L. Sevely and J. W. Bennett in the late 1970s.[34] Mainstream sexologists, however, have consistently agreed with Masters and Johnson's disavowal of female ejaculation. While many researchers now acknowledge the possibility of fluid expulsion during orgasm, questions remain as to what it is. Whipple and Perry insisted that it is not urine and hinted that it might have prostatic fluid as a component. Efforts at replication have been problematic at best. Some research posits that the ejaculate is biochemically distinct from urine.[35] Other studies (including, ironically, an early attempt by a team of researchers that included Beverly Whipple) reveal that the substance emitted from the urethra is indistinguishable from urine.[36]

The two major tenets of *The G-Spot*—the existence of a distinct anatomical area of vaginal eroticism and a concomitant female ejaculate that is biochemically unique—have not been categorically disproved, therefore, but subsequent research has cast considerable doubt on them. The outrage expressed at the time of the book's publication, however, was inspired by its perceived violation of rigorous scientific practice, and its challenge to the reigning theory of clitoral orgasm. Despite the trappings of science surrounding the G-spot research, some within sexology charged that it was not scientific. Whipple and Perry had conducted extensive physiological laboratory work on more than four hundred women. They had devised new techniques, invented new machinery to measure and evaluate, and had, in the Masters and Johnson tradition, filmed a woman ejaculating. Yet some reviewers insisted that the G-spot "facts" were not sufficiently developed to warrant such sensational publicity. In the *SIECUS Report*, researcher Jeanne Warner wrote:

> I feel outrage at what I perceive as the irresponsible, premature assertion of embryonic findings and creative, but carelessly developed, ideas as facts. . . .
> Neither the book nor the authors' research is adequate to support as facts a Grafenberg spot, female ejaculation, a relationship between pelvic muscle strength and orgasm, and either a continuum or types of orgasm.[37]

Sex therapist Bernie Zilbergeld supported the notion of a sensitive vaginal area, but concurred with Warner that publication was vastly premature. Zilbergeld's explanation was the lure of financial gain:

> The smell of a best seller and big money was in the air. A large advance was offered; Perry and Whipple, joined by psychologist Alice Ladas, rushed to get into print, several years before such a move could be scientifically justified. The result is a disaster. *The G-Spot* is full of poorly supported claims and

half-baked ideas, lacking in thought and care, and certain to cause a lot of needless suffering.[38]

Perry and Whipple's extensive use of personal experience was an issue for some of the critics, who charged that the G-spot research was largely of an anecdotal and testimonial nature and not based on biopsy or tissue-culture studies.[39] This is an affront to scientific standards for such critics: "These 'data' are not analyzed or reported systematically, and there is no indication that either their subjects or their anecdotes were systematically obtained."[40] In addition, the presentation of the research was clearly aimed at a mass popular market rather than a scientific coterie. It was quite different in style from the books published by orthodox medical sexologists, such as Masters and Johnson and Helen Singer Kaplan. Written for the layperson in simple prose, it was picked up by six book clubs and even contained a self-help section. Kaplan complained: "That's not theory. That's not in the realm of science. There have been claims and hypotheses but no real research. I can't comment unless I have some studies to look at."[41]

Methodological criticisms, while salient, can also, as was often the case with *The Hite Report*, serve as a smokescreen for different agendas. Some opposition to the G-spot research seems to stem from the conceptual upheaval within the profession that the existence of the G-spot would require. Moreover, the research in *The G-Spot* emerges out of certain traditions of the humanistic branch of sexology—a discrediting connection in the eyes of biomedically oriented sexologists. Whipple, Perry, and Ladas, for example, focus on the importance of strong pelvic muscles in the attainment of sexual health. To this end, they advocate breathing exercises, pelvic exercises, and the use of biofeedback techniques, citing Lowen's bioenergetic theory and Reich's orgastic potency theory. They criticize a medical approach to weak pelvic muscles that utilizes surgery, drugs, or electrical charges, and instead advocate exercise and prevention. In short, they challenge the dominance and superiority of the medical model.

Finally, the G-spot can supposedly be found only through firm and direct sexual stimulation of the woman. Researchers are therefore moving in ethically dangerous waters. The AASECT code of ethics prohibits sexual contact between therapist and client, and this could reasonably be viewed as extending to the researcher and subject. To research the spot, sexologists would have to vaginally stimulate a woman to orgasm—a process that distinctly resembles sexual activity. Some G-spot researchers have solved the problem by having women bring their own partners with them to do the stimulating. Others have had the women sign consent forms agreeing to be stimulated by the researcher. At least one researcher, presumably in the interest of science, has drawn an extremely subtle distinction between sex research and sexual activity, asserting that as long as the experimenter does not become erotically involved, the sexual stimulation of women is acceptable. This sexologist hired twenty-seven women, most of them prostitutes, and vaginally stimulated them "until either the subject reached orgasm or the examiner's fatigue made him stop stimulation."[42] Whether all of these strategies meet ethical standards is unclear and in some cases doubtful, but it seems likely that the need for direct stimulation in conducting the research has inhibited both research on the G-spot and its professional acceptance.

Despite professional resistance, the G-spot at least briefly captured the public imagination. Although Whipple, Perry, and Ladas urged people not to use the research to construct new sexual standards and ideals, one marriage counselor said of the G-spot, "It's going to be like the Grail."[43] This was a red flag for some feminists, who feared that broader ideological pressure would herald a return to vaginal orgasms in order to buttress patriarchal sexual norms, especially since the research reports on the G-spot describe this type of orgasm as "deeper" and "less superficial" than clitoral orgasm.[44] The implication was that Freud was right all along, and vaginal orgasms would resume center stage as the sexual imperative. Some clinicians feared this as well. The preponderance of descriptions of vaginal orgasms as deeper and more satisfying, Jeanne Warner wrote, was evidence of "advocacy" on the part of researchers: "Whether naively or exploitatively, the authors have renewed or bolstered the old expectation, belief, and/or hope that almost all women can be orgasmic with vaginal stimulation alone."[45] These concerns spoke to the larger fear of the creation of sexual ideals for women by scientific expertise.

By the late 1980s, professional resistance to the G-spot had eroded somewhat. Despite the inconclusive or negative results of replication studies, the theory has been incorporated into models of female sexual response. In 1987 Beverly Whipple said, "The feedback I get is from people doing replication work or people using it in their therapy, and that has been very positive."[46] The book has been published in fifteen countries, and its phenomenal success speaks to more than an effective marketing strategy. In fact, the research information has resonated with some women's experience of vaginal orgasm and ejaculation. Whipple said that she has heard from over ten thousand women; five thousand letters flooded in after an appearance on the *Phil Donahue Show:* "It was just 'Thank you, you've really made me feel better,' and it was just outpourings of pages and pages and pages of 'I've never told anybody this but. . . .' And that was very rewarding and affirming and gave me support to go ahead and do something that hadn't been done before."[47]

The public's response, if nothing else, locates Whipple and Perry squarely within the sexological tradition of Kinsey and Masters and Johnson, all of whom received thousands of appreciative letters. And despite their disclaimers about setting up new sexual imperatives, it also locates them squarely within the realm of the experts. Beverly Whipple undoubtedly had women's interests in mind when she told a newspaper reporter, "We are helping people feel they are normal."[48] The fact that in many cases she was right speaks to the continuing power of medical and scientific expertise to affirm or invalidate women's own experience.

Teaching Safer Sex in an Epidemic:
Sexology, Gay Liberation, and AIDS

The AIDS crisis was the third arena in which sexology confronted an organized public and internal dissent in the 1980s. In a manner unprecedented in modern history, the AIDS crisis starkly delineated the ways in which ideology informs issues of sexuality, science, and medicine. First identified in the urban gay male subculture, the disease was virtually ignored by medical and governmental establishments, who saw it as affecting only marginalized groups: gay men, intravenous (IV) drug users, Blacks, and Latinos. It remained of interest only to a small

coterie of scientists until fear grew that it would spread to the heterosexual population. AIDS had afflicted 100,000 people by the summer
of 1989; of that number, half had died. The disease retains an aura of
stigmatization that has shaped medical and cultural discourse.

The early years of the epidemic were marked by both silent inaction
and the crafting of repressive policy. Proposals for interventions such as
quarantine and mandatory testing, for example, were designed with an
eye to punish or control the "undesirable" behavior of people (notably
gay men, drug users, and people of color) who are considered socially
expendable by many. Among conservatives, support for these measures
persisted despite public health evidence that belied their effectiveness
in halting or even limiting the transmission of the human immunodeficiency virus (HIV) that causes AIDS.[49] The virus had boldly highlighted the power and privilege of the groups whom our society values.

Control of the epidemic depends on measures to stop transmission
of HIV, so it is perhaps not surprising that AIDS education has been
a flash point for social conflict. A central focus has been preventive
education programs that address high-risk behaviors such as IV drug
use and specific sexual practices. Ideological struggles over the structure
and content of this education reflect opposing definitions of sociosexual
morality. Clean needle programs compete with "Just Say No!" dogma;
proponents of abstinence and monogamy argue that there is no such
thing as "safe sex," while others insist that since gay "promiscuity" triggered the epidemic, gay men should give up sex altogether. The Catholic
Church remains stubbornly opposed to the use of condoms to prevent
infection, since they also interfere with procreation. Conservatives in
government have advocated widespread or mandatory testing and the
enforcement of antisodomy laws. Fundamentalists have urged quarantine and claimed that AIDS is the wrath of a righteous God. Safer
sex material that explicitly addresses high-risk behavior is consistently
censored and denied federal funding.[50]

In the absence of effective, or in some cases *any*, response from the
professional health care system, the task of organizing educational programs fell to those most affected—the gay community. As AIDS activist
Cindy Patton notes, safer sex organizing was virtually coterminous with

the recognition of the disease, and most educational strategies implemented prior to 1985 grew out of gay liberation and feminist theory.[51] Weary of homophobic advice that urged abstinence, gay men analyzed the emerging data, crafted educational programs, and coined the term "safe sex." The success of these programs in lowering infection rates in the gay male community has been widely noted.[52] When "heterosexual AIDS" became a threat, health professionals moved in and attempted to appropriate safer sex education. "It was as if the professionals had invented safe sex," Patton complains. "Although professional health and sex educators have made important contributions to AIDS education, their work came long after a community under siege had mobilized to protect itself."[53] What was at stake was not simply recognition for effective organizing, but the very style and content of safer sex programs. When professionals began to dictate the dimensions of AIDS education, grass-roots efficacy was undermined while, often, moralism and restrictions were introduced.

For a field bent on establishing hegemony over sexual issues, the AIDS epidemic represented a perfect opportunity for sexologists to consolidate professional expertise. Especially in the early years of the health crisis, the door was wide open for anyone with concern and expertise to assume leadership. Since physicians are notoriously untrained in and uncomfortable with questions of sexuality, sexologists could have moved to the front lines, fashioning educational interventions and directing public policy. Yet, like other health professionals, sexologists came late to the AIDS crisis. An occasional conference presentation constituted the educational response of the field, and these often attracted little interest. A workshop sponsored in Los Angeles by AASECT in 1985 was canceled because only two people showed up.[54] And once sexologists turned to the issues raised by AIDS, tensions and ideological differences flourished. The sexological leadership was divided, the membership was often confused, and the gay community was alienated. In many respects, the AIDS crisis has been a watershed event for sexologists, and the field has demonstrated its inability to unify and exercise a decisive and critical role.

Historical tensions between the medical profession and gay people have generalized to scientific sexology. Yet sexologists and gay people do not constitute mutually exclusive groups. The success of gay liberation enabled many gay sexologists to come out, and the impact of AIDS drew other gay helping professionals into the field. Gay social worker Michael Shernoff, for example, became involved in sexology when he noted that his gay male clients were suffering from an increase in erectile and ejaculatory dysfunction directly related to sexual changes that they were initiating because of AIDS.[55] When scientific sexologists began releasing public statements on AIDS, therefore, a cohort of gay people within the field responded.

The leadership of scientific sexology, represented by such prominent figures as Helen Singer Kaplan, former AASECT president and sex therapist Theresa Crenshaw, and Masters and Johnson, announced public positions on AIDS that were striking in their conservatism. They called for mandatory testing, insisted that safe sex was a myth, and harked back to a traditional sexual morality of celibacy and monogamy. In two notable early incidents, conflict flared. The first involved an editorial written by Kaplan for the *Journal of Sex and Marital Therapy*. "There is no such thing as safe sex," she warned; "immunopositive individuals can never . . . have sex again." She called for mass testing and urged single people "not [to] have sex with individuals in the high-risk group, unless that person *is willing to be tested and cleared*" (emphasis in original).[56]

Opposition to Kaplan's position was swift. Psychologist James Harrison criticized the editorial in painstaking detail. In two letters to Kaplan, he charged that the essay was "incompetent, scientifically and philosophically, and irresponsible ethically," and claimed that "it is doubtful . . . that this article will accomplish anything more than to increase public anxiety and enhance the likelihood of homophobia."[57] Other sexologists echoed these criticisms. Edwin Haeberle of the Institute for Advanced Study of Human Sexuality voiced his concern that the many inaccuracies and the ideological conservatism of Kaplan's editorial would damage the profession's reputation. In *Sexuality Today* he detailed Kaplan's errors, such as her assumption that there was an AIDS test, when in fact no such thing exists,[58] and her statement that "women

who are immunopositive can never become pregnant," which errone-
ously implied that AIDS results in infertility. Haeberle wrote, "I fear
that your editorial will result in undermining the confidence the general
public has so far placed in sexological professionals."[59] Both Haeberle
and Harrison noted that by saying that there is no such thing as safe sex,
Kaplan effectively limited the definition of sex:

> Dr. Singer Kaplan is not only a physician, but a noted sex therapist and medi-
> cal educator. For a person of this public stature to use language so carelessly
> is inexcusable, unprofessional and unethical. The sex therapy movement has
> consistently worked to broaden the understanding of "sex" to refer to mutual
> intimacy and sensual pleasuring, recognizing that much sexual dysfunction
> can be attributed to the equation of sex with intercourse. How can Dr.
> Kaplan say that there is no such thing as "safe sex"?[60]

Yet Dr. Theresa Crenshaw, director of the Crenshaw Clinic in San
Diego, was outspoken in her disavowal of the existence of safer sex and
her valorization of abstinence and monogamy; she called for mandatory testing. An AASECT conference in May 1987 was the forum for
another confrontation over AIDS. Chairing an AIDS plenary that included Kaplan as a participant, Crenshaw called for the "reestablishment
of traditional values" and said, "I don't really mind if the right-wing
leaders want to limit sexual practices to monogamy for religious reasons,
if we want to limit them scientifically and the net result is the same." She
infuriated lesbian and gay sexologists in the audience with her advocacy
of mandatory testing, her alliance with the right, and her insistence that
the only safe sex is monogamy.[61] Some audience members leapt to their
feet to shout Crenshaw down; she threatened to have them forcibly
removed.

Crenshaw's opponents objected to both her conservative and inaccurate presentation and her control over the flow of AIDS information
within the AASECT conference and the membership at large. Michael
Shernoff, one of the originators of the highly successful safer sex workshop called "Hot, Horny, and Healthy," charged that Crenshaw relegated his program to a marginal roundtable position while stacking
the AIDS plenary with conservatives like herself and Kaplan. Shernoff

criticized Crenshaw for failing to respect the educational organizing of the gay community and instead relying on scientific professionals. He yelled from the floor:

> I'm concerned that AASECT is apparently not taking a leadership position on training people to prevent the disease and educate as to what you can learn from the gay men's community's successful efforts. We have a one-hour roundtable tonight, instead of being able to share our expertise on the plenary. So it makes me question the sincerity of AASECT's position to really educate people.[62]

Despite applause from the audience, Crenshaw insisted on controlling the dialogue, which prompted another sexologist, psychologist Margie Nichols, to interrupt the session again by shouting:

> We need to have open debate and dialogue about the appropriateness of your passing off your moralistic, politically reactionary and scientifically unsound views in the name of AASECT. As an AASECT member and the head of an AIDS organization and an AASECT-certified sex therapist, I absolutely object to your representing me. It's important for us to do this. . . . We have to have an open debate and dialogue about what views AASECT is going to represent as an organization.[63]

These internal conflicts were soon eclipsed by the nationwide controversy unleashed by the publication of Masters and Johnson's book on AIDS. Released in early 1988, seven years after AIDS was first diagnosed in this country, *Crisis: Heterosexual Behavior in the Age of AIDS* was the result of a research project conducted by Masters and Johnson and their colleague Robert Kolodny. The trio had surveyed 800 sexually active individuals who fell outside the groups considered to be at high risk for AIDS. Half the people in the sample claimed to have been in monogamous heterosexual relationships for at least five years. The remainder claimed to have had sex with at least six different partners per year for the past five years. The demographics of the groups were consistent with those of Masters and Johnson's other studies; the sample was overwhelmingly white, married, and college-educated.

Masters and Johnson so completely flouted conventional public health wisdom on AIDS that it almost seemed as though this was their strategy to distinguish themselves from other AIDS researchers. They contended that three million Americans were infected with HIV, twice as many as officials of the Centers for Disease Control estimated. They warned that "AIDS is breaking out. The AIDS virus is now running rampant in the heterosexual community."[64] Further, they accused the scientific community of "benevolent deception" and "misinformation."[65] Suddenly they were critical of the "voice of authority" to which they had aspired for two decades. In the face of solid research that revealed the inefficacy of premarital testing for AIDS,[66] Masters, Johnson, and Kolodny proposed that such testing be mandatory. Perhaps their most inflammatory claim was that, contrary to all public health research, HIV could be spread by casual contact. It was theoretically possible, they alleged, to contract the infection from food in restaurants, playing touch football, and toilet seats: "The fact is that it is a possibility, so it is legitimate to be concerned about the risk of exposure of this sort, no matter how farfetched it might seem."[67] And, in jarring contrast to their earlier collegial relationship with prostitutes, they joined in the public scapegoating by calling for "governmental crackdowns on prostitution."[68] Finally, like other conservatives, they urged mandatory testing for special populations, a proposal that has been discredited as invasive, unfeasible, and of little public health benefit.

Within hours after the release of the book, the sex researchers were defending themselves against widespread criticism. Public health officials were outraged at their inaccuracies and decried their decision (not for the first time) to publish immediately and circumvent traditional peer-review procedures. *Newsday* writer B. D. Colen said, "The pair is so shrill in their stance that they make U.S. Surgeon General C. Everett Koop look like a satyr at a bacchanal."[69] Koop himself charged the sex researchers with "scare tactics."[70] Scores of periodicals and newspapers carried articles that blasted the pioneers of sex research. And some of the staidest of AIDS researchers, even some who had been quoted in *Crisis*, publicly disavowed the work. Constance Wofsy, a researcher with Project Aware at San Francisco General Hospital, complained that she opened the book at random and saw that Masters and Johnson had miscited her data (in fact, they had moved a decimal point). She decided then that she "didn't have to consider the book further."[71] Defending the book at a news conference, William Masters was asked to support the assertion that the "AIDS virus is now running rampant in the heterosexual community." He responded, "I simply believe this,"[72] a defense that failed to deflect the vehement scientific criticism. Masters and Johnson compounded their difficulties by adopting their traditional defensive and defiant posture and refusing to release full and clear information on their methodology. Several months after the release of *Crisis*, the *Journal of Sex Research* published a review. The reviewer criticized the design and implementation of the entire research project and, using the authors' own measures, demonstrated that "MJK's conclusions are contradicted by their own data, without regard to the quality of these data."[73]

The popular media were clearly stunned at what seemed to be ideological inconsistency: why were the nation's most radical and pioneering sex researchers, the couple who helped usher in the sexual revolution, heralding abstinence and monogamy? The apparent inconsistency prompted widespread speculation and commentary. *Crisis*, however, simply revealed, in the most public way to date, the profoundly conservative ideology of Masters and Johnson. Like their other popular book, *The Pleasure Bond*, *Crisis* highlighted the sex researchers' overriding commitment to marriage and monogamy. The fact that the book focused on heterosexuals, in an epidemic in which only 4 percent of those affected are heterosexual, demonstrated Masters and Johnson's disregard for the gay male community. Like other prominent sexologists, they dismissed concerns about the civil rights of those who might be infected and instead elevated the rights of "the prospective marriage partner (and of unborn children)."[74] In fact, the shock over Masters and Johnson's position on AIDS merely highlights the error of the assumption that, simply by virtue of their topic, sex researchers are radicals.

Helen Singer Kaplan, too, responded to the AIDS epidemic in a fashion characteristic of her sexual conservatism. Like *Crisis*, Kaplan's book on AIDS is distinguished by public health distortions, scare tactics, and sexual moralism. And, like *Crisis*, *The Real Truth About Women and AIDS: How to Eliminate the Risks Without Giving Up Love and Sex* was routinely panned, despite the popular attention it garnered.[75] *The Real Truth* pandered to public insecurity about AIDS with insinuations, similar to those expressed by Masters and Johnson, that health officials were lying about risk factors and safer sex:

> It is shocking to me to read and hear the false alarms, false reassurances, half-truths, distortions, misleading information, and outright lies that are being dispersed through the media, by some of the so-called "sex education" programs, AIDS hotlines, and counseling services. Even the recent how-to-avoid-AIDS books that I have seen are not telling the whole truth about AIDS.[76]

The book combines attacks on public health officials, gay rights and AIDS organizations, and the American Civil Liberties Union (for its attempts to forestall civil liberties abuses in connection with AIDS) with inaccuracies and distortions concerning AIDS research. *The Real Truth* is shrill and alarmist, a tone exacerbated by the use of italics, exclamation points, and bold-type admonitions that "SEXUALLY ACTIVE WOMEN ARE NEXT."[77] Most sex is too risky in Kaplan's estimate, even with the use of condoms. To ensure safety, Kaplan urges monogamy, frequent HIV antibody testing, and "dry sex," where no potentially viral fluids are exchanged. Like *Crisis*, *The Real Truth* elevates the remotely and theoretically possible to the imminently dangerous. Condoms, along with partners, cannot be trusted; kissing is inadvisable; and "AIDS bugs can 'swim' right into your body."[78] Thus (in the chapter entitled "Great Safe Sex!") she advises partners who get "wet" with each other to get up immediately, wash the exposed body parts with soap and water, and then disinfect with Lysol.

The views of the scientific sexological leadership resonate with the conservative social climate of the Reagan years. The insistence that no sex is safe outside of monogamous relationships is not only false, but conflates sex and intercourse as it elevates marriage and tradition. Heterosexuals become the locus of concern and value for whom the rights of others must be sacrificed. "We cannot protect the civil rights of the ill at the expense of the healthy and the civil rights of those who are not yet infected," claims Theresa Crenshaw.[79] A lack of concern about discrimination against gay people underpins the emphasis on voluntary and mandatory testing, on identifying the "diseased" and separating them from the innocent, as the cornerstone of prevention.

This "us–them" mindset is the justification for free enterprise endeavors such as Safe Love International, a singles service that boasted that its members are AIDS-free. These clubs represented but one aspect of a glut of profiteering schemes that thrive on the fear of AIDS. (Related products include "antiviral" sprays for toilet seats and megavitamins to bolster the immune system.) Now defunct, in its heyday Safe Love promised that membership would facilitate "safe" relationships, since it will "affirm for yourself and others that you are AIDS FREE, insofar as modern science and technology make this possible."[80] This club was distinguished from its more explicitly and crassly commercial competitors by the fact that it was begun by a neuropsychologist, Jim Prescott, who was active in SSSS, and boasted a lineup of prominent sexologists (including Theresa Crenshaw) on its advisory council. Critics both within and outside sexology immediately opposed such groups on the grounds that they are both discriminatory and fraudulent. The antibody tests can be inaccurate, and the variability of the period of seroconversion renders the whole concept of the club problematic. Edwin Haeberle wrote:

> In actual fact, . . . we would have to talk about a whole series of tests repeated perhaps every few months; and even then a "clearance" would only be good, with certain qualifications, on the day issued. In other words, strictly speaking, any such "clearances" are basically worthless. This is the very reason that certain entrepreneurs who have tried to make a fast buck in the testing and clearance business have had to retrench under public and scientific pressure.[81]

Some of the sexologists on the Safe Love advisory committee dropped off when the club's seamy implications became transparent. Yet supporters, undaunted by pragmatic criticisms, were still more cavalier about charges of discrimination. Kaplan predicted: "There will come a time when everyone will have a card. People who don't have a card will be discriminated against. But if we take action to protect these people, it won't be as big a problem."[82]

Feelings run high about remarks on AIDS by prominent scientific sexologists. David McWhirter, SSSS president in 1987, contends that Crenshaw does not represent American sexology and claims that she threatened him with a libel suit after his criticisms of her position on AIDS.[83] Others believe that Crenshaw is simply willing to risk voicing the opinions that many share. Michael Shernoff says, "I think that you'd probably get a majority of people who may not take as extreme a position as Crenshaw and Helen Singer Kaplan, but I think that most sexologists will be much more traditional and centrist."[84] No systematic survey of sexologists' attitudes and beliefs about AIDS has been undertaken, and the field is probably divided.

Once again, humanistic sexologists diverge from the conservative moralism of the scientific leadership. Their emphasis on sexual enhancement has prompted enthusiastic support for safer sex education by the Institute for Advanced Study of Human Sexuality. Ted McIlvenna believes that sexologists should play a vital role in teaching people that they can have, and enjoy, safer sex: "I've been very disappointed in people in the sex field talking about AIDS. They've been taking a conservative stance."[85] In fact, the Institute demonstrates, as others in the "AIDS industry" are discovering, that AIDS work is not only educationally sound, but can be highly profitable. In addition to offering a certificate in AIDS/STD Prevention, the Institute now markets an array of safer sex paraphernalia, including *The Safe Sex Book*, *The Safe Sex Video*, and the Safe Sex Kit.

Although the conservative scientific leadership may not represent the profession, however, it is they who have achieved public prominence and credibility. Crenshaw's talk show devoted to sexual issues runs on the Playboy cable channel; she has appeared in numerous films on AIDS; and she has testified before the Republican Leadership Task Force on Health Care and the House Subcommittee on Health and the Environment. Since her position is congruent with that of the Reagan administration, it was not surprising that she was appointed to the national commission on AIDS. Ultimately, that commission released a report that was stronger than anticipated in, for example, its critique of problems in the health care system and endorsement of federal antidiscrimination legislation. From the start, however, the commission was under fire from health care professionals, minority leaders, and gay activists, who charged that the members were short on AIDS expertise but long on right-wing views. Crenshaw came under particular attack for her general conservatism, her alleged statements that AIDS can be spread by mosquito bites and toilet seats, and her advocacy that children with AIDS be kept out of school. The *Boston Globe* reported that "Crenshaw denied making the remark about toilet seats but said 'the jury is still out' on whether casual contact can spread the virus—a finding disputed by most researchers."[86] And out of thirteen commission members, Crenshaw was ultimately one of five who voted to oppose the recommendation of antidiscrimination provisions.[87]

The contention and disarray that characterize sexology's response to the AIDS epidemic reveal the difficulties it faces in achieving professional dominance. The scientists and physicians who dominate scientific sexology are inclined to a conservatism not shared by others in the field. Humanistic sexologists, who are much more energetic about providing leadership in safer sex education, have been castigated by the scientists for providing "disinformation."[88] Further, gay activists both inside and outside sexology are vigilant in challenging moralism and encouraging the profession to take a progressive stand. In response to the debacle of 1987, gay men within AASECT took the lead in organizing the national conference in 1988, inviting well-respected AIDS researchers to present their findings in San Francisco. In terms of decisive leadership, however, sexology has been found lacking. Crenshaw admits that AASECT has been underutilized by the Centers for Disease Control, public health officials, and federal policy makers: "We, as a whole, are not making recommendations about anything about AIDS at this time. We are not setting policy. It is premature."[89] Given the internal division it may be premature for the would-be profession of sexology—it is hardly premature for the health crisis.

Part Three: The Practice of Scientific Sexology

Sex Therapy and Gender Research

S cientific sexology's two major projects—the provision of sex therapy and research into gender-related issues—were not simply scientific exercises; they grew from sexology's goal of achieving cultural
authority by addressing issues that are among the most profound in
both individual and cultural experience. Sexology benefited from the
cultural upheaval of the 1960s and 1970s by crafting programs to eliminate the superficial symptoms of dissatisfaction while leaving the dominant ideology intact. In particular, as we shall see, it focused on sex
therapy and gender research, both attempts to scientifically define and
engineer "normality." The practice of sex therapy raises questions about
the very nature of sex, sexual excitement, and sexual desire. An individual couple's sexual problems must be approached through larger
questions: "What does it mean when two people have sexual difficul-

ties?" "Is sex separable from the relationship?" "What triggers sexual arousal, and if you've lost it, can you get it back?" Research into gender roles, homosexuality, and transsexualism strikes at the very heart of what it means to be a man or a woman, gay or straight. Questions of sexual development, the formation of sexual identity, the organization and expression of sexual desire, all underpin the professional enterprises of sexology.

Yet sexology's goal of hegemony over these issues has been thwarted by one of its own strategies for professional development: the emphasis on scientific rationality. With a theoretical basis narrowly grounded in the physical body, sexologists were ill equipped to handle many of the dilemmas inherent in the culturally and politically based sex/gender system. One major source of professional trouble was reliance on biomedical empiricism and the absence of a coherent and encompassing theory of sex and gender. Kinsey and Masters and Johnson counted, timed, and measured behavior; sex was distilled into a meticulously detailed yet almost unrecognizable set of physical motions. Eager to establish the field as a respectable science, these sex researchers emphasized the quantifiable and eschewed the theoretical. Cultural influences on sexuality such as race or gender socialization were euphemized as "psychosocial influences" and then dismissed. Sexual politics were avoided, almost disdained. As William Simon and John Gagnon wrote in 1973, "We have allowed the organs, the orifices, and the gender of the actors to personify or embody or exhaust nearly all of the meanings that exist in the sexual situation."[1] Without a theoretical base, research and therapeutic practice in sexology proliferated in an incoherent and sometimes contradictory fashion.

The question of what, if any, theory informs sexological practice is essential for two interrelated reasons. First, sexology contributes to the collective sexual discourse of the medical and psychiatric professions, a discourse that is itself a means of social control.[2] Categories of "natural" and "deviant" not only operate on the personal level to shape individual experience, but underpin the legal system as well. Whether a personal preference becomes a "sexual dysfunction," a "sexual deviancy," or a crime is a political decision often related to its status in the psychiatric community. Since sexologists rarely lobby, sexology's role in perpetuating or challenging certain sex/gender typifications lies in its accumulated research and practice. Second, the field's theoretical framework quite directly affects the type of information and treatment afforded to individuals. Therapeutic intervention will differ, for example, according to whether the therapist believes that sexual desire resides in the brain or is an outcome of certain personal, cultural, and political factors. In the former instance, a pill or some other individualistic intervention may be developed in the hope of eliciting desire, whereas the latter entails a more complex, multifaceted approach.

To some extent, the content and direction of modern sexology are a function of its theoretical impoverishment. Two decades of innovative scholarship on sexuality and gender by feminists, gay activists, post-structuralist critics, and others have not lifted sexology from the mire of sexual essentialism. Sexuality is seen as a universal force or drive residing inside the body in some observable and perhaps measurable quantity. The human sexual response described by Masters and Johnson was a map of that essential instinct. The maxim "sex is a natural force" denotes the biologistic reduction of sex, which has many ramifications. Once sexology located sexuality in the body and identified sexual problems as a "blockage" of instinct, sex therapy, as we shall see, became little more than the practice of developing techniques to coax it out. Gender essentialism within sexology has validated traditional demarcations between men and women, heterosexuals and homosexuals. Treatment programs to convert homosexuals into heterosexuals imply the inherent naturalness of one type of sexual expression and the desirability of attempts to reorganize and channel desire in socially acceptable directions.

Essentialism has occupied prime time within sexology not just because of the profession's traditionally empirical focus but also because it resonates with sexology's bid for legitimacy through supporting traditional values and the dominant ideology. Locating sex in the body makes sex research and therapy simpler and potentially less controversial than practice that acknowledges and encompasses social factors. Sexology can seek the technical interventions of medical cure, rather than confront the possibility that issues of sexuality and gender are fundamentally political and "cure" may entail the necessity of social change. It is financially and professionally more lucrative to prescribe a two-week therapeutic regime, psychopharmaceuticals, or surgery for problems of sexual functioning, sexual desire, or gender identity. Within an essentialist framework, all these interventions are viable.

Yet, ultimately, in the absence of a constructionist theory that explains sex and gender in terms of their social, historical, and political context, sexological interventions are intellectually circumscribed and practically inadequate. As this section will elucidate, it is in the practices of sex therapy and gender research that the theoretical limitations and the ideological contradictions of sexology become most apparent. And it is here, therefore, that we can locate the seeds of the ultimate failure of sexology's attempt at professionalization.

Chapter Six

Repairing the Conjugal Bed:
The Clinical Practice
of Modern Sex Therapy

I know every way is normal.
Tell me which way is right.

female client to sex therapist

Sexology's most visible, lucrative, and widespread enterprise has been sex therapy. The practice of sex therapy serves several functions for the profession. First, it is sexology's most easily marketable commodity and allows for heightened visibility, expansion, and profit. In addition, modern sex therapy is highly medicalized. Sexual behavior and desire are regarded largely as physiological processes; problems in sexual expression, therefore, are treated as diseases. Thus, the reliance on a biomedical model and technological interventions legitimizes the practice of sex therapy as a method of addressing individual and cultural concerns about sexuality and, most specifically, relations between women and men. An analysis of sex therapy reveals much about the conceptual underpinnings and the quest for professional consolidation of modern sexology.

Despite the popular impression that sex therapy is a recent phenomenon, technical interventions into sexual behavior have a long history. The practical study of lovemaking—what Edwin Haeberle terms "erotology"[1]—is embodied in early Eastern sex manuals such as the *Kamasutra*, which can be considered the ancient forerunners of recent best sellers like *The Joy of Sex*. Clay tablets discovered in the Tigris–Euphrates Valley were inscribed with incantations to be used to deal with impotence. The Romans had a series of directives for women concerning intercourse, orgasm, and sexual health. And medieval manuals addressed the role of diet and proper technique in fostering better sex.[2] Aggressive medical interventions into sexual behavior have been implemented for the last century. Clitoridectomies, for example, were performed in the late nineteenth and early twentieth centuries either to curb women's sexual activity or to "cure" them of active or aggressive behavior, and physicians employed a range of surgical techniques and mechanical devices such as metal mittens to "cure" the disease of masturbation. Other physicians of the early to mid-twentieth century attempted through their writing and practices to foster effective and pleasurable heterosexual sex.[3] Helen Singer Kaplan has summarized the history of "expert" advice concerning sexuality—benign and punitive, effective and useless—with the comment that "the electric vibrator represents the only significant advance in sexual technique since the days of Pompeii."[4]

Her remark is an explicit acknowledgment of the dominant tendency in modern sex therapy: the widespread and aggressive application of medical technology to sexual practice. The last half of the twentieth century marks an expansion in the development of clinically sophisticated programs designed to inform, educate, and actively assist couples to overcome sexual problems. The sex therapy that evolved in the late 1960s and through the 1970s had two notable features. First, it represented a major mobilization of empirical and medical research to probe problems of sexuality. Sexual problems and disappointments became defined as sexual dysfunctions to be diagnosed, investigated, and cured. And since the definition of a problem determines the solutions proposed, the range of interventions that have been developed have a biomedical cast. The individual body is located as the site of disease and targeted for reeducation or invasive measures such as surgery or drug treatment. Second, the ideological enterprise of modern sex therapy was undeniably positive and enthusiastic about sex. More specifically, it promoted heterosexual sex, or those techniques, such as masturbation, that sex research indicated could foster more effective heterosexual sex. Sexual mores had changed considerably since the nineteenth century; whereas physicians of that era propagated "cures" for nonreproductive sexuality, the new sex therapy conveyed the ideal of hypersexuality—a "more is better" model for performance.

These dimensions of modern sex therapy were sculpted by social and economic factors that effected changes in sexuality and marriage and affected cultural attitudes toward medicine. The culturally perceived crisis of heterosexuality and the family reached new depths in the 1970s. Since "family" is traditionally assumed to be "nuclear" in our society, it is not difficult to understand the clamor. The American family structure has undergone dramatic renovation in the past twenty years: the rate of marriages has declined while divorce rates have risen, especially among Black couples; heterosexual cohabitation has increased, along with the percentage of births outside of marriage.[5] Marriages in the late 1970s had a 50 percent chance of ending in divorce. Decisions to remain single, or couples' decisions to remain childless, acquired increasing respectability. Feminism and gay liberation widened the parameters of "family" to include same-gender lovers, ex-lovers, and friends. A vision for some, these changes represented a nightmare for others, and a gnawing insecurity for many more. The cultural imperative to grow up, marry, have children, and live "happily ever after" was under siege.

Equally troublesome for many were the relationships between women and men, inside marriage or not. Feminist critiques of gender role constraints and power inequities in heterosexual relations cast a spotlight on what seemed a chasm between women and men. For commentators, the prognosis looked grim. In *Intimate Strangers*, sociologist Lillian Rubin wrote: "More and more we have come to see that we made a bad bargain, if not an impossible one. More and more we have come to recognize that both men and women have been feeling helpless and angry—feelings that get acted out against each other all too often."[6] To critics who drew on the influential theory of feminist sociologist Nancy

Chodorow,[7] it seemed apparent that the different socialization of boys and girls led them on parallel and unequal tracks that rendered future intimacy and commitment problematic. Rather than heterosexual bliss, alienated affection was perhaps the most realistic hope.

Sex played a paramount role in the crises of heterosexuality and the family. The glut of media-disseminated information about sex reflected both a growing openness and increasing sexological expertise. A study of married couples in the early 1970s revealed greater sexual experimentation among white couples of all classes.[8] Many women were empowered not merely to avoid exploitative sex, but to seek out fantasy, orgasms, and thrills. Feminist consciousness-raising groups were forums for both criticizing existing sexual relationships and exploring new sexual terrain. Mainstream books like *The Joy of Sex*, *The Sensuous Woman*, and *My Secret Garden* spoke to a new sexual spirit. By the late 1970s, women had become increasingly active partners, and couples were enthusiastically proclaiming the importance of sex to a good relationship. Yet there was a downside to this emerging hedonism. Escaping sexual socialization proved more difficult than merely shrugging off an old coat. The persistence of the double standard resulted in social opprobrium for many women pursuing sexual freedom. Feminist organizing drew greater public attention to sexual violence as a mechanism of sociosexual control of women. And the plethora of sexual options touted by sexologists and the media—including multiple and extended orgasms— were experienced by some merely in the form of increased pressures.

Sexual malaise and family travails were linked in the popular imagination. As we have seen, sexologists justified their research with claims that more than half of American families were foundering because of sexual problems. It was a powerful tactic precisely because it hit a sensitive nerve. Yet if sexual problems could be blamed for the demise of marriages, the opposite claim was also made. One commentator noted: "Marriage seemed to possess limitless resources for extinguishing the tiniest spark of fun in sex."[9] Ironically, the evolving sexual openness disclosed as much sexual misery as orgiastic revelry. The glaring disjuncture between expectations of an easy sexual pleasure and the realities of failed sex helped create a cultural basis for the successful development of clinical programs of sex therapy. This endeavor was enhanced by the widespread belief that sex was crucial to personal and relational fulfillment.

Public response to the profession of medicine was an important factor in the proliferation of sex therapy programs. In the face of competition from the humanistic sexologists and social movements that arose in the 1960s, scientific sexologists appealed to the popular mystique that ascribed to physicians both the ability and the mandate to solve a myriad of physical as well as social problems. Physicians, enjoying over a half-century of public confidence and optimism, had expanded their areas of expertise.[10] Improved technology and surgical techniques inspired confidence and impressed the public: the first heart transplant was one of the decade's most dramatic media events. It seemed, in those heady times, that the only problem with medical science was that not enough people had access to it.

By the late 1960s, however, the public's infatuation with medicine was certainly tempered. Access was no longer the major issue; increasingly questions were voiced about the effectiveness of many medical interventions. Professional authority was criticized on several fronts. Medicine was depicted as a mechanism of social control by critics like Thomas Szasz and R. D. Laing.[11] The women's movement criticized both male dominance and the use and abuse of power in medical situations where "standard professional practices" cannot simply be accepted as the most appropriate or desirable models for promoting well-being.[12] Analysts claimed that medicine created as many problems as it solved, and criticized the tendency toward "medicalizing" human experiences.[13] It was in this era that a number of alternative therapies, from chiropractic to herbology, flourished.

For individuals with sexual problems, the medical mystique—the "white coat of authority" evoked so often by Masters and Johnson—still held considerable sway. Sex therapy based in biomedical science offered the promise of effective solutions dispensed by neutral, dispassionate practitioners. The lure of the medical "sex expert" could prove irresistible for couples suffering from sexual difficulties who wanted immediate solutions. In a consumer culture where sex had been increasingly commoditized over the decades, sex therapy became a viable and valuable product. Monumental demand led to the proliferation of clinics and private practices across the country.

The Impact of Masters and Johnson

T he obvious pioneers in this field, grounded as they were in medicine and the scientific method, were Masters and Johnson. The publication in 1970 of *Human Sexual Inadequacy*, quickly dubbed "the bible" of sex therapy,[14] was a watershed in the development of the field. As with their data on human sexual response, not all of Masters and Johnson's sex therapy techniques were original. Both Kinsey and Albert Ellis had previously written about the importance of the clitoris in female sexual response. "The squeeze technique" that Masters and Johnson prescribe for premature ejaculation had been developed in the 1950s by Dr. J. H. Semans. And the application of behavioral conditioning to the treatment of sexual problems had been described in 1958 in J. Wolpe's *Psychotherapy by Reciprocal Inhibition*.[15] It was not as innovators, but as respectable, medically oriented researchers with appealingly conservative personae that Masters and Johnson were catapulted to fame as scientific experts both in the public view and within the emerging field of sexology. They became household words in an era when sexual gratification and the search for sexual healing occupied the foreground of cultural consciousness.

Within the field of sexology since 1970, Masters and Johnson's conceptual system has served as the prototype for the diagnosis and treatment of sexual dysfunctions. It is *the* model to which subsequent conflicts, controversies, and theoretical and clinical innovations have responded. Masters and Johnson themselves regarded their early physiological research as crucial to the understanding and treatment of sexual problems.

> When the laboratory program for the investigation in human sexual functioning was designed in 1954, permission to institute the program was granted upon a research premise which stated categorically that the greatest handicap to successful treatment of sexual inadequacy was a lack of reliable physiologi-

cal information in the area of human sexual response. It was presumed that definitive laboratory effort would develop material of clinical consequence.[16]

This hyperreliance on physiology was, as we have seen, a logical component of Masters and Johnson's commitment to the biomedical model and a legitimating strategy for sexology at large. While the quantification of sexuality proved horrifying to many during the Kinsey era, it could be reassuring in a culture that idealizes science. Moreover, as sex therapist Leonore Tiefer notes, "Sexual physiology has a tangibility that 'love' and 'lust' lack, increasing its propriety as a language for public discourse."[17]

On the basis of their laboratory research and their notion of the four stages of sexual response, Masters and Johnson developed the "St. Louis approach" to sex therapy. Only couples are accepted into the treatment program, although initially Masters and Johnson provided surrogate partners for men. The "relationship" is considered to be the patient, and the major goal is to return sex to its "natural context." The treatment program runs for two weeks, during which time the couple lives at a nearby hotel. Therapy sessions are conducted every day, including Sundays, and are directed by a dual-sex team, one member of which must be a physician.[18]

Through their physiological research and their clinical work, Masters and Johnson identified several major areas in which sexual problems were likely to occur. Eventually, these categories were adopted by the third edition of the *Diagnostic and Statistical Manual of Mental Disorders* (*DSM-III*) and are now considered official "mental disorders." For men, the basic sexual dysfunctions delineated by Masters and Johnson include premature ejaculation, primary and secondary impotence, and ejaculatory incompetence, an extremely rare condition in which a man cannot ejaculate intravaginally. Female sexual dysfunctions include dyspareunia (painful intercourse), vaginismus (a tightening of the vaginal muscles that prohibits penile penetration), and several types of orgasmic dysfunctions, broken down into primary or secondary and coital or masturbatory categories.

In contrast to the highly medicalized ambience of the program, Masters and Johnson's actual treatment is an amalgam of behavior therapy and sexual advice and information. In *HSI* they acknowledged that most of their therapy was actually education or reeducation.[19] In the early years of sex therapy, sexual problems were often easily resolved through basic sex education, and sex researchers were fond of imparting anecdotes about couples who failed to conceive or marriages that remained unconsummated for years because of simple ignorance of the mechanics of sexual intercourse.[20] Masters and Johnson's therapeutic intervention seeks to alleviate performance anxiety and reestablish communication between the partners.

Whatever the diagnosis, the Masters and Johnson model begins by prohibiting intercourse between the couple. They then prescribe "sensate focus"—a series of massage-like exercises implemented by the couple in their hotel room. Later in the treatment program, depending on the specific sexual problem, other techniques are taught, such as the squeeze technique for premature ejaculation, or directed masturbation for female orgasmic problems. With this format, they claimed to achieve excellent results. As with their research on the response cycle, however, Masters and Johnson departed from scientific protocol by immediately publishing their results in a text instead of submitting their work to journals that would subject the findings to a review process. This allowed them to claim success without specifying the actual criteria used, and several years passed before they were challenged.

In sex therapy, Masters and Johnson had developed a highly marketable package with several advantages over traditional psychotherapy. First, the very existence of sex therapy programs validated people's hopes and desires for better sex. Suddenly it was legitimate to seek help solely for firmer erections or better orgasms, rather than hope for these improvements as a by-product of a long stretch of analysis. Second, the Masters and Johnson treatment was brief and symptomatic. Based on principles of behaviorism, it considered sex a form of learned behavior. Although this conception was somewhat at odds with their famed dictum that sex is "natural," they posited sexual dysfunctions as simply "bad habits" that could be modified or unlearned. This clearly differentiated their treatment from psychoanalysis, which viewed sexual problems as mere symptoms of a far more complex and largely unconscious psychological process with its origin in early childhood. Finally, marketability was enhanced by the enthusiasm with which Masters and Johnson and other sex therapists proclaimed excellent results. The St. Louis researchers, who conducted five-year follow-up studies and idiosyncratically inverted the normal practice of reporting successes, claimed failure rates as low as 2.2 percent (for premature ejaculation) and 40.6 percent (for primary impotence).[21] Again they failed to specify what constituted success or failure, but the expectation of high cure rates for sex therapy became so commonplace that one commentator noted that many patients seemed to be cured merely by being placed on the waiting list.[22]

Not surprisingly, such unfettered enthusiasm drew mixed reviews in the American therapeutic community. Until that time, psychiatrists and psychoanalysts, operating in the tradition of Freud, were considered the experts on sexuality. Initially, then, these professionals, as competitors, were extremely critical of the Masters and Johnson treatment format, which they characterized as mechanistic, superficial, and dehumanizing.[23] More specifically, they warned that removal of the sexual problem without addressing the more deep-seated pathology would only result in the substitution of another symptom. During these early disputes, a researcher from the Kinsey Institute remarked:

> Some psychiatrists, "particularly run-of-the-mill-ones," have had a tendency to be "uptight" about Masters and Johnson because prior to their advent it was the psychiatrist and the psychiatrist alone who was "Dr. Sex." . . . It was threatening enough to the profession when Masters and Johnson set about with their original research into the nature of sexual response. But now that they have gone into therapy many traditional therapists will be as jittery as the plumbers union is when faced with a possible incursion of blacks into their ranks.[24]

The practice of sex therapy cast into stark relief Masters and Johnson's analysis of sex and gender. Like Kinsey, they envision sex as core physiological response. Sex is what occurs during the four-stage response cycle they outlined in their early research. While they never precisely define the "natural context" to which sex must be returned,[25] it is presumably the state of pure physiological response unencumbered by social or psychological variables. In *HSI*, they write: "For sexual functioning is a naturally occurring phenomenon and cannot be controlled, directed, or even initiated unless it is in some manner related to the natural cycle of sexual response. *No man can will an erection,* but he can relax and enjoy it" (emphasis in original).[26]

This notion of spontaneously occurring sexual energy was developed, in part, to alleviate performance anxiety: since you can't force it to happen, just don't try, and it will. It was a therapeutic attempt to assure clients that, if they could just put aside the worries of the workaday world, a natural sexual energy would spontaneously reassert itself. This was the rationale for the mandatory two weeks in St. Louis: clients were forced to withdraw from work, children, and other possibly distracting influences. The problem is that this approach dismisses the extent to which culture, or the workaday world, not only shapes but is an integral part of our sexuality.

This lack of attention is consistent with Masters and Johnson's tendency to deal peripherally and euphemistically with cultural factors. They speak of female socialization and the sexual double standard as the "psychosocial backdrop," and they discuss "interdigitating biophysical and psychosocial systems."[27] This analysis is again reminiscent of Kinsey's portrait of an essential sexual energy that will naturally emerge in the absence of such distractions as gender, ethnicity, social class, and age. Social factors compete with distilled sexual energy. *HSI* condemns the

> failure to conceptualize the whole of sexual experience for both the human male and female as constituted in two totally separate systems of influence that coexist naturally, both contributing positively or negatively to any state of sexual responsivity, but having no biological demand to function in a complementary manner.[28]

This view of two systems, the biological and the psychosocial, supports Masters and Johnson's tenet that women and men are more similar than different. If women appear to be less sexual than men, it is merely because they are held back by a less robust psychosocial system. Contradicting Kinsey's notion of the lesser sexual capacity of women, Masters and Johnson assert that women's biophysical capacity is far superior to men's. It is not a major issue for them, then, that women often suffer from sexual problems resulting from socialization in a culture that trivializes, devalues, or actively discourages female sexuality. Masters and Johnson's analysis is that "based upon the manner in which an individual woman internalizes the prevailing psychosocial influence, her sexual value system may or may not reinforce her natural capacity to function sexually."[29] Since social relations carry little weight for Masters and Johnson, they have little empathy for women's sexual oppression. Their emphasis on physiology allows them to focus on what they consider women's sexual superiority:

> Yet woman's conscious denial of biophysical capacity rarely is a completely successful venture, for her physiological capacity for sexual response infinitely surpasses that of man. Indeed, her significantly greater susceptibility to negatively based psychosocial influences may imply the existence of a natural state of psycho-sexual-social balance between the sexes that has been culturally established to neutralize woman's biophysical superiority.[30]

In other words, women's biological sex drive is so strong that it will ultimately triumph over any cultural obstacles in its path. Women's sexual oppression and the sexual double standard are culturally normative and "natural," since they operate to neutralize what might be a voracious, out-of-control sex drive. An extension of this thesis could hint that sexual inequality and its consequences are necessary restraints on female sexual expression.

A cogent analysis of gender and power is sorely lacking in Masters and Johnson's sex therapy program. Throughout *HSI* the marriage partners are assumed to be equal, or, as we have seen, the woman's oppression is canceled out by her superior sexual capacity. Their sympathies lie almost exclusively with men, whom they perceive as bearing an unconscionable responsibility for sexual interaction. While they rarely criticize sexual violence or the oppression of women, they constantly rail against the disproportionate sexual burden shouldered by men:

> The most unfortunate misconception our culture has assigned to sexual functioning is the assumption, by both men and women, that men by divine guidance and infallible instinct are able to discern exactly what a woman wants sexually and when she wants it. Probably this fallacy has interfered with natural sexual interaction as much as any other single factor. The second

most frequently encountered sexual fallacy, and therefore a constant deterrent to effective sexual expression, is the assumption, again by both men and women, that sexual expertise is the man's responsibility.[31]

They have cited these errors as the two most devastating examples of gender inequality in sex. In a later interview, they continued this theme by blaming women for irresponsibility in the sexual arena:

MRS. JOHNSON: The double standard is perpetuated by both sexes. People who don't really want to be responsible for their behavior are the ones who hide behind the double standard.

DR. MASTERS: Women are not always ready to accept a single standard either. They still want their own set of privileges. Our culture today is trying to give the female all of the male advantages without the disadvantages. I am opposed to that.[32]

This penchant for alleging equal power between men and women with regard to sexuality is a logical outcome of the emphasis on male/female similarities posited in *Human Sexual Response*, flattening differences in the hope of improved heterosexual relationships.

The relationship between sex therapy and the family is ideologically complex. For conservatives fearful of the new sexual openness, sex therapy represented a liberal threat, an explicit affirmation of the "right" to sexual fulfillment and the pursuit of good sex. This triggered the complaint that "it is the sex therapist who most seriously assaults the traditional institutions of marriage, family and religious values."[33] In fact, however, *HSI* is strongly imbued with Masters and Johnson's marital ideology. They are heavy-handed in driving home the point that their research is directed at salvaging marriages by solving their sexual troubles. The relationship, not the individual, is the patient. They insist on calling the couple "the marital unit." They write that "the ultimate level in marital-unit communication is sexual intercourse,"[34] and a breakdown spells doom. Reversing the causal equation that good relationships lead to good sex, Masters and Johnson claimed that the failure of sex could bring a marriage to its knees.[35] "Usually the failure of communication in the bedroom extends rapidly to every other phase of the marriage."[36] The repeated claim that half of American marriages suffer sexual dysfunction was later challenged by their nemesis, Bernie Zilbergeld, who noted that there is no evidence for this much-touted statistic and implied that it merely functioned to enhance the importance of sex therapists.[37] Yet clearly Masters and Johnson spoke to deep cultural anxieties when they addressed issues of marital discord and sexual incompatibility. They offered the "white coat of authority" to couples often suffering sexual problems in silence and shame.

Undeniably, Masters and Johnson's sex therapy program helped scores of couples improve their sex lives. The brief, symptomatic treatment seemed perfect for those with little experience or information about sex. The mere discovery of the program's existence was enough to instill hope and confidence in some couples. *Inside the Sex Clinic*, for example, published not long after *HSI*, was an anecdotal account of an experience with the two-week St. Louis program. The marriage of Sam and Louise was in decline after years of enduring Sam's premature ejaculation problem. One morning in 1968 Louise saw an article in *Ladies Home Journal* that described Masters and Johnson's program. When Sam came home, she broached the topic with him and they decided to enter sex therapy. That night, they lay awake together until the early hours. "Both of them were calmer and more hopeful about their marriage than they had been since their first year together."[38] Sam and Louise went on to enjoy a not idyllic, but quite functional, sex life. Undoubtedly, this scenario was repeated countless times throughout the country.

Yet a vision of Masters and Johnson's form of sex therapy as more than a band-aid solution is ultimately a false promise. Sensate focus and the squeeze technique are potentially important therapeutic tools, but they don't touch the source of the most intractable sexual problems of heterosexuals: fear, anger, boredom, overwork and lack of time, inequality in the relationship, prior sexual assault on the woman, and differential socialization and sexual scripts.[39] If a theoretical analysis is to account for these issues, sexual politics are inescapable; yet addressing these social relations is anathema to Masters, Johnson, and most other sexologists. In sex therapy, the "cure" is orgasm, not social change. And this is vital, because orgasms can be marketed in a profit-making system, while social change cannot.

Since the marketing of sex therapy depends on claims of effectiveness, the definition of success is carefully sculpted to procure good therapeutic results. Yet controversies over treatment outcomes reveal that the "magic bullet" of sex therapy may not be as powerful as enthusiasts once claimed. Few controlled studies have been conducted to evaluate the efficacy of sex therapy.[40] Many sex therapists report their results in vague categories of "improved" or "not improved."[41] Masters and Johnson, with their five-year follow-up studies, developed reputations as stellar scientists as well as remarkable clinicians. Yet it is on the basis of the scientific validity of their outcome statistics that Masters and Johnson's work has sustained its most serious challenge.

Critiques of the purported effectiveness of sex therapy are vital because they strike at the heart of this controversial and rapidly proliferating field. In August 1980, Bernie Zilbergeld and Michael Evans published a critique entitled "The Inadequacy of Masters and Johnson,"[42] setting off profound tremors in the field of sexology. The psychologists criticized the lack of specific criteria for therapeutic success and failure in *HSI*. Zilbergeld and Evans noted that few sexologists, if any, had achieved the success rates proclaimed by Masters and Johnson. For this reason it was crucial that the St. Louis team specify their outcome criteria: what did they mean by "cure"?

While the explicit challenge was methodological, there was also an implicit criticism of the researchers' custom of publishing without subjecting their work to peer review. The issue came to a head when, at a California meeting, Zilbergeld alleged that William Masters had stated that "therapeutic success was predicated upon a non-orgasmic woman having one orgasm during the two weeks of therapy and one orgasm during the next five years."[43] This explained to many the phenomenally high success rates: for Masters and Johnson, cure equaled as little as one orgasm in several years! Masters denied that he had made the statement, although it was corroborated by several others who attended the meeting. He later released a more detailed set of outcome criteria.

But the damage had been done. Zilbergeld and Evans had challenged the paragons of scientific sexology on the basis of their scientific methodology. By doing so, they were, by implication, attacking sexology itself. They wrote:

We began to have misgivings about the underpinnings of the edifice (Masters and Johnson) have built. The standing and popularity of sex therapy today rest heavily on the study Masters and Johnson did of their treatment results. . . . Our conclusion, in brief: Masters and Johnson's research is so flawed by methodological errors and slipshod reporting that it fails to meet customary standards—and their own—for evaluation research. . . . Because of this, the effectiveness of sex therapy—widely assumed to be high since the advent of Masters and Johnson—is thrown into question.[44]

This was heresy, and the controversy escalated. Although Masters and Johnson avoided comment at first, following a confrontation at the sixth World Congress of Sexology in 1983 they called a press conference to defend themselves against the charges. Prominent sexologists such as Wardell Pomeroy, co-author of the Kinsey studies, came to their defense. But the issue was covered extensively in the press, and many sexologists worried about the erosion of their own credibility. For many, the publicity emphasized sexology's tenuous niche and fueled anxiety about professionalism. Mary Calderone of SIECUS said:

The public wants to find us bad, and that includes some of the media. There is a tendency to snigger. They report that we go around telling each other about our sex lives. We don't do that. None of us are voyeurs. This is a serious business. We've been serious about it for years.[45]

Zilbergeld did not retreat, speculating that Masters and Johnson had concealed their outcome statistics in order to legitimate their controversial work. Unless they reported excellent results, he noted, their whole endeavor would have been open to challenge: "It suggests to me that Masters and Johnson got carried away with their own enthusiasm. . . . Their data are not organized, not specific, nothing that we would call rigorous or scientific." And he criticized the general direction of sexology:

Without naming names, I feel that the promoters of these trends are building an empire, making money and establishing practices. Those motivations are not absent from me, either. But in some sense we have lost control. This whole business about G-Spots and extended orgasms and men waving towels with their penises really represents a profession that cannot police itself. I think it is quite unfortunate. You know, we sex therapists can do a lot of harm.[46]

Zilbergeld, a clinical psychologist, was critical of the clinical therapeutic ethos in general, not just sex therapy. His book, *The Shrinking of America*, was a major critique of the transformation of human difficulties into therapeutic dysfunctions. Yet his attacks on sexology struck a particularly vulnerable spot within the field. *Time* reported that "the foundations of sex therapy . . . are shaken,"[47] and many sexologists rushed to buttress them. Lewis Durham, executive director of TAOS, intimated that the matter was a turf struggle: "We think sexology is a science, but it remains a debatable issue. Psychologists might look down on sexology and say they can handle sexual problems. And there's also the factor of professional jealousy."[48]

The rapid proliferation of sex therapists through the 1970s accounted for much of the anxiety over the question of effectiveness. It was a largely unregulated field flourishing because of a reputation for quick and easy cures. Scores of practitioners, many lacking formal training, hung out "sex therapist" shingles and began treatment.[49] Often their interventions consisted of little more than the dispensation of advice and St. Louis–style homework assignments. Many other therapists were trained mental health professionals who integrated the newer sex therapy techniques into their practice. Whatever their philosophy, most sex therapists were deferential to the groundbreaking Masters and Johnson model. Even the west-coast team of Hartman and Fithian utilized Masters and Johnson's methods within the more eclectic range of techniques characteristic of humanistic sexology.

Although Masters and Johnson themselves decried the potential for malpractice in the field of sex therapy, the very nature of their program was conducive to exploitation. Largely atheoretical, with no psychodynamic framework or theory of the unconscious, to many the St. Louis program appeared little more than a series of exercises. The very simplicity of the program, so valued by Masters and Johnson, lent itself to simplistic adoption. Yet by the mid-1970s other major figures had emerged within scientific sexology who would both add depth and help steer sex therapy toward new ground.

The New Sex Therapy: Beyond Masters and Johnson

D r. Helen Singer Kaplan, M.D., Ph.D., from Cornell University–New York Hospital Center, broadened the field of sex therapy in several ways. By synthesizing the Masters and Johnson program with psychoanalysis, she expanded the repertoire of techniques, incorporated a theory of the unconscious, and therefore allowed for the encompassing of more practitioners under the rubric of sex therapy. Further, she reconceptualized Masters and Johnson's sexual response cycle to include the "desire" phase and thus developed a theoretical model that could accommodate the sexual dysfunction of the 1980s—disorders of sexual desire.

Kaplan was unaware of Masters and Johnson's research in St. Louis when she began her work in 1964. She has said that her involvement in sex therapy developed from her focus on psychosomatic medicine: "It was the opportunity to be creative in a neglected field. It's easy to be an expert in sexuality because it's so neglected."[50] Having written several texts on sex therapy and developed what she termed "the new sex therapy," Kaplan is considered one of the leading experts in the field.

The new sex therapy represents a synthesis of the therapeutic traditions of behaviorism and psychoanalysis. This is most apparent in its approach to etiology. Kaplan views sexual disorders as emerging from either remote or immediate psychological determinants. So, like Masters and Johnson, she initially focuses on the situation immediately preceding the sexual problem. This technique reflects the behavior modification ("stimulus–response") concept of behavior, wherein altering the initial stimulus condition changes the subsequent behavior. She is, however, critical of programs like Masters and Johnson's that view sexual difficulties only in the context of the present. Kaplan's psychiatric training is evident in her concern for the more remote determinants of sexual dysfunctions, and she views sex therapy as an opportunity "to deal with the deeper determinants of the problem, with the unconscious conflicts, the relationship problems and with the underlying guilts and anxieties which often are revealed in the course of sex therapy."[51] Thus, Kaplan's new sex therapy is an amalgam of psychiatry, behaviorism, and experiential sex exercises.

As a physician, Kaplan retains the aura of science and the emphasis on sexual medicine established by Masters and Johnson. She incorporates many of the medicalized categories of sexual dysfunctions, such as vaginismus, premature ejaculation, and orgastic dysfunction. In fact, she served on the revision committee for the *DSM-III*, which included many of these sexual problems under the category of psychosexual disorders. As a physician, she views sexual problems as diseases. She requires medical evaluations of all clients, and will prescribe drugs for the treatment of certain dysfunctions.[52] She emphasizes that sex therapy is the new "sexual medicine," and her published works resemble classic medical textbooks.[53] She uses many of the behavioral therapeutic techniques, such as directed masturbation and the squeeze technique, but she also utilizes more long-term psychoanalytic treatment.

Despite the introduction of a more psychodynamic analysis, Kaplan's analysis of sex and gender is remarkably similar to Masters and Johnson's. She also emphasizes sex as a biological process, yet moves a step beyond Masters and Johnson in her emphasis on the reproductive purpose of sex. In *The New Sex Therapy*, her initial premise is, "The human sexual response is a highly rational and orderly sequence of physiological events, the object of which is to prepare the bodies of two mates for reproductive union."[54] Kaplan's emphasis on the physical body approaches the style of sociobiology, where form and function are congruent with some naturally unfolding schema. She told an interviewer: "Just as the bodies of males and females are complementary and fit together for the purpose of reproduction and survival, the brains of males and females are somewhat different physically. Perhaps that's so our behavior patterns can fit together as beautifully as our bodies do."[55]

Kaplan believes in a male sex drive that "is much more difficult to suppress" and "is so compelling that it's less subject to inhibition by learning than the female's."[56] If the origin and nature of gender differences reside in the body, so, for Kaplan, do love and attraction. She attributes the feeling of romance to a universal, biological component and claims that men are naturally attracted to women with unwrinkled skin: "That's why women wear makeup and try to look young. And it's foolish not to recognize the universal appeal of the younger woman. I think it's ludicrous to say this is due to advertising or social conditioning."[57] In an analysis reminiscent of Kinsey's Kaplan believes that "the more closely you express your biological heritage, the more content you'll feel."[58]

Her idealization of the physical body, coupled with the virtual dismissal of the power of culture to affect sexual expression, results in the same therapeutic impoverishment that characterizes the Masters and Johnson program. Biological sexuality is depicted as a true, essential state that can triumphantly emerge in the absence of cultural distractions. She explains, "It is the aim of sexual therapy to allow couples to experience the natural unfolding of their sexual responses, free from the inhibitory influences which can, because of the hierarchical construction of our nervous system, impinge on these from numerous sources."[59] These sources can be conscious or unconscious, remote in origin or immediate. "Indeed, in the matrix of our sexually confused, constricted and conflicted society and in the cradle of our intensely emotional and provocatively incestuous families, negative affects and conflict almost invariably come to contaminate the pure pleasure-craving sexual instinct."[60]

The goal of sex therapy is to help this pure, untouched sexual energy emerge. Of necessity, sex therapists practicing from this perspective will intervene in a highly individualistic fashion, since the goal is to excavate the client's biological response. Like Masters and Johnson, Kaplan acknowledges cultural factors, but with little more than a passing nod. Likewise, sexual politics are given short shrift, and sometimes ignored completely. *The New Sex Therapy* frequently describes women's sexual difficulties, but focuses on individual pathology. Cultural pressures and the double standard are mentioned but the true implications ignored.

Women are particularly vulnerable to rejection anxiety. Habitual responses such as, "*I have to hurry and have an orgasm or he will be disappointed with me,*" or, "*My breasts are not big enough to excite him,*" or "*I can't take this much time; he will be impatient,*" "*I can't ask him to go down on me, he will be repulsed,*" have destroyed the sexual adequacy of countless women.

The roots of such insecurity may have their origin both in the patient's childhood relationships, particularly if love and acceptance were contingent on pleasing the parents and "performing" for them, and in sexual misinformation which engenders unrealistic expectations. (Emphasis in original.)[61]

Like many sex therapists, Kaplan equates male and female sexual oppression. Women, she notes, suffer the destructive effects of a society that casts them in a subservient and dependent role. But, she quickly adds, "The male is no better off. He is heavily burdened by the 'male role,' which carries with it the need to perform, to compete, and to excel."[62] There is virtually no analysis of power differences and the social privilege inherent in the male role.

Significantly, the new sex therapy includes a psychodynamic theory of the unconscious, which allows for a broader analysis of sexuality and, eventually, of sexual desire. Yet the allure—along with the marketability—of brief, symptomatic treatment is maintained. Kaplan emphasizes that the first therapeutic strategy is to circumvent deeper problems and work directly to improve sexual functioning. Intrapsychic conflicts are addressed only if initial, limited interventions fail. A pertinent description in *The New Sex Therapy* illustrates the overriding emphasis on physical functioning to the exclusion of underlying difficulties or sexist dynamics within the marriage:

Although I recognized that Mr. A's premature ejaculation was probably related to his unconscious hostility toward women, I did not interpret this as long as it did not present a specific obstacle to therapy. I did so only when the husband's hostility gave rise to resistances which interfered with treatment. It may be speculated that the husband's ambivalence toward his wife made him reluctant to "give" her good sex at this point. His unconscious conflicts surrounding women impeded his gaining ejaculatory continence by motivating him to arrange his work schedule so that he could not "find time" to perform the prescribed exercises. When this became apparent, he was confronted with his avoidance of the exercises and the presumed unconscious reasons for his behavior were actively interpreted. However, no such interpretations were offered during the initial phase of treatment; at that stage, the wife was merely instructed to repeatedly stimulate her husband's penis and stop just before he was reaching orgasm. The patient was admonished not to think about his wife during this experience, or about past sexual failures, or to let himself be distracted by any other thoughts, but to focus his attention exclusively on his genital sensations as he experienced mounting excitement and impending orgasm.[63]

Sex therapists' belief that they can liberate a surging sexual energy, untouched by cultural or developmental factors, ensures that sex therapy will remain a limited intervention.

As the field of sex therapy matures in the late 1980s and early 1990s, sexology's diverse and interdisciplinary body of practitioners often embellish basic programs with updated twists and nuances. The synthesis of behaviorism and psychodynamic theory remains the staple of the field. In addition, sex therapists may use explicit erotic material, sex toys such as vibrators and dildoes, group therapy and marathons, "intimate showering," and various forms of bodywork. The range of bodywork techniques is both enormous and beset by controversy. As noted earlier, nude group therapy sessions, massage therapy, sessions in hot tubs, sexual encounters with surrogate partners, and sexual touch between therapist and client are all therapeutic interventions that some sexologists will vehemently defend, although nudity and some forms of touch have been proscribed by the AASECT code of ethics. The range of treatments is largely acontextual, retaining the problems with sex and gender associated with Kaplan and Masters and Johnson.

Two promising developments within sex therapy are the use of scripting theory and the application of principles of feminist therapy. Scripting theory originates in part in the intellectual tradition of the symbolic interactionists and, on the more popular therapeutic level, in Eric Berne's principles of transactional analysis therapy. The notion of scripts refers to early life decisions that are fashioned into a predictable, stylized form of behavior.[64] Sociologists William Simon and John Gagnon, whose *Sexual Conduct* was a pioneering text emphasizing the social origins of sexuality, have expanded the scripting concept and applied it to sexual behavior. In this perspective, people use scripts developed through experiences in early childhood and adolescence as guides that tell them how to behave in sexual situations. Sex therapists can assess "dysfunctional scripts" and help the client to modify or change them. Simon and Gagnon posit three levels of scripting: "cultural scenarios (instructive in collective meanings), interpersonal scripts (the application of specific cultural scenarios by a specific individual in a specific social context), and intrapsychic scripts (the management of desires as experienced by the individual)."[65]

Applying script theory to sexual issues reconceptualizes sexuality. Particularly in the Simon and Gagnon model, sexuality is removed from a privileged site as a natural, immutable drive. Instead, the juxtaposition of social, interpersonal, and intrapsychic factors shape sexual expression. Significantly, this approach emphasizes the power of culture in constructing sexuality. The danger in script theory is that it may be used narrowly to rescript client behavior, with the emphasis remaining on the individual. In such cases change is limited to the individual modification of a problematic script, and the role of culture is deemphasized. Script theory can also be misinterpreted as conveying the notion of a role or image that can be easily refashioned or shed to reveal a "true" self or essence underneath. Despite these possible limitations, sophisticated uses of script theory could potentially propel sex therapy toward greater complexity and effectiveness.

If the role of culture is in danger of being minimized by some scripting theorists, it is actively reasserted by feminist sex therapists. Although a tiny voice within sexology, feminist sex therapists have developed critiques of several aspects of current sex therapy, focusing on power, gender, and the patriarchal infrastructure of the field. Leonore Tiefer was one of the first feminist sexologists to publicly analyze the ideological underpinnings of sex therapy. In articles and at conferences, she has pointedly elucidated gender bias within sex therapy.

> Sex therapy is not infrequently sexist for several reasons. (1) when it accepts only the genital, intercourse-oriented definitions of dysfunctions as treatable; (2) when by its kneejerk use of behavioral techniques it ignores the gender dynamics of the couple; or (3) perhaps worst of all, when, in cotherapy treatment, it thoughtlessly models a male–female relationship that serves to suppress development and liberation.[66]

In this view, sex therapy accepts as normative those models of sexuality that spring from a male-centered imperative. Penile–vaginal intercourse is the norm in treatment modalities; inabilities are termed "dysfunctions," while differences are labeled "deviations" or, more politely, "variations." Thus, the sexual dysfunctions codified in the *DSM-III* as mental disorders are inhibitions of the sexual response cycle that render intercourse difficult or impossible: vaginismus, dyspareunia, premature ejaculation, orgasmic disorders, and impotence. Since data from Kinsey, Masters and Johnson, Shere Hite, and other sexologists have strikingly illustrated that only a minority of women experience orgasm or their most powerful sexual satisfaction from coitus, this single-minded emphasis on intercourse tends merely to accommodate male sexual desires.

The role of culture in the differential sexual socialization of men and women is central to a feminist analysis. Sexual interaction can be accurately understood only within the context of the social and economic oppression of women. Power inequities in society must inevitably surface in sexuality. In a critique of sex roles and sexual dysfunction, sex therapist Wendy Stock has analyzed the influence of gender stereotypes on sexual relationships and functioning.[67] She describes how women's learned passivity often circumscribes their ability to enjoy sex, let alone aggressively pursue satisfying sexual activities. Conversely, the emphasis on physical orchestration, control, and performance in the male sexual script requires men to be ready and willing sex machines. The impact of these divergent expectations on heterosexual relationships and sexuality has been minimized by sex therapists, who traditionally focus on the behavioral level. Yet both Stock and Tiefer address the practical dilemma facing sex therapists who seriously acknowledge feminist analyses: is it possible to integrate a broader critique with specific therapeutic techniques for the actual practice of sex therapy? In the absence of major social change, it is important to assert a theory that can acknowledge the power of culture while simultaneously offering pragmatic interventions for change. An overhaul of sex therapy with this in mind could entail a broadening of the assumed parameters of sexuality as well as the inclusion of therapeutic interventions that deal directly with gender roles. Stock, for example, recommends supplementing standard sex therapy techniques with remedial training for women in such areas as self-esteem, emotional expression, assertiveness, communication, and body awareness.[68] Feminist psychotherapy, which emphasizes the role of social, political, and economic factors in individual problems, can provide a useful model for integrating gender politics and psychological treatment in sex therapy.

Disorders of Desire

I nherent in the process of medicalization is the inclusion of an ever-increasing number of problems under a medical rubric. For the specialty of sex therapy, this process is reflected in the widening parameters for the diagnosis of behaviors and conditions as dysfunctions. By the middle to late 1970s, a quiet revolution in the presenting sex problems of clients was under way. Sex therapists began to recognize differences between the sexual problems reported by their clients and the cases they had seen earlier in the decade. The quandary was formulated by many as, "Where have all the easy cases gone?" "Easy cases" were those where the problems were essentially "technical difficulties," often the result of ignorance or misinformation. Typically they responded well to the simple behavioral methods developed by Masters and Johnson, accurate information, advice on technique, direct treatment programs, and even self-help books. Later in the decade, however, many clients were seeking the help of sex therapists for a less tractable problem—lack of interest in sex. The difficulties were presented in different ways: sexual boredom, low libido, sexual malaise, and even sexual aversion and sexual phobia.

The emergence and visibility of desire issues would prove significant in revealing sexology's commitment, despite evidence of ineffectiveness, to a highly medicalized model of definition and treatment. Unlike problems of erectile failure or inability to achieve orgasm, problems where sex therapists could focus on individual technique and functioning, the absence of sexual desire itself provoked a crisis in a profession that had boasted quick and simple cures. Yet sex therapists responded rapidly, extending their biomedical perspective to encompass the new complaint. They coined a term, and low sexual interest became a sexual dysfunction called inhibition of sexual desire (ISD). ISD was included as a mental disorder in the *DSM-III*, and sex therapists claim that it is now the most widespread sexual dysfunction and the one that is the most resistant to treatment.[69] For women, ISD is the most frequently diagnosed sexual dysfunction, constituting 30 to 35 percent of female diagnoses.[70]

With its rapid ascendance to the status of mental disorder, ISD became the medically legitimated equivalent of "Not tonight, dear. I have a headache."

It was perhaps inevitable that sexologists in the late twentieth century would address desire as a major medical problem. Historically, physicians have played a significant role in defining the existence, appropriateness, and ideal object of sexual desire or passion. And, most important, physicians have attempted to codify changing social expectations about desire into the presumed "truth" of medical discourse. Desire must be understood both as an individual experience and as a category of social rules and expectations whose dimensions evolve and change historically. And physicians, sexologists, and clergy are some of the actors who help chart those changes. Further, there is a complicated, reciprocal, and not very clearly understood relationship between the internal, individual experience of desire and the development of desire as a cultural construct. While it is true that individuals can experience physical signals that we identify as sexual yearning, historical research indicates that broader societal notions of desire are based not merely on biological or even psychosocial impulses, but on ideological beliefs about sexuality and gender. Critics are currently debating the ways in which ideology might be psychologically incorporated to sculpt internal expression of desire.

Permission for any individual woman to experience desire, discuss sexuality, initiate a sexual encounter, or present herself as passionate varies historically and culturally. Carl Degler has documented the variability in nineteenth-century medical advice literature regarding desire in middle-class women. One theme speaks to the strength of women's passion; another articulates the stereotypic Victorian view that women approach sex "with shrinking, or even with horror, rather than with desire."[71] Further, Nancy Cott has related variations in the dominant ideology about women's passion through the eighteenth and nineteenth centuries not to changes in individual and interpersonal sexual experiences, but to cultural shifts in metaphoric systems about the nature of women. Passionlessness, she argues, transformed women's image in the nineteenth century to one of spirituality, away from the eighteenth-century view of women as lustful creatures prone to sexual excess.[72]

Clearly, there is no linear relationship between medical advice literature and the sexual behavior and experiences of individuals in a society. Yet historical analysis of the variability in medical prescriptiveness is significant for two reasons. It belies the notion, so integral to medical discourse, that theory about desire simply reflects the internal, universal expression of the biological impulse of individuals. The content of medical literature is not based on essential truth but is itself shaped by social, economic, and political factors. Second, it underscores the role of cultural ideology in the construction of individual experiences of sexual desire. Not simply a biological urge, sexual desire is a culturally constructed composite. Any theory must account for a range of variables, among them the body, the historical era, the economic system, dominant ideologies of both sexuality and gender, and race and ethnicity.

While much of the medical literature one hundred years ago approvingly documented women's indifference to sex, contemporary sexologists have noted a similar attitude with dismay. Helen Singer Kaplan was the earliest major theorist of ISD and set the tone for much of what followed: a biomedical approach characterized by a view of sexual desire as a drive whose presence indicates health and whose absence signals a dysfunction that should be treated by therapy or drugs. By the late 1970s, Kaplan had developed a "triphasic" model of sexual response that identified the desire phase, excitement phase, and orgasm as separate physiological entities. This new schema allowed for the differentiation of dysfunctions specific to each phase. Within sexology, this was considered a major conceptual advance over the Masters and Johnson four-stage model, which could not encompass a theory of desire at all. For the treatment of ISD, Kaplan adapted her earlier therapeutic program into the new "psychosexual therapy," an amalgam of behavioral, psychodynamic, and pharmacologic intervention.[73] This integrated approach was deemed vital for ISD sufferers, who are considered to be more deeply troubled and therapeutically intractable than others seeking sex therapy.

As is consistent with her essentialism, Kaplan believes that "sexual desire resides in the brain."[74] Although her therapy is heavily psychoanalytic, its underpinnings are strongly biological. "Sexual desire," she wrote, "is an appetite or drive which is produced by the activation of a specific neural system in the brain, while the excitement and orgasm phases involve the genital organs."[75] As in earlier sex therapies, sex (or, in this case, desire) is located in and thus reduced to, the physical body. Like Freudian libido theory, this notion suggests that desire is endogenous and inevitable, unless blocked or repressed by intrapsychic conflict. Again, sexuality is flattened out to an internal, or at most interpersonal, dynamic.

Sexological discourse in the 1980s was heavily dominated by disorders of desire. The alleged pervasiveness and intractability of these dysfunctions have inspired a literature representing diverse theories and clinical techniques. Systems theorists, psychoanalysts, behaviorists, object relations clinicians, and biologists have all contributed to the growing landscape around desire dysfunctions. Subsequent to Kaplan's theories, some sexologists have more strongly asserted the role of cultural learning as a determinant of desire. Simon and Gagnon's scripting theory suggests that "it is just as plausible to examine sexual behavior for its capacity to express and serve nonsexual motives as the reverse."[76] Social and contextual variables are integral to the notion of scripts. Similarly, Barry Bass has criticized the assumption of most sex therapists "that sexual desire is the expression of a physiological need that varies with the biological make-up of the individual, much like the wide variability reported in individual requirements for sleep."[77] Bass suggests that the concept of low sexual desire is an unnecessary hypothetical, even mythical, construct. Most individuals, he notes, who describe themselves as experiencing little sexual interest find their sexual desire flourishing once their "conditions for good sex" are discovered and implemented.[78] Sex therapist Bernie Apfelbaum has criticized the broader therapeutic milieu of sex therapy, whose emphasis on sexual enhancement techniques increases the "pressure we all are under to 'always say yes.' "[79]

The tendency persists, however, for many sex therapists to view desire as a surging energy that can be switched on or off. The focus of treatment is to discover and cancel the "turn off" mechanism. Despite lack of supporting evidence, laboratory research is dominated by a search for hormonal determinants.[80] And, logically, this perspective has led to the development of pharmacologic agents to turn desire back on. For a time, Wellbrutin, manufactured by Burroughs-Wellcome, was the rising star of drug therapy for ISD. An antidepressant that was accidently discovered to have aphrodisiac qualities, Wellbrutin was tested by Theresa Crenshaw on 57 men and women with ISD. Sixty-three percent of the patients on Wellbrutin reported significantly increased libido, compared with 3 percent on a placebo. A follow-up revealed 46 percent improvement on the drug, and 22 percent improvement on placebos.[81] The drug was touted as providing new hope for patients "who had failed every other form of sex therapy before Wellbrutin."[82] This new hope faded when Wellbrutin was discovered to trigger seizure activity in patients. Given the strong biomedical emphasis within sex therapy, however, analysts note that the search for pharmacologic "cures" for desire disorders will likely increase.[83] Despite the lack of empirical evidence for its effectiveness, clinicians are prescribing testosterone for premenopausal women who complain of low sexual desire.[84] And, in a predictable countercultural move, humanistic sexologists at the Institute for Advanced Study of Human Sexuality have developed a natural oat extract called Exsativa that they claim enhances women's desire.

Focusing on a sex *drive* while ignoring social and contextual factors that affect sexual interest has led to theoretical dilemmas for sexology. The quest for a pill, whether Wellbrutin or Exsativa, that will magically induce sexiness lends itself to bizarre fantasies about the effects of such agents. A *Phil Donahue Show* featuring Theresa Crenshaw and one of her patients who had used Wellbrutin, Sharon, contained the following exchange:

PHIL DONAHUE: Sharon took Wellbrutin. We thank you for stepping forward courageously here to tell us about your own experience with it. You took the pill and how long—what, were you probably in the library when you had erotic feelings, I don't know?

AUDIENCE: (*laughter*)

PHIL DONAHUE: Share with us, if you will please, what happened.

SHARON: Well, actually I was studying because I was going to college at the time. So, yeah, it did kind of, ah—erotic feelings came on me very suddenly.

PHIL DONAHUE: Was it suddenly?

SHARON: Yes, as a matter of fact, it was suddenly.

AUDIENCE: (*laughter*)

PHIL DONAHUE: So you're really going to have to plan who you're with, aren't you?[85]

The humor here derives mainly from the separation of sexual feelings from the social situations and cues that usually trigger and shape them —an incongruity that is inherent in the notion of chemotherapy for sexual desire.

More conventional sex therapy also suffers from an individualistic, acultural theory of desire. The sex therapy canon is replete with case studies in which dynamics of gender roles or social class are glaringly apparent as potential etiologic factors, but are ignored by the therapist. Kaplan, for example, describes the case of Dora.[86] Dora came to therapy with her husband, Dick, because of her total lack of desire and her partial avoidance of sex. We learn that Dora is furious at Dick: "The couple met when he was at a prestigious medical school and she was attending a city college. When they first met he did not hide the fact that he considered her to be inferior to him in intellect and social position." Yet Dora pursued Dick relentlessly, despite his frequent gibes that "he could do better."[87] Eventually they married and, in time, the relational balance shifted so that she ceased to find him attractive while he pined after her.

Kaplan attributes Dora's lack of desire to "her intense hostility toward her husband" and "unrecognized anger at men which had its genesis in an unresolved oedipal wish." The prescribed sensate focus exercises only generated more negative feelings in Dora, leading Kaplan to conclude that Dora was "simply too angry and had no wish to give up her anger." Therapy was unsuccessful, and the couple divorced bitterly. Perhaps there was no way that this marriage could, or should, have been "saved." Yet one cannot help but wonder about the outcome had the intervention probed the couple's feelings about social class and gender expectations, rather than locating the problems within Dora's intractable psyche.

Not only do disorders of desire present sex therapists with problematic treatment results; they also pose difficult conceptual and ideological problems. One major area of controversy concerns the definition of ISD. The syndrome of ISD suffers from the same conceptual murkiness as premature ejaculation: how fast is too fast, how low is too low? What, specifically, is low sexual interest? Is it based on quantity of sexual activity or quality? Who decides normal frequency? The *DSM-III* category of desire disorders is vague, but it implies that the person must be distressed, or that there must be an inherent disadvantage to low sexual interest. "Inherent disadvantage" is a euphemism that typically refers to the anger of a spouse. Since it frequently happens that one partner wants to have sex more often than the other, the existence of ISD as a medical diagnosis can serve as a trump card in relational power struggles over this issue: one partner can simply accuse the other of having a disease. In addition, the reliance on individual distress as a major diagnostic criterion for ISD places sexology in the same definitional quandary as transsexualism does. Both depend on self-diagnosis, since there are no tests that can measure whether one desires "enough" or feels "sufficiently" male or female.

ISD is a syndrome with contradictory implications for the profession. There has been some concern over the high failure rate in the treatment of ISD.[88] Sex therapists had grown accustomed to claiming treatment success and having sexual problems resolved by the utilization of a simple technique. ISD posed a threat to sexology's reputation (and legitimacy), and as the numbers of these clients increased, so did the threat. On the other hand, ISD represented a vast new market. In an era that suggests that happiness, even identity, depends on sexual expression,[89] people who are sexually indifferent rather than enraptured might well feel inadequate and do something about it. So although there was professional concern about the treatment of the syndrome, sexologists did not shrink from the task. They turned the armamentarium of clinical medicine on sexual boredom and indifference and (1) made it a disease, (2) conducted massive biomedical research into its etiology and treatment, (3) developed new treatment programs that proved to be significantly longer-term than earlier programs, and (4) implemented the use of drug treatment in certain cases. Thus, a widespread human problem of flagging sexual interest within marriage had been medicalized, enabling sexologists to tap a potentially unlimited market. It is a striking example of the changing ideological construction of sexual norms over the century that, in the 1980s, low interest in sex would be considered a major problem within sexual medicine. Yet it is not surprising, since lack of sexual desire is a devastating economic threat to a field based upon the treatment and enhancement of sexuality.[90] Sexual disinterest puts sex therapists in the awkward and fruitless position of trying to sell the proverbial bicycle to the proverbial fish. From a marketing perspective, then, inhibition of sexual desire is the quintessential dysfunction for the field of sexology.

Yet ISD may represent the weak link in the field of sex therapy. Its conceptual tenuousness combined with its ideological nature may undermine the already shaky foundations of a profession that seeks to be apolitical. Much of the literature reports that desire disorders typically emerge as a result of anger or hostility toward the spouse. Kaplan notes, "Fear or anxiety is the major etiologic factor in all the sexual dysfunctions, but anger at the partner is also a highly prevalent cause for the loss of sexual interest. . . . Regardless of the origin of the anger, it is not possible for most persons to feel sexual desire for 'the enemy.'"[91] Similarly, other studies of ISD in women demonstrate that power struggles and lack of respect are major dynamics.[92] Yet without an analysis that can account for factors such as power and gender roles within marriage, sex therapists tend to view the problem intrapsychically (offering clients like Dora a solution that locates the problem in unresolved oedipal conflicts) or interpersonally (prescribing sensate focus). Further, the biomedical approach of focusing on the individual is safer for sex therapists, since potential causes of sexual disinterest such as hostility, power struggles, or simple boredom from long-term monogamy may prove more threatening to the "marital unit," and to a profession that hopes to achieve status and authority by salvaging marriages.

There are a myriad of possible causes of sexual disinterest. Performance anxiety, anger, boredom, fear, trauma from sexual assault, lack of time, cultural pressures to have or not have sex, and the DINS syndrome (dual income, no sex) are among many cited. Yet there are several pieces to the puzzle of ISD that emerge thematically in the literature but that sex therapists fail to connect: (1) it is often not possible to feel sexual desire for someone with whom you are angry or engaged in a power struggle; (2) although the numbers are changing, women still account for most diagnoses of ISD; (3) traditional sex therapy techniques have been expanded to include longer-term relationship therapy, but the focus is still individualistic; and (4) in most reports, ISD is not responding as well to sex therapy as the other dysfunctions and produces a failure rate close to 50 percent.[93] Taken together, these factors suggest the extension of male-dominated culture into the bedroom. Some of the consequences of women's lesser power can be inability to initiate and direct sexual interaction, deference to men, and residual pain and anxiety from earlier sexual abuse. It is not inconceivable that anger at a lifetime of subordination might dampen a woman's sexual enthusiasm for her male partner. Similarly, female sexual socialization, with its emphasis on passivity and dependence, often results in profound conflict for women about sexual arousal and behavior. And ambivalence routinely results in lack of interest and alienation. Sex therapy that eschews an analysis of the etiology of sexual problems in gender and power differences can be only partially effective, at best. The intractability of many cases of ISD in the face of biomedical treatment merely highlights feminist arguments that sexual liberation is a broader vision, and will not occur until it is achieved in society at large.

In contrast to sexologists, who assume that, for both men and women, desire inevitably lurks beneath the surface, feminist theorist Jessica Benjamin, in a reformulation of Freud's infamous question, "What does woman want?" has asked, "Do women want?" or "Does woman *have* a desire?"[94] She and other feminists cite sociopolitical and developmental factors to explain how, in a rigidly gendered, patriarchal society, female desire itself is problematic. Women, who have largely been excluded from sexual subjectivity themselves, have instead traditionally been cast as objects for male desire. The phallus reigns supreme as the symbol of sexual agency and desire. In a culture in which power and authority, and hence an active sexual desire, are male prerogatives, it is logical that the individual experience of desire would be affected. For these theorists, women's desire is not simply a biological urge to be liberated under the right conditions. The question of desire entails an understanding, not just of biology, but of a complex construction of gender inequality in which differences are psychically reinscribed in the developmental context of the family and the larger culture.

In a feminist interpretation of psychoanalytic theory, Benjamin posits that in order for a child to have subjectivity and agency, necessary components of desire, he or she must have two things: a safe space in which to experience desire as coming from within, and a recognizing other, someone to recognize the desire as one's own. Recognition is a response from the other that makes meaningful the feelings, intentions, and actions of the self. To be a subject requires recognition of one's subjectivity by another subject or agent. In the Western nuclear family, only boys are allowed both. Their mothers provide a safe space (i.e., nurturance), and their fathers recognize them as like themselves (i.e., as having desire). Girls are denied the recognizing other, for in order to recognize the other, one must have power and agency oneself. Mothers, whose only real power is power over their children, are not able to recognize the daughter. Girl children identify with a largely powerless and desexualized mother. In Benjamin's view, the girl child's solution to this problem surfaces later in life in the heterosexual woman's search for ideal love in which she allows a man to carry all sense of agency for her. Her submission to him and to his will and agency is an attempt at finally getting the identificatory love that she missed with her father. Benjamin believes that only when cultural and familial changes allow women a sense of agency and men an identificatory connection to their young children will girls have the capacity to develop a desire of their own.

The implication of this and other feminist theories is that profound social, political, and developmental changes are crucial to engendering ongoing desire in women. Social change that ascribes the power of recognition to the mother would also engender a cultural metaphor of female sexual agency. Technical adjustments, individualistic therapy, and drug treatments offered by sexologists are just not sufficient. These theories are emphatic, moreover, in their insistence on the political dimension even of the psyche. Feminist therapist Jade McGleughlin, for example, asserts that the strong sense of community offered by the women's movement can provide for adults the sense of intersubjectivity that supports sexual agency and desire for women.[95] The women's movement of the 1970s, she notes, allowed women a safe space to experience desire as coming from within them. In addition, it elevated women to subject status with the power to recognize others. These feminist theories illustrate that the issue of desire involves complex interconnections of the individual psyche, development, relational components, and social dynamics.

In an interesting connection with another issue of concern to feminists, sexual desire disorders are frequently referred to as sexual anorexia, in an analogy to the eating disorder anorexia nervosa. Sexologists often compare sex to eating, in an attempt to present it as a simple, biological, "natural" behavior. Yet both are human activities imbued with cultural meaning and, for women in particular, fraught with symbolism and often danger. The sociopolitical context has rendered both eating and sexual expression potentially and frequently oppressive to women. And the destructive effects in both areas have been medicalized by professionals who have transformed sociopolitical problems into individual, medical dysfunctions.

In ISD, sexology faces the largest obstacles to its goal of improving and promoting sex between men and women, particularly within marriage. Without a richer analysis that examines historical changes in ideas about sexuality and desire, and affords a critique of marriage, the family, and power relations between men and women, sex therapy will likely be helpless to solve problems resulting in a loss of interest in sex. And sexology is now faced with the realization that increasingly sophisticated research techniques, new multiaxial diagnostic tools, surgical interventions, and drugs are all inadequate to the task. ISD does not respond to the early, simple tricks of sex therapy. Hydraulic feats (as described in the following section) will not necessarily spark a desire for sexual activity, and the age-old search for an aphrodisiac has not been realized in the techniques of sex therapists. Unless sexology incorporates a cultural, historical, and political analysis, disorders of desire may be its nemesis.

The Dilemmas of the Medical Model

How successfully is the medical model of sex therapy managing its clients' more traditional complaints? The major structural weaknesses of sex therapy are revealed in the very texts of the field. First, mechanically individualistic techniques typically miss the causes of the difficulties. Sex therapists have historically recognized a pattern to the etiology of female sexual dysfunctions. Helen Singer Kaplan wrote:

Prominent among these obstacles . . . are their attitudes toward helplessness, passivity, and dependence on the man, which lead to fears of being abandoned and rejected by him. Feelings of guilt and shame about sexuality in general and clitoral eroticism in particular are also exceedingly common in sexually repressed women.[96]

Since passivity, dependence, and sexual guilt are all socially acquired attributes, sexual difficulty can be merely one of the ramifications of female gender socialization. Anger, hostility, and lack of trust are repeatedly cited in the literature as causes of sexual problems in relationships. Yet it is precisely issues of this type that resist superficial therapeutic treatment. Kaplan notes, for example, that women "whose sexual response is blocked by deep hostility or conflict" are "*not* helped by these brief, experientially oriented methods" (emphasis in original).[97] Literature demonstrates that the institution of marriage itself is often inimical to the mental health of women,[98] the convergence point of gender stereotypes, sexual expectations, and economic and social pressures that can easily blossom into rage, power struggles, and, as Stock notes, "a virulent environment for healthy sexual functioning."[99]

Even sex therapy that is psychodynamically oriented fails to address institutionally based origins of sexual problems. The individual manifestation of symptoms such as performance anxiety, lack of interest in sex, bad timing, or unconscious sabotaging of opportunities for satisfying sex is undeniable. The "cure," however, is only partly individual. Instead of persistently focusing on the individual, sex therapy must incorporate a broader analysis and truly address painful and intractable sexual problems. In sex therapy with individuals, clinicians can work not just with psychodynamic constructs that locate the origin of problems within the nuclear family, but provide a more comprehensive cultural analysis of both the family and the psychic incorporation of social structures.

In the above-mentioned case of Mr. A, Kaplan recognizes hostility toward women as an underlying component of his premature ejaculation but chooses to ignore this interpretation as long as Mr. A's hostility does not impede the goal of ejaculatory competence. If she were to help the patient bring this hostility to consciousness and work to integrate it, might she not serve him better—to say nothing of his wife, their relationship, and society in general? Sex therapists sometimes ascribe a woman's sexual problems to "deep hostility toward the father." Such hostility could be interpreted to a woman both in terms of her individual relationship to her parent and as a problematic connection that has developed and been supported by differential and difficult gender relations in the broader context of a patriarchal society. A woman's sexual passivity, interpreted as the internalization of her mother's low self-esteem, could be framed to include the ways in which individual women and mothers are taught to devalue each other in a climate of misogyny and social inequality. In the absence of broader analysis, therapists misleadingly imply that such problems are a matter of individual pathology. But by casting the interpretive net more widely, sex therapists could help clients understand, and empower them to overcome, social, political, and economic obstacles to individual happiness.

Second, sex therapy literature reveals the iatrogenic dangers of a medicalized approach to sexual dilemmas. As evidenced by their meteoric ascent to best-seller status, sexological texts by the major sex researchers have been a primary source of sex education for countless individuals. Their success dramatically illustrates the hunger for accurate information in a culture that sensationalizes or obfuscates sex. Yet with its rigidly normative standards of sexuality, the widespread dissemination of sex therapy information has itself been cited as the cause of sexual problems.[100] The role of the texts often extends beyond the dispersion of knowledge to serving as yardsticks by which individuals measure their own sexual feelings and experiences. Such texts have assumed an ever-increasing importance in the social construction of sexuality. In 1977 sex therapists Joe LoPiccolo and Julia Heiman wrote:

> It is ironic that the new availability of physiologically accurate information concerning female sexuality, which should reassure couples about their sexual adjustment, is having exactly the opposite effect in some cases. Somehow the popular media have transformed "women are sexual and can have multiple orgasms" into "real women must be hypersexual and must have multiple orgasms." Hopefully, the present generation of therapists will not be acculturation agents, but will instead be a countercultural force, reassuring such couples that they are not in need of therapy.[101]

In fact, the media alone do not bear the responsibility for fashioning a new sexual tyranny. There are obvious and compelling reasons for sex therapists to relish and maintain their status as "experts" with a role in determining sexual behavior.

A complex social and economic system underpins LoPiccolo and Heiman's hope that sexologists will eschew the role of "expert." A primary factor sustaining the cultural status of the sex therapist within white, middle-class American society is simple demand. Sam and Louise, along with scores of other couples and individuals, seek the services of sex therapists every year. It is impossible to untangle the myriad cultural determinants of sexual problems, but many people want, or have been taught to want, help with their sex lives. The Masters and Johnson gospel that sex is our natural birthright tapped a market of people eager to find theirs. Since, in our society, the most legitimate sexual discourse is medical, sexology offers a seemingly neutral, nonmoralistic program for treatment. It is one of the few options for individuals who have difficulty feeling or being sexual. Sex therapists, it would seem, are simply providing the services that they have been asked to provide.

As a medical intervention dominated by "experts," however, sex therapy is subject to the same questions raised by sociological critiques of the general medicalization of our culture.[102] Increasingly, behaviors that were once considered moral or legal problems, like excessive drinking, overeating, or certain sexual activities, now fall under the medical purview. For alcoholics, drug addicts, or individuals like Sam, defining their problem as medical may decrease its stigma: it is much more acceptable to have a medical problem than to be morally bankrupt or sexually inept. The term "frigid," for example, widely used before the 1970s not just to denote sexual unresponsiveness but to convey a host of negative stereotypes of women, has virtually dropped from the lexicon. And, in the area of sex, medical discourse legitimates requests for certain treatments or interventions that, in another era, might have been judged lascivious. In sex therapy, for example, sex purchased from an unknown partner is deemed surrogate therapy rather than prostitution.

However, there are also disadvantages stemming from the application of medical science to sexuality. In its attempt to develop dramatic procedures that would win public confidence, scientific sexology relies on a paradigm conceptualizing disease states triggered by specific agents and countered by aggressive treatments. The medical model targets the human body as the site of dysfunction and intervention and does not account for the broader social and political context.[103] From this perspective, as we have seen, many human problems are considered to be diseases and practitioners attempt to implement individual cures. In the area of sexuality this has meant the development of various sex- and gender-related dysfunctions and dysphorias. The culmination of this movement was the inclusion of a myriad of sex-related issues within the updated *DSM-III*. The 1980 revision includes such conditions as "gender identity disorders," "sexual masochism," "inhibited sexual desire," "inhibited female orgasm," and "ego-dystonic homosexuality."[104] Reified into diseases, sexual issues or problems can be fought with conventional medical therapies such as drugs and surgery. Drugs and electroconvulsive therapy, for example, are used in the treatment of low libido.[105] Chemotherapy is commonplace in the treatment of gender identity dysphoria or transsexualism; in the area of sexual anxiety, drugs may be used to complement psychological counseling.

Medicalization may bring mixed results for individuals and the culture, but it has undeniable benefits for sexology's professional aspirations. When a social issue is defined as a public problem, negotiation takes place over who is to define and frame the terms of discussion until a profession or organization establishes undisputed "ownership."[106] Sexology, which does not exert hegemony over sexual issues, has hoped, by reliance on a biomedical model, to achieve authority and legitimacy by its command over a medicalized discourse of sex.

Given the inherently political nature of the medical system, it should not be surprising that the practice of sexual medicine is vulnerable to the dynamics of gender politics. The cultural emphasis on men rather than women as active sexual agents has meant that the most energetic expansion of practice has been directed to male problems and illnesses. It is now possible, for example, for men to have penile implants resembling hydraulic pumps that will enable them to have erections. Or they can have a less expensive silicon rod implant, which gives the penis a permanently rigid form. The New England Male Reproductive Center performed more than four hundred surgical implants in five years. If the cause of impotence is organic, the fees are covered by insurance, and the director of the Center reports few complications. One implantee noted, "Now I can work a 14-hour day, come home, and still have sex."[107] Leonore Tiefer, however, criticizes the growing reliance on penile prostheses, which have become culturally normative despite recent evidence of high rates of postoperative infection and mechanical failure.[108] Similarly, an experimental treatment for impotence involving intrapenile injections of smooth muscle relaxants such as papaverine was implemented in a few clinics in the early 1980s. Despite lack of follow-up and inadequate documentation of effectiveness, the injections are now common practice. Potions and interventions to enhance male sexuality seem to have almost unlimited market potential. At least one practitioner charges clients a hundred dollars a shot, does not teach them to self-inject, and makes them pay for a year's treatment in advance.[109] Since these new techniques have more to do with societal ideals about sexuality and male prowess than with physiological deficiency, the potential for abuse and the lack of data on effectiveness do not deter practitioners or diminish business.

The proliferation of medical technology in the field of sexology continues apace despite lack of equitable access, major questions about efficacy, and repeated failures. Many instruments have been designed to facilitate the diagnosis and treatment of sexual problems. Devices such as the vaginal photoplethismograph measure the amount of lubrication in the vagina to evaluate the sexual response level, while the nocturnal penile tumescence (NPT) monitor is designed to record the "architecture, amplitude, and duration" of erections during the night.[110] NPT is regarded as having "brought sexual psychophysiology into new stature in the medical and psychological fields," despite studies that call into question the disgnostic accuracy and the relative costs and benefits of the procedure.[111] The dildo camera, vaginal photoplethismograph, and postmortem searches for the G-spot represent the continuing evolution of medicine's ability to explore and conquer the inner body in the quest for knowledge, scientific truth, and clinical intervention. This emphasis on the physical body supersedes attention to material or cultural circumstances, gender, age, race, and ethnicity.

Medical advances in the exploration of the body may in fact alienate individuals from their own bodies. This is particularly true for women, who have been subjected to expert diagnoses for centuries. Even the existence of female orgasm was medically questioned until confirmed by early sex researchers' empirical observation of uterine contractions.[112] And the course of the vaginal–clitoral orgasm debate has been charted, until recently, by men. Albert Ellis described the research in this area by the early sexologist Robert Latou Dickinson. In 1948 Dickinson examined a woman to determine the comparative sensitivity of her clitoris and vagina. She described no sensitivity when he touched her inner vagina with a blunt probe. When he touched her clitoral area with the probe, she described great sexual sensitivity, but referred to it as emerging from her vagina. Ellis concluded:

> Bobby always smiled when he told this story—to emphasize the point that many women *think* or *believe* that they get intense vaginal stimulation when, really, they only have been stimulated clitorally. His point seemed well taken: not only do most "normal" women primarily get clitoral sensation, and ultimately orgasm but they *assume* the source of this feeling as vaginal. Forgive them, Bobby would smile: they know not what they feel! (Emphasis in original.) [113]

This type of technical intervention can foster a woman's mistrust of her own bodily experiences and a reliance on medical authority and machinery. The vaginal photoplethismograph was described as measuring "arousal that is not seen in the mind." [114] A typical clinical technique is to hook up a woman to the photoplethismograph, show her erotic material, and monitor her response. Frequently, women who register some vaginal lubrication will report a lack of arousal. The clinician will then correct the woman, advise her that she is, in fact, sexually stimulated, and provide her with the proof from the monitoring device. It is a quintessential reduction of sex to the biophysical, where lubrication equals arousal.

Thus, sexology is experiencing some tension with respect to the clinical practice of sex therapy. It depends on the dramatic, near-miraculous "cure" rates of those heady days in the early 1970s to convince potential consumers of its authority and expertise. Yet, increasingly, sex therapists are reaching a therapeutic dead-end. Ironically, this conundrum is exacerbated by the very strategy sexology has chosen to enhance its credibility and effectiveness: the emphasis on biomedical technique. The medicalization of sexual problems has allowed for a discourse free of moralism and blame, and, for many, opened the possibility of seeking help for sexual issues. Yet medical technique is embedded in a generally invisible matrix of values and attitudes that uphold traditional ideas about sexuality and gender. Sex therapy is therefore striated with implicit mandates about appropriate sexual expression and roles. Finally, contemporary sex therapy, with its emphasis on physiology and pharmaceuticals, is too narrow in scope. Science and medicine are ultimately ineffective in achieving viable and comprehensive change in sexuality, which is so profoundly grounded in social relations. Yet, given that scientific rationality is considered vital for professional consolidation, it is likely that sexology will sacrifice effectiveness for perceived legitimacy.

Chapter Seven

Boys Will Be Girls:
Contemporary
Research on Gender

Whenever you find a number of
different explanations coming
from the medical profession, then
you know we don't know
what we're talking about.

Dr. Helen Singer Kaplan

In the 1960s, while many scientific sexologists were responding to widespread difficulties in heterosexuality and marriage by implementing clinical programs of sex therapy, others moved in a different direction. The second major endeavor of scientific and medical sexology was gender research. In response to shifts in traditional gender roles throughout the century, sexologists have viewed scientific research as an avenue to the "truth" about gender differences and similarities. In its clinical application, gender research is an attempt to shape cultural constructions of gender in the mold of scientific fact. In addition, sexologists believe that a resolution to the cultural dilemma of heterosexuality can emerge from a scientifically based understanding of gender. John Money, one of the most prominent gender researchers, wrote of the need for a new science within sexology that would be named "genderology": "All behavior that is sex-classified or sex-coded, regardless of its genesis, ultimately impinges on pair-bonding and the failure or the success of men and women in their relationships together."[1] Gender research thus reflects Kinsey's fondest hope that harmony between the sexes would flourish if men and women understood each other.

This concentration on gender issues was congruent with sexology's attempt to establish cultural authority by addressing issues of profound social anxiety. As with sex therapists, the ultimate agenda of gender researchers is to understand and enhance heterosexual relationships. This would be accomplished in two ways: by seeking to understand the origins and development of masculine and feminine behavior and by attempting to explain gender "failures." The enormous emphasis on persons who behave in "gender-anomalous" ways—for example, homosexuals and transsexuals—derives from the notion that "normality" can be understood by studying "deviancy." This quasi-covert agenda underlies the voluminous research in these areas. The upheavals in traditional gender norms in the last half-century clearly indicate the need for a new vision. The goal of gender sexologists is to help chart the new boundaries in a scientific fashion.

The establishment of expertise and authority in the area of gender would signal a level of successful professional consolidation for sexual scientists. Over the decades, then, sexologists have attempted to assert control over the definitions and parameters of maleness, femaleness, homosexuality, and heterosexuality. This chapter will explore the implications and measure the success of scientific sexological research on gender. For this terrain is contested. Sexual orientation and gender are evolving historical, social, and political concepts, and medical and scientific definition is but one element in their social construction. Thus, it is important to include other social actors and locate sexology's endeavors in the larger historical and political context of gender research.

The notion of two immutable and opposed genders, male and female, is one of the most widely assumed and hotly debated organizing principles of our culture. Attributions of gender are the first step in our social interactions. Individuals often report acute anxiety in the company of transsexuals or other gender-anomalous people until it can be ascertained "which way" they are going.[2] Likewise, it is assumed that, early on, people grasp which gender category is theirs and develop an appropriate behavioral schema to which they will forever adhere. Potential transgressors face a dizzying array of admonitions regarding the proper conduct of "real men" and "real women." Clothing, mannerisms, career choices (and options), and even, according to popular culture, food preferences, serve as some of the cultural signifiers of gender. Traditional gender typifications represent the promise of a safe and orderly world. They are, according to John Money and Patricia Tucker, "the glue that holds a society together."[3]

Societal norms regarding gender and sexuality are highly routinized in a symbolic gender system. Stereotypic expectations hold fast in the popular imagination, despite more than two decades of gradually relaxing behavioral parameters.[4] Similarly, appropriate sexual identity and behavior are strongly linked to gender. Males are expected to be *men:* tough, strong behavior is not enough unless they are also attracted to women as sexual partners. Thus, heterosexuality is a major component of "normal" gender expression, and, by extension, a primary concern of social scientists.

Sexologists have attempted to scientifically delineate some of the dimensions of sex and gender. John Money has popularized the concepts of gender identity (one's sense of oneself as male or female), gender role (the outward expression of maleness or femaleness), and sexual preference (one's choice of sexual partner).[5] In sexological terms, male gender identity, masculine gender role, and a sexual preference for women are normatively linked. The combination of female gender identity, feminine gender role, and a sexual preference for men constitutes the typical heterosexual woman. This is the normative, but by no means the only, model.

Historical Background

Modern sexologists have been instrumental in refining many popular gender concepts, and they are generally considered experts in the area. Their work, however, is largely an extension of social science research on femininity and masculinity that has proceeded since the early part of the century. As with sexological gender research, it was rapidly changing expectations for both women and men that provided the impetus for early psychological research on "sex-appropriate behavior." The shift away from the Victorian social structure of "separate spheres," the gender shake-up of World War I, the impact of the early feminist movement, and the effects of the depression in the 1930s (which has been dubbed "the greatest single historical crisis in the institutional basis of the traditional male role")[6] provided the backdrop for research on gender. Eminent social scientists in the research tradition that came to be called the Chicago School produced studies that suggested a social rather than biological basis for sex differences. Yet it was many forgotten women academics, such as Helen Thompson, Jessie Taft, and Elsie Clews Parsons, who at the turn of the century successfully undermined, in the social sciences at least, the theoretical hegemony of biological determinism in gender differences.[7] The pioneering work of these women, in conjunction with the men whom they influenced, such as W. I. Thomas and George Herbert Mead, challenged traditional beliefs that gender differentials in social status were biological imperatives. While not dismissing biology, their research increasingly explored the role of environment and socialization in the establishment of masculinity and femininity.

In the mid-1930s, however, more functionalist researchers took a major step in the quantification and reification of gender by formulating ideal personality types for men and women. In their influential *Sex and Personality* (1936) Lewis Terman and Catherine Miles posited that normality depended upon adherence to clusters of sex-related characteristics.[8] Their work was funded by the Committee for Research in Problems of Sex, the same Rockefeller-backed organization that sponsored the early Kinsey research, and their empirical methods reflected the era's faith that scientific research could solve contemporary social ills. For Terman and Miles, gender differences often seemed to be the key. "In every culture," they note in the preface, "they help to determine the accepted patterns of family life, of education, of industry, and of political organization."[9] As in so much research on sexuality and gender, there was an implicit belief that understanding maleness and femaleness would unlock the secrets of the social order.

Several aspects of Terman and Miles's theories prefigure sexological research. First, they identified gender-typed behaviors as essential, stable, and ahistorical components of the self.

> Masculinity and femininity are important aspects of human personality. They are not to be thought of as lending to it merely a superficial coloring and flavor; rather they are one of a small number of cores around which the structure of personality gradually takes shape. . . . The M–F dichotomy, in various patterns, has existed throughout history, and is still firmly established in our mores.[10]

This gender essentialism constituted the very foundation of their method; they needed a stable research object if they were to measure it effectively. Second, they fused gender-appropriate behavior with sexual identity. This was one more example of the theory that asserts that "real" men and women inevitably choose sexual partners of the opposite gender. But it also underscored the subtextual agenda in gender research—the leap from investigation of maleness and femaleness to an emphasis on "deviates."

> Along with the acceptance of M–F types of the sort we have delineated, there is an explicit recognition of the existence of individual variants from type: the effeminate man and the masculine woman. Grades of deviates are recognized ranging from the slightly variant to the genuine invert who is capable of romantic attachments only to members of his or her own sex.[11]

Like much contemporary gender research, Terman and Miles's work embodies the belief that painstaking quantification of gender differences and development will reveal how to achieve normality and avoid deviance. Much of *Sex and Personality* speaks to issues of "inversion" and, as is consistent in this culture, specifically male homosexuality. And, like modern sexologists, they crafted composites that described variations among inverts themselves, who are slotted dichotomously into "active" and "passive" classifications.

Third, Terman and Miles's equivocation over the roles of biology versus social factors in the development of gender and sexual identity prefigures the research of gender sexologists such as Richard Green and John Money. Much gender research is characterized by the construction of elaborate psychometry or intricate path analysis wherein the researcher is compelled to admit the inadequacy of truly confirming data about the etiology and development of gender and sexuality. At this point gender researchers modestly claim a small piece of empirical turf for themselves and look wistfully to future research. Terman and Miles, for example, awaited "with special interest the results of biochemical studies of homosexual subjects."[12]

Finally, Terman and Miles foreshadowed contemporary sexological research by devising not only the notion of "masculinity–femininity" (M–F), but a personality test to measure individual capacity and range as well. Tests to quantify and measure maleness and femaleness are central to much of gender sexology. Throughout the next decade, more of these scales were developed and integrated into the vastly expanding compendium of personality and psychometric tests.[13] Thus, Terman and Miles helped to form the intellectual and theoretical Zeitgeist within which modern gender sexology would develop.

Gender research in the 1940s and 1950s was impelled by the ongoing social anxieties wrought by World War II. By the mid-1950s the sociological theorist Talcott Parsons had applied his concept of "role" to the issue of gender,[14] embedding the notion of sex role in functionalism, the dominant social theory of the decade. This ensured the analysis of gender issues, not as power relations, but as roles and identities to be learned, accommodated, and negotiated within the context of marriage and the family. Family conflicts over work, children, and sexuality were viewed as inadequacies in socialization and the enactment of gender role, rather than as struggles complicated by men's domination of women. It was, as critics note, a theory that fitted in well with the social conservatism of the 1950s, and that went unchallenged in the absence of a viable feminist movement.[15]

It is feminists and lesbian and gay activists who have problematized the normative constructs of sex and gender and attempted to popularize alternative notions. Feminists, challenging mainstream social science research, have demonstrated that gender stereotypes are social relations rooted in history, culture, race, and the political and economic era.[16] Although the specific signifiers of gender may change historically or cross-culturally, gender remains a characteristic marked by inequality and power differentials. Indeed, cultural misogyny and male dominance are central features of an adequate examination of gender. In her analysis of the "principle of consistency," Barbara Ponse demonstrates the way in which gender identity, gender role, and sexual preference have been ideologically linked in the heterosexual configuration and then assumed to be "natural."[17] All other combinations, such as homosexuality or transsexualism, are considered deviant, unnatural, or perverted, and relegated to the depths of the sexual hierarchy.[18]

Political organizing by sexual minorities since World War II has served several functions. The coalescence of groups organized around gender variance or erotic desire, such as gay people, bisexuals, sadomasochists, and transsexuals, heightens the visibility of nonconformance to the "principle of consistency" and challenges the heterosexual imperative. Second, these groups have highlighted the political nature of the sex/gender system and exposed the network of oppression based on gender, sexual desire, or sexual practices.[19] Gay liberation has challenged the historical notion that homosexuality is a "disease" and has elucidated the power and privilege that accrue to those who are heterosexual. Finally, texts by sexual minorities have added depth and sophistication to mainstream theories of sex and gender. Explicit refutations of the "naturalness" and "inevitability" of heterosexuality and "gender-appropriate" behavior, these chronicles reveal the inadequacy of theories that unilaterally align gender identity, gender role, and sexual preference and instead demonstrate the varying permutations and combinations of sexual and gender expression. Drag queens, butch dykes, transvestites, dominatrixes, femmy butches, sissy boys, faeries, clones—all emerge, an amalgam of possibilities and, significantly, social and political agents. As Gayle Rubin wryly notes, "Sexualities keep marching out of the *Diagnostic and Statistical Manual* and on to the pages of social history."[20]

The texts of "erotic dissidents"[21] are important lessons in both sexual theory and sexual politics. Esther Newton and Shirley Walton, for example, have added and refined concepts to clarify and enhance sexual communication.[22] Erotic identity (how one images oneself as erotic object), erotic role (one's position or means of expression during sex, such as "top" or "bottom"), and erotic acts (particular acts that are sexually arousing) are concepts that speak to the panoply of sexual diversity. Even within the traditional heterosexual paradigm, these constructs show that one could be butch, femme, top, bottom, fetishistic, or transvestic in an array of configurations that can render sexual encounters with any potential "other" either hot or mundane.

Since repercussions for erotically complex or variant behavior range from economic discrimination to violence and murder, the political economy of sex and gender is foregrounded in lesbian/gay analyses. In a discussion of lesbian relationships in the 1950s, Joan Nestle writes:

> I was forced to understand that sexual style is a complicated mixture of class, history, and personal integrity. My butch-fem sensibility also incorporates the wisdom of freaks. When we broke gender lines in the 1950's, we fell off the biologically charted maps. One day many years ago, as I was walking through Central Park, a group of cheerful straight people walked past me and said, "What shall we feed it?" The "it" has never left my consciousness. A butch woman in her fifties reminisced the other day about when she was stoned in Washington Square Park for wearing men's clothes. These searing experiences of marginality because of sexual style are crucial lessons.[23]

These "lessons" of violence and derision emerge from a society that is profoundly anxious about evolving sex/gender ideologies. The cultural discourse on gender in the 1990s features a multiplicity of conflicting themes. Certainly the feminist movement and lesbian/gay liberation have succeeded in widening the boundaries of acceptable style and behavior. Yet the political underpinnings of a two-gender system remain. Patriarchal society is organized by the gender hierarchy, and the resurgence of reactionary ideology in the form of sociobiology speaks to its tenacity. In *Sexual Suicide* George Gilder articulates an extreme view:

> The differences between the sexes are the single most important fact of human society. The drive to deny them—in the name of women's liberation, marital openness, sexual equality, erotic consumption, homosexual romanticism—must be one of the most quixotic crusades in the history of the species.[24]

"Gender Choice," a kit that claims to boost a couple's chance of conceiving either a boy or a girl, boasts a thriving market, despite FDA disclaimers that it is a "gross deception."[25] Its market derives from the fact that, despite evolving norms, this culture is organized around, and obsessed with, gender. Both individually and institutionally, people struggle to respond to the renegotiation of gender roles. As the meanings of gender evolve, the shock waves are felt throughout the workplace, family life, and individual relationships. New questions—for example, questions about how dual-career couples can negotiate childrearing—can stimulate creative solutions that speak to women's and men's connection to both children and work, or reactionary efforts to reestablish traditional parenting strategies. It is in this cultural context of sex and gender anxiety that modern American sexology has developed, moving along two distinct trajectories.

Gender Sexology

S exology's discourse on gender is complex, focusing less on examinations of male–female differences and more on areas such as homosexuality and transsexualism, which are deemed to reveal, indirectly, gender "truths." Theories on the origin and development of gender-based behavior abound. Similarly, researchers span the ideological spectrum in their attitudes toward gender variance. Yet a general pattern can be detected. First, the gender discourse is based on heavily normative standards. Despite research emphasis on gender transpositions, the cultural norm is always the arbiter of what is "appropriate," "natural," and, ultimately, "good." There is an unarticulated assumption that men should be stereotypically masculine, women stereotypically feminine, and both heterosexually oriented. Deviations from this standard of normality are received with varying degrees of tolerance. Clinical programs to convert gay people into heterosexuals, and to teach stereotypic gender behavior to children, reflect the lack of true respect for and acceptance of variation.

The second aspect of the gender discourse is the tendency toward essentialism. Gender identity is defined as a core, enduring characteristic of the self that is immutable after the age of eighteen to thirty-six months. Gender researchers like John Money, Richard Green, Robert Stoller, and Anke Erhardt agree that gender schemata are the result of a multivariate interaction between biology and culture, but there is increasing emphasis on biology and an insistence that gender patterning is locked into the brain. Money's gender development theory is based on his belief that "the biology of learning includes learning that becomes imprinted and immutable."[26] Prenatal influences set the gender stage for particular vulnerabilities to environmental stimuli. Behaviors that are gender-specific as a result of prenatal and neonatal hormonal coding include roaming, competition, intruder aggression, and parenting.[27] The presence (or absence) of certain stimuli can, Money believes, have effects on gender that are permanently encoded into the brain. He warns:

> Among human beings, the hallowed social policy of prohibiting, preventing and punishing erotosexual rehearsal play in late infancy and the juvenile years may interfere with the genital component of identification and complementation to a degree as yet barely suspected. Social failure to endorse healthy masculinity and femininity in erotosexual rehearsal play may very well permit this aspect of development to become permanently and irrevocably stunted —misrepresented or transposed in the brain.[28]

The strongly biological cast of these gender theories and the physiological immutability they posit bode ill for feminists and others who seek to widen gender expectations. Money, for example, makes the leap from his theory of gender identity to justifying inequitable social relations:

> If you're a woman with passive dependence bound deep in the core of your female schema, you will be as uncomfortable wielding authority as if you grew a full beard. People can no more be expected to decode behavior that has been locked into the core of their gender schemas than a Chinese woman whose feet were bound in childhood could be expected to walk naturally.[29]

In this view, both tradition and biology will ultimately triumph. The implication of this interactive model of gender development is that if prenatal development proceeds normally, and the child then receives clear gender training, an unambiguous gender identity will evolve and the individual will be happily masculine or feminine. Psychologist Frank Beach says: "The child should easily learn the 'appropriate' behavior and enjoy performing it. Sex differences in the brain may influence the facility with which the individual learns and experiences positive affect involved in fulfilling the socially defined gender role."[30]

This model displays an obsessive concern with gender signifiers—clothing and mannerisms—to the exclusion of the signified. No attention is given to the meaning of "atypical" gender behavior for specific individuals. In clinical gender-retraining programs, children repeatedly insist that their cross-gender behavior is the result of having fewer options to express themselves in their "appropriate" gender role. Girls in particular express wishes to pursue traditionally male-defined careers, to be boisterous and adventurous, to be freed from the constraints of femininity. One young man who had been enrolled in psychiatrist Richard Green's "sissy boy" program later recounted his appreciation that his mother encouraged his early creative dressing up. When Green skeptically noted that most mothers would not "push their sons in the direction of fashion design," the man reaffirmed his gratitude and indicated that he had told her, "I thank you, mother, for not bringing me up in another environment and for subjecting me to the finer things in life."[31] Gender sexologists are disinclined to hear that "cross-gender behavior," "gender transpositions," or "sexual deviance" can be positive, affirming experiences for those who live them.

The essentialist writings of sexologists such as John Money are characterized by vagueness and allusion. Neuroendocrinological research on gender differences has been so painstakingly criticized and deconstructed by feminist social scientists and others that unequivocal acceptance is problematic.[32] Sexologists consequently vacillate between explanations based on nature and culture. For example, Richard Green's *"Sissy Boy" Syndrome*, a failed attempt to explain gendered behavior scientifically, ends simply in mystical speculation. Failing to relate behavior such as cross-dressing or homosexuality to socialization, Green begins to hint at the possibility of a "vital force" that continues to elude scientists. Ambivalence about nature versus nurture has been so striking in John Money's work that he has been accused of "loose thinking dangerously dressed up as 'good science.'"[33] In a revealing argument, Money attempts to dismiss the culture–nature conundrum by weight of sheer definition. It is erroneous, he claims, to divide pre- and postnatal influences and attribute them to biology and culture respectively, since social influences enter the brain and are therefore also physiological. "That which is not biological is occult, mystical, or, to coin a term, spookological."[34] By conflating the biological and the social, and by dismissing the case for a cultural construction of sex and gender, Money can thus justify a reductivist, biologically deterministic argument.

The third, related component of the gender discourse is the lack of attention to culture, power, and privilege. Sexology's dismissal of feminist and lesbian/gay scholarship is particularly evident in gender research. The privilege of men and the male role is virtually ignored. Rarely is it considered that inequities of power, options, and access might play a role in cross-gender behavior. In a recent interview, June Reinisch, the director of the Kinsey Institute, explained the influence of her background on her current predilection for psychophysiological research: "I was delighted to discover that there might be biological reasons for my being a tomboy."[35] Biological fundamentalism usurps the realization that, without culture, there would be no content or meaning to gender. It is culture, for example, that supplies the content to gender: that assigns nurturance, passivity, cooking, and clerical work to women; applauds independence, aggression, firefighting, and mechanical skills in men; and thus celebrates the tomboy and excoriates the sissy. In fact, it is impossible to analyze gender intelligently without an analysis of misogyny, or to analyze homosexuality without considering homophobia.

The inattention to gender politics means that little critical analysis is directed to the fact that these gender programs are aimed almost entirely at men. Male homosexuals, sissy boys, and male-to-female transsexuals are the prime targets for research and intervention. As justification, gender sexologists rightly assert several rationales: tomboyishness in girls arouses less cultural hostility than sissyness in boys; parents more readily bring cross-gender boys in for treatment; and "while many girls express a wish to be boys because of the apparent cultural benefits, it is the rare boy who regularly cross-dresses and expresses the wish to be a girl. On the other hand, there are far more sexually atypical adult males."[36] In this analysis, then, it is understandable, even acceptable, for girls to aspire to the higher social status of males, especially since they do not evolve into sexual deviants. Gender scientists readily embrace these superficial rationales without probing their sociopolitical underpinnings.

The almost obsessive focus on homosexuality and effeminacy in men and boys can be seen as resulting from the confluence of several factors. Historically, male homosexuality has been more vulnerable to social control than lesbianism. In part, this was a function of the cultural inability to fathom the lesbian potential. In addition, Jeffrey Weeks notes that in the nineteenth century male homosexuality was viewed as merely another version of uncontrolled male lust, and thus decried by social purity campaigners.[37] Structurally, homophobia functions to buttress the system of heterosexual privilege. Specifically, Eve Sedgwick points out that not only does male homophobia serve to control gay men, but, since all men are vulnerable to homophobic accusations, it operates to supervise and regulate the relationships of heterosexual men as well.[38] Such a system of reprisals is deemed necessary to curb homosexuality, which can be seen as subverting both heterosexual and male privilege and power. Finally, contempt for male homosexuality can be interpreted as explicit misogyny. The desire to eradicate the "feminine" in men is paramount. The literature on male homosexuality, transsexualism, and sissy boys reveals that mannerisms perceived as feminine are intolerable to researchers. Contemporary gender research contains strong currents of sexism and homophobia.

Gender research within sexology has two major foci: homosexuality and transsexualism (later expanded to gender dysphoria syndrome). Both areas of research required not only an expansion of sexology's interests but an incursion into others' turf. Research on and therapy for homosexuals had traditionally been the purview of psychiatry, and there was resistance within psychiatric circles to this challenge to their hegemony.[39] Similarly, psychiatrists were initially critical of what would become one of the most profitable business endeavors within medical sexology—the establishment of sex-change clinics to "treat" the newly defined disease of transsexualism.[40] In addition, sexological research into the two minority groups of homosexuals and transsexuals was thought to have an important consequence for sexology's primary constituency: through the study of "deviants," scientists could garner a clearer understanding of "normal" maleness and femaleness and the relationship between the two.

Sexology and Homosexuality

P erhaps the most significant impact of sexology on homosexuality
was its role in the invention of the category itself. Michel Foucault,
Jeffrey Weeks, and others have detailed the shift in the late eighteenth
and early nineteenth centuries from a focus on specific sexual behaviors to one on sexual identities or individual "conditions."[41] Whereas,
earlier, religion and the law took note of *acts* of sodomy, the new medical
discourse recognized a distinct kind of *person*—the homosexual. Historians have differed on the significance of medical labeling: did it create a
subculture that organized around the new concept of homosexual identity, or was medicalization a response to, and an attempt to define and
control, preexisting sexual communities?[42] Although evidence indicates
that the determinative role of medical literature in shaping homosexual
activity and identity was limited, medicalization shifted the locus of
moral authority to the medicopsychiatric profession, and much early
research focused on descriptive and etiological studies of this new individual. This newly medicalized condition was variously conceptualized
as a disease or, as in the case of Havelock Ellis, an anomaly akin to color
blindness.[43] Whatever the specific diagnosis, homosexuality was seen as
an individual condition, and interventions were subject to the current
theories and treatment modalities of medicine and psychiatry.

The new category of "the homosexual" brought new complexities.
The advantage for society was the safety implied by the existence of a distinct type of person who was homosexual. Since deviance was allegedly
marked and separate, an "us–them" philosophy was possible. A related
advantage for sexologists was the creation of a new population of research subjects and, later, clients. But practical and theoretical dilemmas
were introduced with the new conceptual category. Primary questions
centered on definitional boundaries: who were the individuals who were
homosexuals, and how did they get that way? The texts of the early sexologists offered an array of complicated, sometimes contrived, theories,
which form the backdrop for modern sex research on homosexuality.[44]

Although it is a hallmark of modern sexology that gender identity,
gender role, and sexual preference are at least nominally distinct, early
sexological theories of homosexuality amalgamated sex and gender.

Physiological characteristics and cross-gender mannerisms were targeted by sexologists as essential features of "inverts," "the intermediate sex," or "the third sex." Carroll Smith-Rosenberg describes the role of the early sexologists in the struggle over "the social and sexual legitimacy of the New Woman" in the late nineteenth and early twentieth centuries.[45] Bourgeois women who were educated, independent, unmarried, and desirous of male privilege became symbols of female rebellion and a crisis of gender. It was precisely for their aspirations to male power and privilege that these women were targeted by the Viennese neurologist and sexologist Krafft-Ebing as "Mannish Lesbians."[46] In an analysis that is remarkably predictive of some late twentieth-century research, Krafft-Ebing argued that homosexuality was characterized by cross-gender behavior in early childhood. In one of his case studies he reported: "Even in her earliest childhood she preferred playing at soldiers and other boys' games; she was bold and tom-boyish and tried even to excel her little companions of the other sex. She never had a liking for dolls, needlework or domestic duties."[47] This conflation of sexual variation, gender role, and social status was common in the sexological gender discourse throughout the century. It is, as Smith-Rosenberg notes, a metaphoric system in which "disease again bespoke social disorder."[48]

Gender rebellion thus became a primary signifier of the homosexual condition. There remained questions about the origins of this condition, for it was vital to the social order to understand how it might be "caught" and whether it might be prevented or cured. Krafft-Ebing promulgated the notions of congenital and acquired inversion. Masturbation, the *bête noire* of the nineteenth century, was seen as a major cause of acquired inversion.[49] For Havelock Ellis, inversion was rooted in biology, and the male or female invert suffered from some genetic or chromosomal abnormality.[50] Yet Ellis distinguished between inversion, which was biologically inevitable, and homosexuality, which was an acquired characteristic. The homosexual woman, for example, was viewed as simply having a weakness or a predisposition to seduction by female inverts, who were considered to be congenitally deviant.

The ramifications of etiological theories are clearly political and remain controversial among gay activists as well as sexologists. Biological determinism, as in Ellis' notion of the invert, can be the basis for an appeal to social tolerance: an individual who is powerless to change should not be subjected to legal or moral censure, or to therapeutic attempts at change. And if homosexuality is congenital, then there is no social threat of seduction or conversion. This is the social agenda behind some sexological theories based on biology,[51] and, significantly, their essentialism resonates with the personal experience of many gay people, for whom sexual desire and attraction are so powerfully compelling and consistent that they feel as if they were "born this way." Yet the essentialist sword can cut both ways. Biological theories of homosexuality can also connote a sense of "wrongness" or disease. Since heterosexuality is normative, homosexuality can be considered unnatural and abnormal, whether it is biological or not. Thus, essentialism within a culture dominated by a medical discourse can raise the specter of disease and thus prevention, a theme evident in the work of Krafft-Ebing and hinted at by contemporary scientists such as Gunter Doerner.[52]

A theory based on "acquired" or socially mediated factors can also engender responses aimed toward prevention or cure. If homosexuality is not innately programmed, some believe, it should be possible to determine the developmental factors involved and eliminate them. This, in fact, is the impetus behind some modern sex research that seeks to identify and modify factors thought to be related to homosexuality, such as cross-gender behavior. If we can derail a boy from "sissy" behaviors, some hope, we can avert future homosexuality. Social learning theory is also interpreted by some as highlighting the threat of homosexual seduction, and thus may increase efforts at social control. If one is not born homosexual, in this view, vulnerable and impressionable children should be protected from deviants who might want to convert them. Over the decades, psychoanalytic therapy, hypnotherapy, and aversion treatment have been directed toward eliminating homosexual behavior, reshaping desire, or liberating "blocked" heterosexual expression. Such theories about homosexual etiology, which appear to be less biologically determined and which introduce the role of culture, still reflect essentialist thinking, in that there is the presumption of an immutable sexual force that, at birth, begins to be shaped by the exigencies of individual and social learning. Such thinking still typically views homosexuality as a perversion of normal development and as an identity whose meaning is stable through time.[53]

Sex research is always shaped by the cultural context, and the social relations of gender and homosexuality are characterized by inequality. Political considerations are present in any discourse on homosexuality, since gay people, as a persecuted minority, are vulnerable to the ideological ramifications of research hypotheses. Unfortunately, modern research on homosexuality is often conducted by scientists committed to the pretense of "neutrality," who either ignore the political implications of their work or fail to act in behalf of those whom they study. Research on homosexuality has flourished in the last several decades, but given the myriad conflicting social and professional pressures surrounding it, it is indeed a mixed bag.

Homosexuality in the Laboratory

The two institutional pillars of scientific sex research both embarked on major research projects into homosexuality beginning in the 1960s. The Kinsey Institute for Research in Sex, Gender, and Reproduction and the Masters and Johnson Institute, although dissimilar in methodology and research focus, have viewed the study of homosexuality as a logical step in their scientific investigations into human sexuality. Both institutes have published massive texts presenting their findings. In 1979 Masters and Johnson released *Homosexuality in Perspective*. The Kinsey Institute has been more prolific over the years. It has published *Homosexuality: An Annotated Bibliography* (1972), *Male Homosexuals: Their Problems and Adaptations* (1974), *Homosexualities: A Style of Diversity Among Men and Women* (1978), and *Sexual Preference: Its Development in Men and Women* (1981).

Research into homosexuality has been the major research endeavor of the Kinsey Institute since the late 1960s. Kinsey himself had planned, after the release of his works on male and female sexuality, a publication on homosexuality, but he died before realizing this goal. The Institute went in a different research direction after his death, but returned to the subject in 1967, aided by funding from the National Institute of Mental Health.[54] Like Kinsey himself, the Institute researchers have found many friends in the gay community because of their liberal acceptance of homosexuality.

The theoretical orientation of the Institute's work on homosexuality has been predominantly sociological. Their data come from ethnographic studies and survey research in major gay communities in the United States, the Netherlands, and Denmark, as well as extensive fieldwork with lesbians and gay men. The Kinsey Institute research is framed by the societal reaction (or "labeling") theory of deviance. This perspective criticizes the notion that certain behaviors are deviant per se and instead focuses on the processes by which such acts come to be labeled as deviant by society.[55] Martin Weinberg has noted that his research on homosexuality is more related to his training as a sociologist than to sexology.[56] A focus on the social context and how people deal with stigmatization clearly distinguishes the work of Weinberg and Colin Williams from that of psychoanalysts, who view homosexuality as an illness. In *Male Homosexuals*, the authors state, "The paramount problems faced by homosexuals are a function of the social and cultural contexts within which they pursue their sexual expression."[57] By deriving its approach from labeling theory, the Kinsey Institute shifted the research emphasis at least somewhat from lesbians and gays and addressed the sociopolitical context. This has led to a fairly consistent liberalism in its publications, which frequently call for "tolerance" and "the day when homosexuality is no longer regarded as a 'sin' or a 'sickness' but rather as another important form of human diversity."[58] The books pragmatically advise homosexuals to find homosexual roommates and not live with their parents, and admonish therapists not to attempt to convert homosexuals to heterosexuality.[59]

In its ethnographic inquiries into the gay "lifestyle" and its developmental research on the origins of homosexuality, the Kinsey program mirrors the research goals of the early sexologists who sought to explain who was homosexual and why. Both assume the uniqueness of a homosexual person, despite Kinsey's admonition that "the world is not to be divided into sheep and goats."[60] Significantly, the Institute's research is unable to delineate developmental differences between gay people and non-gays. Traditional etiological theories simply did not hold up under their longitudinal studies. Yet the research did uphold the connection between homosexuality and cross-gender behavior posited by the early sexologists.

The major tenets about homosexuality advanced by the research of the Kinsey Institute are as follows:

1. Homosexuality is not deviant per se, but must be viewed within the broader social context in which it is perceived with hostility.

2. There is no such entity as "the" homosexual, but rather a range of homosexual lifestyles. The Institute has chosen to refer to "homosexualities," and has developed a typology of expressions of gay behavior.

3. Contrary to traditional developmental theories of psychiatry, there are no significant differences in the families of heterosexuals and homosexuals. Specifically, there has been no support for the "dominant mother, absent father" syndrome advanced by psychiatry as the etiology of male homosexuality.

4. Among both lesbians and gay men, there is a significant link between nonconformity to stereotypic gender roles and the development of homosexuality.

This was the major finding of the Institute's most recent book, *Sexual Preference*:

> While gender nonconformity appears to have been an aspect of the development of homosexuality in many of our respondents, it was by no means universal, and conversely, gender nonconformity does not inevitably signal future homosexuality. Nonetheless, according to our findings, a child's display of gender nonconformity greatly increases the likelihood of that child's becoming homosexual regardless of his or her family background and regardless of how much the child identifies with either parent.[61]

For lesbians and gay men, assessing the Kinsey Institute research is problematic. It is tempting, in a virulently homophobic culture, to praise any scientific treatise that is as progay as the Institute studies. In the finest tradition of Havelock Ellis, *Homosexualities* proclaims that "few homosexual men and women conform to the hideous stereotype most people have of them."[62] The studies methodically document that, cultural stereotypes to the contrary, there are no psychological differences between homosexuals and heterosexuals. In retrospective analysis, Weinberg notes that, given the detrimental social consequences of the myriad developmental theories about homosexuality, the very inconclusiveness of the Kinsey studies serves an important function.[63]

Yet gay activists have not been blind to the shortcomings of the Kinsey Institute research. Major criticisms include the inevitable focus on white males; sampling difficulties, such as the pitfalls of generalizing from respondents concentrated in San Francisco to gay people living in more homophobic areas; the unwieldy nature of the five-hour interview; and insufficient attention to demographic data in their final analysis.[64] A review in *Gay Community News* went to the heart of the issue, describing the flaws listed above as "secondary considerations":

> There is no need to worry about diction when we should be worrying about asking the wrong question. The question is not, "*Why* are there homosexuals?" but rather "*What* is a homosexual?" That is a question science cannot answer, because there is no such thing as a homosexual. (Emphasis in original.)[65]

Sexological research, however enlightened, unquestioningly supports the idea of homosexuals and heterosexuals as two distinct and mutually exclusive brands of human beings, rather than understanding sexual orientation as a fluid concept.

The latest release from the Institute shows a tendency toward biologism. Although the authors carefully state that their study contained no data that would allow them to determine any possible biological etiology of homosexuality, they nevertheless make numerous speculations and state: "Our findings are not inconsistent with what we would expect to find if, indeed, there were a biological basis for sexual preference."[66] In addition, they review the research of the late 1970s that attempted to isolate a biological cause of homosexuality. They conclude that there is mounting evidence for a physiological, and specifically hormonal, determinant of homosexuality and report a growing momentum of support for this theory within scholarly circles. This drift toward biological determinism is congruent with the new biomedical and physiological emphasis at the Kinsey Institute under the directorship of June Reinisch.[67]

The Kinsey Institute authors hypothesize that the scientific determination of a physiological basis for homosexuality would loosen societal
oppression. Like Masters and Johnson and Kinsey himself, they equate
the biological with the "natural" and think that proving that a behavior
has physiological origins will undermine the basis for social, political,
and moral condemnation. Alan Bell and his colleagues write:

> Those who argue that homosexuality is "unnatural" will be forced to recon-
> sider their belief, because something that is biologically innate must certainly
> be natural for a particular person, regardless of how unusual it may be.
> People might ultimately come to the conclusion that everyone is unique,
> biologically and socially, and that natural physiological factors will make it
> inevitable that a certain percentage of people in any society will be funda-
> mentally homosexual regardless of whether they are momentarily (or even
> continuously) engaged in heterosexual behaviors.[68]

The latest theoretical tendency of the Kinsey Institute researchers is a
disappointing shift away from their earlier commitment to research on
homosexuality from a societal reaction perspective. Although they still
criticize discrimination against lesbians and gays, they have shifted their
lens back to the individual rather than the social environment. Their
current references to biology, physiology, and "natural" sexual behavior
reflect less their sociological roots and more the medical ideology of
Masters and Johnson.

Masters and Johnson's research on homosexuality reflects their belief
in the biomedical model and the primacy of physiology in understanding human sexuality. Sociological and psychological research is helpful,
they believe, but "unless these two areas are supported by basic science
and pre-clinical work, it's going to fall right back into the old traps
of speculative hypothesis."[69] In 1964 they began their physiological research on homosexuality, and they published *Homosexuality in Perspective*
in 1979. The research for *HIP* took longer than that for either *Human
Sexual Response* or *Human Sexual Inadequacy* because, essentially, it is a
"homosexual composite" of both. It contains data on the physiological
sexual response of homosexuals as well as information on the treatment
of sexual dysfunction and dissatisfaction.

Masters and Johnson's initial goal had simply been to study and report on the physiological sexual response of homosexuals. They added the second component when, after years in the laboratory, they concluded, "No real differences exist between homosexual men and women and heterosexual men and women in their physiological capacity to respond to sexual stimuli."[70] This finding, by itself, produced yawns within sexology. Helen Singer Kaplan responded that any medical person would have known that there would be no physiological differences, and added, "Nobody would have thought penises would react any differently—the penis doesn't know what brand of sex it's having."[71] Anticipating criticism, Masters and Johnson had expanded their work, and also expanded their potential market to include clinical interventions with homosexuals and research into the sexual fantasies of both heterosexuals and homosexuals.

Perhaps the most controversial aspect of the book was its report on clinical programs to convert homosexuals into heterosexuals. In a two-week intensive therapy program that emphasized reeducation and sensate focus techniques, Masters and Johnson treated sixty-seven lesbians and gay men who had expressed a desire to function heterosexually, and claimed success in changing all but 35 percent of them. In addition, although they essentially maintain that homosexuality is learned behavior, they, like the Kinsey researchers, opened the door to possible physiological determinants, concluding that in some instances "hormonal predispositions may interact with social and environmental factors to lead toward a homosexual orientation."[72]

The research biases in *HIP* reflect the ideology of all of Masters and Johnson's work: a belief that physiological data will reveal essential "truths" about human sexuality; an ethos that stresses the superiority of marriage and commitment; and a liberal tendency that emphasizes individualism and free choice while minimizing the importance of the sociopolitical context. Their research sample reveals the same inadequacies as their earlier investigations. The majority of subjects were white and of high socioeconomic and educational levels. In addition, they chose subjects whom they defined as "committed"—that is, homosexuals who had lived together for at least one year. This was clearly an ideological decision, since in *HSR* they had demonstrated that physiological response was not affected by marriage.

Masters and Johnson are unclear about the purpose of their research on homosexuality. On the one hand, they insist that increased scientific evidence will alter cultural conceptualizations of homosexuality: "Now that it has been established that homosexual men and women are not physiologically different, it is also reasonable to speculate that in the near future, a significant measure of the current onus of public opprobrium will be eased from the men and women with homosexual preference."[73] Yet they quickly retreat from confronting homophobia and take refuge in their alleged professional and scientific neutrality. In the preface they caution that *HIP* "must not be construed as a statement of social, legal, or religious position," and in the conclusion they emphasize: "It is not our intention to assume a role in interpreting or implementing moral judgment. These privileges and their accompanying awesome responsibilities are not within the purview of a research group devoted to psycho-physiologic aspects of human sexuality."[74]

The sex research institutes of both Kinsey and Masters and Johnson acknowledge the environment of social and political oppression of lesbians and gay men, yet they fail to deal with the implication that this is also the context in which their work will be received. Masters and Johnson were particularly naive in believing that their data showing that homosexuals and heterosexuals had the same physiological responses during sex would decrease homophobia. In fact, a *Newsweek* poll revealed that in July 1983, 58 percent of respondents said that homosexuality should *not* be considered an accepted alternative lifestyle, up from 51 percent in June 1982. Like their insistence on the similarities between women and men, it reflected their belief that people can understand and accept each other only when they are proven to be the same. Differences are unacceptable, alienating, and intolerable.

Although Masters and Johnson are theoretically consistent in their emphasis on the "sameness" of gay and straight individuals, sexology faces a theoretical tension in research and clinical work on homosexuality. It is both economically and politically practical to focus on the differentness of gay people. This widens the potential market for sexologists in terms of research on the establishment of sexual identity, the development of preventive measures, and clinical treatment programs. Ideologically, it aligns sexology with an antigay dominant culture—a move that could effect broader acceptance and credibility for the aspiring profession. Conversely, an overemphasis on difference is untenable in a field that largely professes a liberal stance toward homosexuality. Further, many sexologists are themselves gay, and subgroups of the profession, such as humanistic sexology, have a legacy of gay advocacy. Indeed, one market strategy encourages sexologists to deemphasize difference, since practitioners cannot afford to alienate their constituency. Sexologists must walk a fine line that casts homosexuality as a disease or even a benign abnormality while simultaneously offering the hope and compassion that will attract clients. Given the widespread but erroneous conflation of sameness and equality, sexologists like Masters and Johnson are in the tricky position of espousing ideological liberalism by positing the similarity of gay and straight people while also offering a cure. They bridge the inconsistency by deferring to the "choice" of clients who seek out a conversion program because of their own desire to change sexual orientation.

HIP had two major effects within popular culture: it validated notions of a cure for homosexuality and, by comparing the love-making techniques of homosexuals and heterosexuals, functioned as a sex manual for heterosexuals. Some of its findings were extrapolated by the media into the conclusion that gay people had better sex than heterosexuals. This emerged from the finding that heterosexuals tended to be more goal-oriented in sex, moving rapidly and predictably into intercourse, whereas the homosexual sample tended to "move more slowly through excitement and to linger at plateau stages of stimulative response."[75] According to Masters and Johnson, same-sex couples have the advantage of better communication, the "it takes one to know one" principle that is reflected in their own dual-sex teams. In addition, they have suggested that poor sexual communication between the sexes is built on the assumption of male sexual expertise. Thus, they advocate in *HIP*, as in their other publications, that in the interest of better heterosexual sex, men should give up the position of sex expert and women should take more sexual responsibility.

The homosexual conversion programs have been more controversial within sexology and the gay community. Shortly after the publication of *HIP*, the *New York Times* ran a front-page story announcing "New

Treatment for Homosexuals."[76] Despite Masters and Johnson's claims that homosexuality was an acceptable lifestyle, their implementation of a treatment program to convert gay people conveyed legitimacy to homophobic attacks. The inherent superiority of heterosexuality was implicit in that they developed no programs facilitating the "free choice" of heterosexuals to convert to homosexuality.

The search for a cure for homosexuality has deep roots in the history of American psychiatry. Homosexuality had been listed as an official category of mental illness in the first *Diagnostic and Statistical Manual* (1952) of the American Psychiatric Association, lending official credence to the profoundly antihomosexual sentiment of Western culture. In the 1940s, analysts began voicing optimism about the potential to "cure" gay people.[77] Irving Bieber and Charles Socarides rose to prominence in the 1960s with their oedipal and preoedipal theories of the pathological development of homosexuality. Socarides claimed that psychoanalysis could cure up to 50 percent of "strongly motivated obligatory homosexuals."[78]

By the early 1970s, however, gay activists had begun to challenge the very definition of homosexuality as a pathological condition. After several years of bitter political dispute, the board of trustees of the American Psychiatric Association removed homosexuality from the *DSM-III*. As a compromise gesture, ego-dystonic homosexuality was included in its place. This measure has remained controversial into the 1990s, and gay activists, gay psychiatrists, and their supporters have lobbied to remove the classification. Most members of the APA's Advisory Committee on Sexual Dysfunction remain supportive of the new diagnosis, however. Several of these members are prominent sexologists, such as Helen Singer Kaplan, Harold Lief, and Joseph LoPiccolo. The links between psychiatry and sexology ensure the perpetuation of the ideology of disease and cure within sexual science, and the conversion programs are merely an extension of a historical struggle.

Yet Masters and Johnson are virtually oblivious to this history of sexual and gender politics. They write that there are "any number of good reasons" for gays to convert to heterosexuality, including concern for job security and increased social respectability.[79] In the 1990s, AIDS would presumably be one of those "good reasons." For women, "the lesbian role was described as preferable because women reported that it was not only more sexually stimulating, but it was psycho-socially more enhancing to the individual. Women in this study consistently reported that they experienced far more freedom of self-expression during their commitment to a lesbian orientation." Therapy focused on convincing a woman that a man could be retrained to provide her "with some opportunity for the self-expression she had grown to appreciate in her experience with lesbian society." Treatment included communication training of the male partner, to attempt to raise him up to the level of "receptivity of communicative exchange"[80] to which the woman had been accustomed in her lesbian relationships.

Masters and Johnson's medical strategy is to change the individual, not society. Their conversion program could serve as legitimation for their research focus on homosexuality, since it yielded clinical tools for returning social and sexual "deviates" to the mainstream. It would also buffer their more culturally challenging enterprise, which was to offer homosexuals treatment for sexual dysfunctions within homosexual relationships. Both treatment programs could significantly expand the market for professional sex therapists, but it was their "cure" for homosexuality that received the most attention.

In the early 1980s, the homosexual "cure" brought sexologists and the gay community head-to-head. The two modalities of intervention and treatment were conversion of adult homosexuals to heterosexuality, and retraining potentially gay children, most notably "sissy boys," in more "gender-normal" behavior. Conceptually, the cures reflect a mix of biological determinism and cultural acquisition theories. The premise that homosexuality is developmentally acquired, combined with research that correlates adult homosexuality with childhood gender anomaly, fosters a sense that being gay is a composite of environmentally induced characteristics such as effeminate mannerisms. Conversion to heterosexuality, then, is merely a function of changing mannerisms and behavior patterns. Hypnotherapy, aversion therapy, and other behavioral techniques are employed to that end. On the other hand, the programs operate on the notion that the core nature that will ultimately be released is heterosexual. Helen Singer Kaplan, a maven of homosexual conversion programs, stated that, with effective therapy, "very often a man's latent heterosexuality will blossom."[81]

Kaplan's work is a striking example of the role of sexologists in pathologizing behavior that is not culturally normative. Having integrated her theory on homosexual conversion with her work on inhibited sexual desire, she considers homosexuality a pathological deviation of the desire phase because it entails "desire for an object or situation which does not interest the majority of persons."[82] She crafted the diagnosis "situationally inhibited sexual desire," which is described as appropriate for people who experience "little or no desire in situations which most persons would find erotic, i.e., an intimate sexual relationship with an attractive partner of the opposite gender."[83] In this view, homosexual desire is considered sick simply because of its minority status.

Gay psychiatrists have challenged conversion programs on the grounds of both their homophobia and the questionable effectiveness of their techniques. As with sex therapy, critics have argued that sexologists provide little or no outcome data to support their extravagant claims of success. Emery Hetrick, president of the Institute for the Protection of Lesbian and Gay Youth, said: "Neither Kaplan nor any of the other cure people have ever demonstrated that their achievement is anything more than the most transient and circumstantial kind of performance."[84] Kaplan, however, incensed many members of the gay psychiatric community by implying that their criticisms were motivated by self-interest:

> The gay psychiatric community insists that there is no such thing as successful treatment when success is measured by capacity of heterosexual pleasure markedly increased over homosexual pleasure. They deny it, yet everyone who has focused on that issue in therapy has seen it. The gay psychiatric community feels threatened by this concept. They would have to look upon themselves as possibly having a pathological condition if they don't deny it.[85]

Since the conversion programs are premised on contempt for a sexual minority, any effective professional opposition must affirm gay sexuality as a viable option. Currently this strategy is most effectively pursued by openly gay sexologists such as David McWhirter and Andrew Mattison. Trained in psychiatry and psychology respectively, McWhirter and Mattison nevertheless moved beyond the paradigms of homosexual pathology to conduct a sophisticated research study on the everyday lives of male couples. In a model predicated on stage theory, McWhirter and Mattison discuss issues relevant to gay men such as intimacy, sexuality, trust, and risk taking in relationships. Thus, they have abandoned the traditional sexological emphases on determining what causes homosexuality and how to prevent it, instead sketching a lively and compassionate view of how men structure their relationships together. In *The Male Couple: How Relationships Develop*, the authors discuss their own initial internalized homophobia and then proceed to locate their work in a context deeply hostile to gay male relationships. They recommend not only that support systems for gay couples be strengthened, but that gay couples be recognized as legitimate family units, and that this recognition be widely visible, particularly to young gay persons.[86]

The Male Couple is a pivotal text in sexological research. Its acceptance of gay sexuality is reminiscent of some of the earlier work on homosexuality produced by the Kinsey Institute. But the courage of the authors in coming out is unprecedented since the era of Magnus Hirschfeld, who once faced the charge that his own research on homosexuality was self-serving.[87] McWhirter and Mattison comment on this fact:

> Not many years ago, the very fact that we are a male couple ourselves would have been an issue used by some to discredit our study. Fortunately, as the times and attitudes have changed, most people recognize that our status as a male couple actually gives the research a more firm footing in truth. . . . It would have been more difficult for nongay researchers to obtain the same degree of accuracy we achieved.[88]

The emergence of openly gay sexologists is a promising step toward more helpful and sophisticated research on homosexuality.

As a whole, the research on homosexuality conducted by the scientific sexologists is characterized by a superficially liberal tolerance that frequently masks a deeper strain of fear and prejudice. Care is taken to emphasize that homosexuality is an acceptable alternative lifestyle and to criticize societal discrimination against gay people. As noted, both the Kinsey Institute and Masters and Johnson publications wistfully hypothesize that their contributions to the scientific study of homosexuality will result in a loosening of social strictures. Yet most gender sexologists hide behind their scientific status and refuse to utilize their research to alleviate the oppression of the very population they have been studying. Shortly after *HIP* was published, for example, Masters and Johnson refused to comment on the antigay Briggs Initiative in California. "We just don't feel qualified to answer," they told the audience.[89]

Moreover, the research creates frightening possibilities for lesbians and gay men. Despite the Kinsey researchers' hopes that societal oppression might erode with evidence of a biological basis for homosexuality, they concede that, in fact, the opposite is just as likely. More often than not, biological determinants trigger a momentum toward eradication, not acceptance, of a minority position. The Kinsey writers acknowledge:

> Already we have heard the suggestion that pregnant women be closely monitored—that those carrying boys be regularly checked for fetal androgen levels and that where hormone levels are low, there be medical intervention to supplement them artificially. And some homosexual adults have allegedly been "cured" by brain surgery to destroy "inappropriate" sexual response centers.[90]

Similarly, the clinical work of Masters and Johnson, Kaplan, and others implies that it is both possible and appropriate to cure homosexuality through therapeutic intervention.

Research on homosexuality is merely one enterprise by which scientific sexologists attempt to understand sex and gender. The connection is perhaps made most explicitly in *Sexual Preference*, which reports a link between homosexuality and early gender nonconformity. The authors conclude in the epilogue, "A principal issue raised by homosexuality in both males and females has to do with what it means to be a man or a woman."[91] Although sexologists generally urge a loosening of cultural stereotypes of masculinity and femininity, their work stands on a continuum alongside that of more open gender engineers—sexologists who have developed and implemented programs for the surgical reassignment of sex.

Sexology and the Rise of Transsexualism

On December 1, 1952, the *New York Daily News* ran a banner headline, "Ex-GI Becomes Blonde Beauty." It propelled into public view for the first time one of the most dramatic medical procedures of modern times—the sex-change operation. George Jorgensen had trav-

eled to Denmark, undergone hormonal and surgical treatment, and returned to his home town as Christine. Although history and mythology
are replete with accounts of cross-gender behavior, the first reported sex-
change operation occurred in Germany in 1931.[92] Two decades later the
Jorgensen case marked both the beginning of public awareness in the
United States and the first step toward what would eventually become
a major enterprise of medical sexologists.

The routinization of sex reassignment was accomplished with amaz-
ing rapidity. The process took off in the United States in the 1950s, and
by the 1970s had consolidated into a thriving medical industry. Medical sexologists were able to legitimate their gender treatment within
the popular consciousness, as well as secure their professional turf in
this area over the opposition of psychoanalysts (who accused them of
collaboration with psychosis) and the legal system (which threatened
prosecution for mayhem—the surgical removal of healthy tissue).

Many factors account for the speed with which sexologists established their authority in this realm. First, they grounded themselves
within scientific medicine and so benefited from the already established
cultural authority of the medical profession. The process of medicalizing
gender issues involved the development of new diagnostic labels, tools
for evaluation, and techniques for clinical and surgical intervention. In
addition, interested professionals organized by establishing clinics and
professional associations.

Medical diagnosis of cross-gender fixation consolidated in the mid-
1950s. A U.S. endocrinologist described the Christine Jorgensen phenomenon as a unique illness that he later termed "transsexualism."[93]
Harry Benjamin, widely considered the forefather of medical research
and intervention regarding transsexuals, was Jorgensen's physician when
she returned to the United States. Benjamin saw his first transsexual
patient in 1948 through a referral from Alfred Kinsey.[94] His work on
hormones through the 1920s and 1930s sparked his interest in the syndrome, which he thought emerged from a biological substrate. By 1966
he had published the classic text in the field, *The Transsexual Phenomenon*.
The syndrome thus had acquired a name and an emerging theory.

The new diagnosis and treatment were quickly incorporated into the
medical landscape. Johns Hopkins Hospital had already established a

Gender Identity Clinic Committee, and in 1960 the hospital performed
a bilateral reduction mammoplasty—the removal of both breasts—on a
woman who expressed a desire to be a male.[95] The Erikson Educational
Foundation was founded in the late 1960s and united the field by serving
as a clearinghouse for the burgeoning medical specialty, disseminating
information, making referrals, sponsoring conferences, and funding research and gender identity clinics. By the early 1970s, transsexualism
was an accepted syndrome, buttressed by a vast medical armamentarium
of research, publications, and treatment programs. Gender sexologists
formed the Harry Benjamin International Gender Dysphoria Association in 1977 and developed a code of treatment standards and a charter.

The second reason for the field's quick and widespread public and
professional acceptance was that the gender identity sexologists had
tapped a major cultural insecurity about shifting gender roles. Transsexuals were individuals who claimed to be one sex trapped in the body
of the other sex, in a society where it was increasingly unclear who
or what either sex was supposed to be. As noted earlier, social science
gender research throughout the century aspired to quantify and delineate maleness and femaleness in a context of anxiety about what constituted "appropriate" development and behavior. Transsexual research
was the next logical step. One gender researcher referred to transsexuals
as "natural experiments" who would promote an understanding of "the
development of masculinity and femininity in all people."[96]

Sexologists' remarkable success in achieving legitimation for sex-
change surgery, then, can be evaluated in light of two major considerations: the valorization of medical science and the rapid proliferation of
medical technology, and the role of ideology in facilitating the adoption of new techniques. The public had already integrated—indeed, had
come to expect—miracles from modern surgery.[97] The established direction of mainstream surgical medicine was metaphorically captured by
the television series entitled *The Six Million Dollar Man*. Transplants and
artificial organs could produce the "totally replaceable body"[98] ending
the quest to elude inevitable mortality. Similarly, the goal of medical
sexology, as represented by transsexual surgery, was the transcendance
of what, in Western culture, is perceived as the most fundamental dichotomy: that of maleness and femaleness. On close inspection, then,

sex-change surgery was no more unorthodox than the endeavors of medicine at large.

The proliferation of advanced technology has, nevertheless, raised critical questions about spiraling costs and unequal access to care. Transsexual surgery can be evaluated through this same lens. It is not sufficient, as we will see, to judge the appropriateness of sex-change operations solely on the basis of their alleged individual success. Nor is it helpful simply to question the individual motivations of gender sexologists. Their integrity ranges widely, from Harry Benjamin's compassionate advocacy for "one of the world's most neglected minorities,"[99] to the unscrupulous profiteering of "surgery mills." Nor should new technology be considered simply from the perspective of what we are *able* to achieve. Rather, technologies are received into a culture with a constellation of social and political relations. In addition to the traditional public health questions of costs and benefits, it is appropriate to examine the cultural context of new techniques.

What are the implications of sex-change surgery within the broader landscape of gender relations? What message does the new technology convey, and what ideology does it uphold? In a society anxious about gender diversity, the creation of "transsexualism" sent a legitimizing message that categories were distinct; roles and statuses were quantifiable. Sexologists offered the promise that gender, which was increasingly the locus of political rebellion and organizing, was subject to control and predictability. The creation of the new disease of "gender dysphoria" individualized social disorder. It allowed for the distancing of cultural conflict and signaled that gender diversity was not a collective problem requiring society to confront rigid stereotypes and inequality; it was the dilemma of individuals with a dysfunction. The very trappings of medical science serve to mask the ideological functions of gender sexology. The development of a theoretical canon, the accruing of scientific "facts," and the creation of a biomedical lexicon provide a smokescreen of authority that is difficult to challenge. Yet by these very endeavors, sexologists function as "moral entrepreneurs" in the same fashion as physicians.[100]

If sexology drew on the cultural authority of medicine to enhance the legitimacy of transsexual surgery, it is also true that transsexual surgery enhanced the legitimacy of sexology. The field benefited both from popular awe at the drama of high-tech medical advances and from the belief that sexology could offer a "cure" for gender rebellion. Throughout the 1970s, gender identity clinics proliferated, and surgery rates soared throughout the country, as sexologists made it increasingly easy for individuals experiencing some type of gender role distress to surgically alter their bodies to accommodate social mores. In 1977 Dr. Ira Pauly predicted that sooner or later every physician in the United States would be consulted by a transsexual seeking help.[101] Research, in fact, documents a steady rise in requests for transsexual surgery.[102] The Erikson Educational Foundation estimated that, by 1976, approximately a thousand sex change operations had been performed,[103] and by 1979 twenty major medical centers across the country offered the procedure at a cost, at that time, of between five and ten thousand dollars.[104] Gender scientists sought structural validation for their programs by attempting to have them covered by third-party payments or by Medicaid.[105] In some states they were successful, which provided the financial infrastructure to expand their market.

The scientific confidence that fueled this rush into surgical treatment faltered slightly in the late 1970s. Despite attempts to rationalize the syndrome of gender distress, the diagnosis essentially rested on self-reports and signifiers of gender such as mannerisms and appearance. The catch-phrase of transsexuals was that they felt like one sex trapped in the body of the other sex. Sexologists waited for this phrase, or a facsimile of it. Soon they began hearing a master narrative repeated by surgical candidates who had studied the literature thoroughly and were prepared to jump the therapeutic hurdles set up by gender scientists. In addition, physicians' evaluation of the candidate's appearance became a critical diagnostic component. One physician said, "We're not taking Puerto Ricans any more; they don't look like transsexuals. They look like fags."[106] And the founder of a New England Gender Identity Clinic said, "You can tell a drag queen because she looks like Diana Ross. A transvestite looks like your Aunt Mary from New Jersey."[107]

Diagnosis has moved away from the quantification that is typical of medicine and into the realm of phenomenology. An individual's success at getting surgery rests on his/her ability to convince a physician that there is an internal incongruence between emotional perceptions and physical reality. This process is more successful if the client can successfully perform in the cross-gender role. And although some physicians perform sex-change operations after a brief office evaluation, most gender clinics require a period of time spent "passing" in the new gender. Applicants have been rejected for surgery because they are not convincing (e.g., too tall, too hairy, too broad-shouldered, too abrupt in their mannerisms), and clinics are reluctant to consign them to a gender twilight zone. Other clinics are less scrupulous.

Despite their ostensible purpose of screening out poor risks for surgery, the diagnostic procedures in fact serve two major functions. First, they offer a measure of security to surgeons worried about lawsuits. Performing sex-change operations can be risky, since not only are the techniques relatively experimental, but these are radically irreversible procedures. This was precisely where professional consolidation attempted to provide a buffer. The development of policies and guidelines, such as the Standards of Care developed by the Harry Benjamin International Gender Dysphoria Association, provided surgeons with a medical rationale. The inclusion of transsexualism as a mental disorder in the *DSM-III* provided additional therapeutic support. One psychiatrist commented that the new classification "has legitimized gender dysphoria . . . in that it is now a legitimate psychiatric diagnosis. . . . The psychiatrists have been getting more acceptance now that they are validated by the *DSM-III*."[108]

The second covert function of the rigorous diagnostic process is that it enforces a highly regularized version of transsexual personality, attitudes, and behavior. By allowing very little latitude in transsexuals' behavior and aspirations, the procedure socializes transsexuals into their new gendered life and affords the medical profession control over cross-gender transitions. A male-to-female transsexual interviewed in a Boston newspaper suggested that the challenge to traditional values was itself the etiology of gender dysphoria:

> the upbringing given him by his professional parents is described perfectly in an article appearing in *Ms.* magazine's recent men's issue. Eric objects strenuously to the article's formula for raising sensitive, non-sexist men. "It reminds me so much of my upbringing. A child has to realize who it is.

Don't take away his burp gun and say, "Go over there and play with the non-sexist toys." I grew up with non-sexist toys and I grew up with a non-sex! I think parents who are trying so hard to make their children sensitive end up robbing them of the identity they very much need." [109]

Much of the literature on transsexualism reveals that, both before and after surgery, transsexuals tend to adhere to extremely rigid portrayals of gender, approaching caricatures of masculinity or femininity. [110] In part, this fetishization of gender can be explained by the overwhelming distress that these individuals have experienced concerning their identities. It has been suggested, however, that the medical sexologists themselves account for some of the stereotypic behavior. One transsexual said, "Shrinks have the idea that to be a transsexual you must be a traditionally feminine woman: skirts, stockings, the whole nine yards." [111]

Sexologists' attempt to regulate the sex and gender expressions of transsexuals sometimes meets with resistance. Although transsexuals know that compliance with the medical guidelines can ease the route to surgery, their own support groups offer advice, shortcuts, and an alternative normative experience. Anthropologist Anne Bolin notes that the informal rituals and folklore of transsexuals themselves are crucial in influencing the way the (male) transsexual becomes a woman. And she documents transsexual resentment of medical gatekeepers who are thought to be less interested in their clients than in their own professional and financial status. One transsexual complained about the typical presurgery requirements:

You will be told you will have to convince two "mental health specialists" that your feelings are real and you are emotionally stable, that you must work at a job for which you were not trained since your job skill will not be transferable, you must save a year's wages or more for the surgery since insurance companies define it as voluntary, cosmetic, non-essential surgery, that you must do all this while conforming to the doctor's idea of a woman, . . . not necessarily yours, and that even if you meet all the requirements and go ahead with the surgery you'll be no happier than you are now—in effect, all the hassle will produce no net change in your life so why do you want to bother? And through it all, you'll get the impression the "professionals" not only know less about the subject than you, they're more interested in protecting their malpractice insurance than your well being.[112]

The actual process of surgical sex reassignment requires a vast array of medical and medical-support services. Typically, the individual approaching sex conversion undergoes a period of psychological counseling, hormone treatment, and cross-living. During this time, ancillary services include electrolysis to remove the beard and speech therapy for male-to-female transsexuals (hormones lower the voices of female-to-male transsexuals). For the male-to-female, surgery entails the construction of a vagina from the outer skin of the penis. For the female-to-male, the process is more difficult, and more varied. Often, these individuals stop after double mastectomies. Others have hysterectomies as well, and some attempt the surgical construction of a penis. Phalloplasty has been so unsuccessful that many surgeons discourage it, although the individual who is persistent can usually locate a physician who will attempt it. The actual reassignment surgery often consists of more than one operation (female-to-male conversions may require three or four), and most gender scientists have found that after the initial operations the individual undergoes even more cosmetic surgery, such as removal of the Adam's apple, in search of a more suitable "presentation of self." Postsurgical complications can include bloated limbs, repeated infections, adhesions in the vaginal canal, hemorrhaging, depression, and sometimes suicide.[113]

In 1979 Johns Hopkins Hospital, which pioneered in gender surgery in the United States, halted its surgical program after a long-term study failed to demonstrate any objective improvements in the recipients' lives. This was a dramatic challenge to the belief that had legitimated sex-change surgery—that gender crises do not respond to psychotherapy, only to surgical conversion. Jon Meyer, a psychiatrist at Johns Hopkins, said, "What we have found is that both operated and non-operated transsexuals improved roughly to an equal extent and that, in fact, the non-operated group's improvement was statistically more significant. . . . Surgical intervention has done nothing objective beyond what time and psychotherapy can do." The decision to stop the operations was made quietly, and publicity was avoided.[114] The study triggered rounds of methodological criticism, was described as "appallingly flawed," and prompted an investigation by the American Psychiatric Association,[115] yet other sexologists now challenge the effectiveness of surgical sex reassignment as well.[116] Nevertheless, the gender market is far from crashing. In fact, it is indicative of the embeddedness of sex-change surgery that the Hopkins and other critical studies were not sufficient to diminish either supply or demand. In 1980 over one thousand sex change operations were performed in the United States.[117] In 1987, rates were estimated at three to six thousand worldwide.[118] Issues of gender identity and techniques of surgical reconstruction continue to be a major concern of the scientific sexologists.

The controversy over Meyer's data raised the thorny question of how to evaluate surgery for which there is no physiological need. Although gender sexologists are divided on the question of etiology, there has never been a demonstrable organic basis for transsexualism. As noted, diagnosis leans heavily on psychology, appearance, and self-report. As Richard Green once joked, "I guess, like love, transsexualism is never having to say, 'I'm sorry.'"[119]

The creation of the dysfunction called transsexualism represents the epitome of the medicalization of a broader sociopolitical crisis around gender. As is true of medicalization in general, there are some very tangible advantages. For individual transsexuals, it presents the possibility that they suffer from a disease rather than a moral failing or sexual deviation. Sexologists have offered a much more sympathetic ear than psychoanalysts, who were virtually unswerving in their belief that transsexualism represents sheer perversion. Finally, the publicity around the new diagnosis has eased the social stigma somewhat. For some transsexuals, sex reassignment does indeed alleviate their distress. For a significant number, who at the critical juncture of ten years post-op either request reassignment back to their original sex or commit suicide, it proves to be a colossal mistake.[120] Yet the new disease of transsexualism has also served to legitimate the traditional system of gender stereotypes, where boys will be boys who may never deviate. Medicalizing gender distress closed down more possibilities than it opened up.

Despite the notion that sex reassignment surgery brought about a "sex change," gender scientists' creation of the disease of "transsexualism," in response to gender confusion and transgression, in fact created a third gender. The ultimate goal of transsexuals is to be released from an inappropriate body, a mistake and encumbrance of nature, to the freedom of their "true" gender. Yet there are both practical and conceptual barriers. It has been widely documented that the label "transsexual" becomes an organizing principle that helps confused and distressed individuals make sense of their lives.[121] Although transsexuals hope the category will be merely transitional, in fact it is an exceedingly difficult identity to escape. For a variety of reasons, many transsexuals never achieve surgery. Some are unable or unwilling to clear the obstacles imposed by sexologists, and most are daunted, if not deterred, by the expense of the process. This leaves a large percentage of transsexuals in a gender netherworld where the medical category itself becomes their identity.

Even those transsexuals who attain surgery can find it hard to be perceived as other than "transsexual." They face the philosophical and political question of whether a person born into one physical gender can ever validly claim to belong to the other. In terms of gender, transsexuals represent the ultimate separation of biology and acculturation. Many people resist the notion that an individual born and raised as a biological male could be transformed, in adulthood, into a "real" woman. The notoriety of transsexuals is another factor that consigns them to the third gender. People like Jan Morris and Renee Richards are typically considered "transsexuals" first, and women second. Many transsexuals resist participating in public educational events, since they know, as one noted, that "it is almost impossible for a transsexual to achieve respect if the fact of their transition becomes general public knowledge."[122] Finally, even when transsexuals are "passing," there are always problems of autobiography, genitalia, or incongruous physique that maintain transsexualism as a subtextual identity. In the way that the category of "berdache" served as an intermediate gender for Native Americans, "transsexualism" is the medically negotiated third gender for modern Western culture. Transsexualism exists in our culture because there is no possibility beyond dichotomous gender identification.

Transsexualism and the Reification of Gender

S ex, gender, and sexual behavior are complex and interrelated phenomena, so little understood that technical interventions have created as much confusion as they have eliminated. Sexologists have profoundly shaped the medical categories of homosexuality and transsexualism. John Money's delineations of gender identity, gender role, and sexual preference, for example, allowed for certain helpful distinctions. A traditional stereotype about gay people was that they all wished to be the opposite sex. And although all cross-dressers are widely considered gay, transvestites are quite vehemently heterosexual. But although the new conceptual schema was educational, it reified the categories into static imperatives. The descriptive terms hardened into diagnostic tools that, it was presumed, would clinically distinguish among gender-divergent individuals. Yet, ultimately, the goal of medicalizing gender diversity into recognizable, predictable, and controllable identities has proven ephemeral. Although transsexualism is now considered a discrete entity distinct from homosexuality, some gender researchers estimate that 30 to 35 percent of those diagnosed as gender dysphoric are really intensely homophobic gay people.[123] Unable to achieve self-acceptance in a hostile social climate, these individuals instead seek to alter their bodies.

The sex/gender schema of sexologists is ultimately an attempt to impose order on the inherently disorderly universe of gender and sexual behavior. It upholds the social dictum that there are, and can only be, two genders, despite the existence of many societies that have anywhere from three to five gender categories.[124] And it demands the internal consistency and permanence of gender identity, gender role, and sexual preference. A serious glance at either the professional literature or the writings of sexual minorities reveals the incredible flexibility of sex/gender patterns. Several male-to-female transsexuals, for example, have become lesbians after surgical conversion, and one postoperative male-to-female said, "I thought I was a homosexual at one time; then I got married and had a child so I figured I was a heterosexual; then because of cross-dressing I thought I was a transvestite. Now [postoperatively] I see myself as bisexual."[125] The gender establishment is, however, resistant to such diversity and can threaten to withhold surgery if normative patterns of sexuality and gender are not upheld. One preoperative transsexual who was discussing her inclination to engage in a lesbian relationship after the sex change was asked by a shocked psychiatrist, "Why do you want to go through all the pain of surgery if you are going to be with a female lover?"[126]

Although transsexualism can only be understood as a political, rather than a medical, issue, the feminist movement has been divided over the phenomenon. In the mid-1970s, when sexology and the mainstream media were at the peak of their enthusiasm for sex reassignment surgery, some male-to-female-transsexuals began to frequent feminist events. In many cities, transsexuals undoubtedly became involved in the movement with no fanfare and no consequences. In some areas, however, the disclosure of transsexual identity was accompanied by bitter controversy. One such occasion was the employment in 1977 of a transsexual by Olivia Records, an all-women recording company. Since Olivia has a prominent presence in the women's community, the debate was nationwide. Support for Olivia's action was countered by outrage. One woman wrote: "I feel raped when Olivia passes off Sandy, a transsexual, as a real woman. After all his male privilege, is he going to cash in on lesbian feminist culture too?"[127]

In Boston in 1978 community forums and angry exchanges in the monthly women's newspaper, *Sojourner*, were precipitated by transsexual participation in "women-only space," such as the Cambridge Women's Center and the Cambridge Women's School. An ad hoc group, identified as Participants of the Greater Boston Women's Community Discussion on Male-to-Constructed Female Transsexualism Within the Women's Movement, called on transsexuals to identify themselves if they were in "events, organizations, spaces, and businesses which are identified as 'women-only.'"[128] This seems to have been an attempt to deal with confusion by clarifying identities. Other feminists viewed it as both offensive and irrelevant to the underlying issues raised by transsexualism:

> Eliminating our local transsexuals will not eliminate these issues. Feminists have criticized patriarchal, linear logic because it is blind to the interplay of contradictions, to dialectics. Yet here we are, shouting at complexity and

hoping it will be frightened away. The world refuses to package itself into neat little boxes.[129]

Feminists were unsuccessful at shouting away complexity simply because, at bottom, transsexualism raises some of the most profound issues of sexuality and gender, biology and socialization. The linchpin of the women's movement is an analysis of the historical manifestations and social consequences of gender. The intellectual and political lens of feminism is focused on "woman." Yet the category of "transsexual" and the emergence of real people who were genetic men claiming to be women threw the very meaning of the term "woman" into disarray. What did it mean, feminists wondered, to have a male-to-female transsexual in a consciousness-raising group? Or organizing at a rape crisis center? Can one simply claim to be a woman after a male childhood? How significant was the absence of a female biography, women's socialization?

It was shaky ground, both theoretically and politically, for a movement based on the social construction of gender. Transsexualism was one of several barometers that revealed the theoretical tensions within feminism. Not surprisingly, transsexualism proved extremely threatening to those feminists with a vision of creating a women's culture. These women, who were separatists or, in Alice Echols' term, "cultural feminists,"[130] harked back to essentialist versions of gender, but with a feminist revisionism. There are, cultural feminists argued, immutable differences between men and women, and it is irrelevant whether this is the result of biology or socialization. Women, however, are the superior gender by dint of inherent gentleness, nurturance, and peacefulness. Transsexuals were the wormy apple in this Garden of Eden.

Cultural feminist theory necessitated a complete rejection of transsexualism. It was ludicrous, from this perspective, to believe that the (male) medical profession could create real women. Yet cultural feminists were unable to separate a critique of the sexism inherent in the work of gender scientists from an attack on transsexuals personally. Transsexuals were "artifactual" females, they charged. In *The Transsexual Empire*, cultural feminist Janice Raymond accused transsexuals of colluding in a patriarchal plot to undermine the women's movement, and ultimately, women themselves. If men could be transformed into women, she warned, that would "make the biological woman obsolete by the creation of man-made 'she-males.'" [131]

Many feminists, though confused about the meaning of transsexualism, were nevertheless amused or outraged by the cultural feminist posture. Drawing boundaries around the concept of a "real" woman was a mistake that could ultimately backfire. The agenda of feminism, after all, included challenging such definitions. For many it was clear that the gender rigidity of society should be the target of feminism, not transsexuals themselves. And one writer wryly condemned the conspiracy theory by acknowledging her inability to "imagine that thousands of jocks are taking this up as a kinky new way to get to women." [132] These feminists spoke to the need for a political critique grounded at the social level of people's everyday lives. As a movement, feminism needed to respect the myriad forms of gender struggle that individuals experience in this culture.

Similarly, gay liberation articulated a political analysis of transsexualism that recognized oppression based on sex/gender difference and attempted a deeper understanding of sex/gender combinations. Unlike the feminist movement, gay liberation has consistently offered a haven to transsexuals, who often feel assured of safety in gay-identified space. As minorities, transsexuals and homosexuals represent a challenge to traditional notions of maleness and femaleness. By examining the *meaning* of gendered behavior and sexual activity, sexual minorities have fashioned a vision that allows for creativity. In an ethnographic analysis of drag queens, Esther Newton describes how cross-dressing becomes a social comment on the normative sex/gender configuration:

> The effect of the drag system is to wrench the sex roles loose from that which supposedly determines them, that is, genital sex. Gay people know that sex-typed behavior can be achieved, contrary to what is popularly believed. They know that the possession of one type of genital equipment by no means guarantees the "naturally appropriate" behavior. . . . The gay world, via drag, says that sex-role behavior is an appearance; it is "outside." It can be manipulated at will. [133]

The notions of "gender bending" and "genderfuck" suggest a system where roles and identities are not rigidly and permanently bound to tradition. They take into account the potential of individuals to experiment and change, at the same time that they acknowledge the necessity of cultural support for that flexibility. As lesbian activist Pat Califia writes:

> Those of us who are working for a world without gender privilege need to ask ourselves how we want to accomplish this. Do we want a society where the similarities between men and women are emphasized, and people are discouraged from expressing or eroticizing their differences? Or do we want a society of pluralistic gender, where people can mix and match the components of their sexual identities? I personally would rather live in a world where every man could be a woman, or might have been one yesterday—and vice versa.[134]

Despite some differences, both feminist and gay analyses would urge sexologists to work as fervently to increase possibilities around gender expression as they do to eliminate them.

Gender Treatment Programs for Children

In their analysis of both transsexualism and homosexuality, many gender sexologists embraced an approach of childhood intervention that was far from Califia's utopian model. They regarded the early years as prime time for training in gender-appropriate behavior. Ira Pauly, a noted gender sexologist, said:

> Even in 1977 we know precious little of how little boys and girls grow up to be—and feel like—men and women. . . . They [transsexuals] are giving us tremendous information about gender identity—what young parents need to know. It's information that's useful to every single human being in interacting with his or her own children.[135]

From studying transsexuals, scientists developed gender treatment programs for children who were perceived, usually by the parents, as having gender identity problems. The precursors of the "sissy boy" program of the 1980s, these programs were aimed at boys, reflecting the greater historical obsession with promoting and maintaining stereotypic masculine behavior in males. The clinics emphasized prevention of both adult transsexualism and homosexuality. George Rekers, a prominent gender scientist, outlined the rationale for implementing treatment for gender disturbances in boys:

1) to relieve the boy's current maladjustment, social isolation, and personal suffering;

2) to prevent the severe psychological and social maladjustment problems in adulthood that accompany the transsexualism for which the boy is at high risk;

3) to prevent transsexualism, transvestism or homosexuality per se as the most probable adulthood diagnostic outcome in the absence of treatment, and

4) to respond to the parents' legitimate requests for professional intervention.[136]

Essentially, these criteria legitimated traditional gender stereotypes and the social ostracism of those who do not conform. The acceptance of childhood gender clinics was fueled by cultural fear and by the oppression of sexual minorities, both of which were exacerbated by two theoretical inventions of sexology: the idea that gender identity is consolidated between the ages of eighteen to thirty-six months, encoded into the brain, and impossible to change, and the idea that transsexualism in adulthood is unresponsive to any treatment but surgical sex reassignment. Sexology, in other words, cultivated the fear, that if you didn't catch him in childhood, he would grow up to be a full-fledged pervert. Thus, intervention in a child's development was justified by Rekers because "intervention in deviant sex-role development in childhood may be the only effective manner of treating (i.e. preventing) serious forms of sexual deviance in adulthood."[137]

Despite monumental problems in defining and diagnosing appropriate versus inappropriate gender role behavior, sexologists in this area too proceeded to quantify and medicalize the issue of gender using traditional, stereotypical concepts of femininity and masculinity. Based on these typifications, they developed testing instruments and treatment techniques. At the Gender Identity Research treatment program at UCLA, children were given psychological tests that included the Family-Doll Preference Test, the Parent and Activity Preference Test, and the Family Communication Task. All are based on traditional concepts of male dominance and rigid gender behavior. The Parent and Activity Preference Test is described by Richard Green, the program's director:

> A series of twenty-eight two-card sets of pictures, one depicting a mother and the other a father in an activity, is presented to the child. The activities pictured in the two cards may be gender-typical, e.g., father sawing wood paired with mother sewing (eight such sets); gender atypical, e.g., mother fixing a car paired with father dusting (eight such sets); gender-typical for one parent; e.g., both sewing (eight such sets); or gender-neutral, e.g., both reading (four such sets).[138]

Treatment programs for children who display cross-gender preferences on the diagnostic tests are based on principles of behavior modification. The child is given a same-sex therapist with whom to identify, but much of the program is implemented by the parents. Essentially, they place the child in a token-economy system, whereby the child is rewarded for exhibiting gender-appropriate behavior, and fined for not doing so. For a boy, parents make a list of stereotypically masculine mannerisms, toys, and activities and pay attention to him only when he is acting within that gender paradigm. Frequently, however, this method achieves only a superficially mechanical solution. Green wrote:

> One four-year-old boy, for example, was fond of carrying a purse. Wherever he went, he would dangle a purse from his forearm and carry it with his arm flexed at the elbow and hand turned upward. The boy then substituted a small brief-case for the purse. The parents saw this solely as modeling after his father. The boy carried the briefcase in precisely the manner in which he carried the purse. His appearance to other children remained decidedly feminine.[139]

Although the UCLA gender scientists refrain from simplistic etiologies of gender disturbances that place sole blame on a dominant mother, treatment strategies include advocating parental role shifts. Green writes:

> Parental-role division may be such that the boy sees his mother as prime provider of rewards, protection, and sustenance. The father's role may be

undermined, overtly or covertly, in the boy's presence, so that he comes to view the male role in a negative manner. Again, the special nature of the boy's behavior may be used as leverage to effect some redistribution of influence. Some fathers are men who have considerable difficulty in overcoming their passivity and have married women whose assertiveness complements their own retiring personality. However, in our experience, these *are* couples who perhaps at first uncomfortably and somewhat stiltedly, but later naturally, can modify role relationships. (Emphasis in original.) [140]

There is very little literature on masculine girls. The treatment for girls consists essentially of modification techniques of the same type as those used with feminine boys. However, girls who behave in a manner that is stereotypically considered masculine—strong, active, and aggressive—do not arouse the same disapproval that feminine boys do. As any grammar school child knows, tomboys are O.K., sissies are not. Consequently, very few masculine girls are taken to gender clinics. As noted earlier, Green wrote in 1974, "Because tomboyishness usually arouses no concern in parents and society very few tomboys are brought for evaluation." [141] The typical manifestation of gender disturbance in girls is a desire to do activities that they believe only boys can do—for example, playing sports and having male-identified careers. A sample interview with a girl at the UCLA clinic was revealing:

DR.: What are other appealing things about being a man?
GIRL: I don't know. I feel I am a boy because I like to do things like a boy. I act like a boy. I think like one.
DR.: In what way?
GIRL: Because I compare me to how my father thinks. I always did think like a boy. I always thought of getting a job, you know, I always thought of being an archeologist, and I always just had that sort of attitude.[142]

The presumption that homosexuality is pathological is perpetuated by childhood gender discord programs. As we have seen, such programs were inspired by fears of future transsexualism. But in his latest book, *The "Sissy Boy Syndrome" and the Development of Homosexuality*, Richard Green clarified that research had revealed that these boys were really prehomosexual rather than pretranssexual.[143] And, although the stated research goal of the UCLA programs is "to identify the relationship between these boyhood [cross-gender] behaviors and adult sexuality,"[144] it is clear that the not-so-latent agenda is to retrain the boys and subvert homosexual development.

The "sissy boy" study is an offshoot of Green's earlier research presented in *Sexual Identity Conflict in Children and Adults* (1974). For fifteen years, Green followed two behaviorally divergent groups of boys: some who could be called feminine, and some who were stereotypically masculine. Again, the distinctions were based largely on cultural signifiers. The masculine boys enjoyed sports, played with trucks, and dressed in boys' clothes. "Sissy boys," on the other hand, preferred girls' activities and made statements about wanting to be a girl. The boys were evaluated by monitoring playroom preferences, by psychological tests, and by ratings of physical behavior. For example, evaluators who were unaware that they were seeing only boys viewed videotapes of the children running and throwing a ball, and made judgments about whether a child was a boy or a girl. Green emphasizes that raters failed to consistently label the "sissy boys" appropriately. The prospective study attempted to determine what social factors, such as quality of relationship with mother and father and reinforcement of the "sissy" behavior, either cause or influence "femininity" in boys. In addition, the effects of behavior modification therapy were assessed. In the end, however, the socialization factors were inconclusive and the therapy was ineffective, leaving Green to hint at biological determinism. Ironically, Green took a leading role in urging the American Psychiatric Association to declassify homosexuality as a mental illness in 1973.[145]

Although Green employs the same behavior modification programs, he distances himself from the motivations of gender researchers such as the virulently homophobic George Rekers, whose goal is to promote "real masculinity, which should be affirmed in every young man in order to prevent them from being strongly tempted by the sexual perversions."[146] The UCLA treatment program has two rationales. First, boys who experience social derision because of their "feminine" behavior are entitled to therapeutic intervention that might enable them to increase their social repertoire. Second, since "feminine" boys are far more likely to mature into gay or bisexual men, the research will develop predictive skills by sketching "the portrait of a boy with greater than average probability of evolving with an atypical sexual identity."[147] As Green notes, "the treatment intervention did not abort the development of homosexual arousal."[148] Green's motivation is to eliminate "feminine" behavior, which has been correlated with gay development, "until society evolves to the point of accommodating greater latitude in the boyhood expression of currently 'sex-typed' behaviors."[149]

Proponents of the childhood gender clinics have steadfastly defended the programs. The more liberal sexologists, like Green himself, say that it is unfortunate that society is so intolerant, but that it is justifiable to seek to change the individual, since society will not easily be changed: "Feminine boys experience considerable social hardship," Green insists. "They are teased, ostracized, and bullied. While we might prefer that society immediately change its often irrational values of what constitutes desirable gender-role behavior, realistically, there is more basis for optimism in helping a single person to change."[150] Yet they virtually ignore the efforts of feminism and gay liberation to challenge stultifying gender stereotypes and to offer support and alternatives. The transcripts from Green's "sissy boy" study reveal the fear and isolation of many of the boys because they have no healthy models of being gay. One boy said that, although he had always known he was gay, that status was repugnant to him. When Green asked him why, he explained:

> Partly because all the images I had of homosexuality were very negative. . . . There was an extra charge on it too, which did come from my family, which was a real fear of disapproval from my parents, and a feeling of shame, and a lot to do with the disapproval of my parents, as well as just no positive role models. You know, the gay people that I saw in society were all very negative to me and I felt very, very repulsed by them.[151]

Yet, repeatedly, Green fails to offer an alternative analysis, or inform the boys about the gay movement or the many gay organizations for young people. If the goal of the gender programs were truly to reduce "distress," they could provide their clients with information about the gay community and about the groups and newsletters specifically for "sissies." Mel Horne addressed the alternatives in "Once I Was a Sissy, Now I'm a Gender Discord Boy":

Behind the seemingly genuine concern for the well-being of sissies, and a liberal attitude toward the gay male lifestyle, lies a tragic disregard for the nature of that society whose standards of masculinity and femininity are those toward which the sissy is being coerced. Masculine sexuality, male gender identity and male gender role do not constitute some neutral territory into which sissies can be herded without serious consequence: indeed, they form the foundation of a way of being in the world that has resulted in the degradation of women and in the relentless subjugation of all human and non-human forms of existence. . . . I recommend this simple advice. Direct all sissies-in-the-making . . . to the nearest feminist counselor. The alternative is a wasted life wondering what went wrong.[152]

It would be misleading to conclude that "sissy boy" research is a nefarious plot bent on the eradication of male homosexuality. Undoubtedly some boys feel that they have been aided by the program. The questions that repeatedly arise, however, are how to measure success and how to balance both individual and social ramifications. Is it a success for a boy to stop wearing a dress and pick up a gun? If a "sissy boy" grows up to be gay, is it a failure of the treatment program or a failure of a society that irrationally condemns homosexuality? Is it a success if, by subverting the effeminacy of a small boy, we have sent a broader social message that homosexuality or any gender variation is bad? Ultimately, the inconclusiveness of the "sissy boy" research is but a symptom of the fundamental problem. Like all sexological research on homosexuality, the study assumes the existence of inherently different types of people: the homosexual and the heterosexual. Many feminist and gay writers, in addition to the occasional sexologist, have challenged this notion. In a recent interview, researcher Martin Weinberg acknowledged his realization that "people move all around on the Kinsey scale. They really are fluid in their sexual orientations."[153] The most serious methodological problem for gender researchers of homosexuality, then, is the elusiveness of the research subject.

The difficulty for gender sexologists of securing an adequate sample of cross-gender children to participate in their programs is an indication that they have formulated "solutions" to a problem that they have helped create. In 1974 Richard Green wrote that his program was focusing on feminine boys because of the difficulty of finding enough masculine girls. Yet when he published his "sissy boy" study in 1987, he admitted that aggressive recruitment was necessary to secure the sample of boys as well. The study sample was finally garnered through letters to mental health professionals, newspaper articles, and television appearances, "since 'feminine' boys do not parade in with their parents on a daily basis to a medical center."[154] Richard Green and his colleagues obviously did not manufacture the difficulties experienced by children who do not conform to gender expectations, yet clearly they have had to create a demand for their program. And publicity and active recruitment for programs that promote stereotypic behavior both suggest to parents that untraditional behavior is pathological and provide a medical validation for the perpetuation of rigid gender roles.

Conclusion

G ender research represents yet another strategic attempt of sexologists to legitimate their services and establish a market by addressing the larger cultural dilemma about definitions of masculinity and femininity. Moored within the scientific establishment, gender sexologists were seemingly untouched by the social movements in the 1960s and 1970s that called for a loosening of rigid gender strictures. Rather, by aligning the profession with the dominant ideology, the gender industry reified normative, oppressive constructions of gender roles, and encouraged these values in the individuals they treated. As inhibitions of sexual desire may be the weak link of the scientific treatment of sexual dysfunctions, however, transsexualism may represent the weak link of the medical gender industry. In its brief, frenetic, and lucrative history, the field has largely failed in its endeavor to channel gender rebellion and regularize gender typifications. Concepts such as "gender dysphoria" and the gay and "sissy boy" conversion programs loom large as medical interventions in the cultural terrain of sexuality and gender. Yet sexologists have not achieved hegemony over alternative definitions. As with sex therapy, the problems of gender distress are social and political, and will not ultimately respond to purely technical and medical solutions. The narrowness of sexological gender research renders it unable to prevail.

Conclusion

Sexual science is coming of age. . . .
People's credibility has increased.

PAUL ABRAMSON
editor, Journal of Sex Research

Working in the area of sexuality is
a risk; what I'd like to do is take the
risk out of it. If the field is given
legitimacy, everyone can work in it.

PAUL ABRAMSON

Sexual science and sexual scientists
are devalued.

DON MOSHER
*former president, Society for the
Scientific Study of Sex*

Words like "risk," "credibility," and "devalued" pepper the discourse of
sexologists. Annual gatherings continue to feature upbeat reassurances
about the triumph of sexual science over the forces of sexual ignorance
and repression. Yet several years after the celebratory optimism of the
sixth World Congress of Sexology, the sexual landscape in the United
States is increasingly complex and contradictory. The AIDS epidemic
has energized political organizing and won widespread recognition for
sexual minorities such as prostitutes and gay people. But while AIDS
has necessitated freer sexual discussion, it has also prompted euphemisms and hyperbolic warnings that sex equals death. The epidemic has
inspired research that, perhaps for the first time since the publication of
the controversial Kinsey reports, reveals the divergence of private sexual
behavior from public morality. Silences have been broken, for example,

about the extent of extramarital affairs among women, homosexuality in the Black community, and bisexuality among married men. Yet a new sexual cynicism, influencing both gay and heterosexual relationships, is reflected in exhortations not to trust anyone until the test results are in. As we move into the 1990s, freedom of sexual expression is perhaps more embattled than at any time since the early 1960s. For sexology, the challenge is to secure an authoritative and profitable niche in the area of human sexuality at a moment of fear and uncertainty.

Certainly sexologists are not strangers to changes in the sex/gender system. The field is accustomed to accommodating and addressing the vagaries of an evolving sexual discourse. As we have seen, sexologists investigating sexual attitudes and behaviors in the 1940s faced a different set of research imperatives from those in the 1970s. Yet the current insecurity and increasing social conservatism, coming after two decades of growth in sexology, have prompted a pause for reflection and reassessment in the field. Some sexologists have taken note of changes in their practice. Sex therapist Sandra Leiblum, for example, admits that the optimism and enthusiasm that greeted Masters and Johnson's work has abated: "Few of us are claiming miraculous two-week cures for chronic problems."[1] And sex therapist Joe LoPiccolo has challenged many of sex therapy's sacred tenets in a lecture he entitles "Lies Sex Therapists Tell."[2] Sexual scientists have also begun to comment more widely on the development of the field itself. And, as the epigraphs to this chapter reveal, their self-assessment is characterized by a familiar paradox: the belief that the profession's triumph is right around the corner, and the simultaneous awareness that sexology is still the stepchild of the sciences. Thus, questions about legitimacy, professional risk, and credibility ring truer than ever in sexual science.

This discussion of sexology's negotiation of the sex/gender system centers on an analysis of its strategies to professionalize, achieve cultural legitimacy, and establish a market, making a case for a multidimensional assessment of its successes and failures. Important as internal activities are, I have subordinated questions about whether sexology meets all the theoretical criteria for a profession (as opposed to being a quasi discipline or even a subfield of medicine) to the more salient questions about professionalization. Why do occupations aspire to professional status?

How do they assume a certain content and direction? How do they establish their credibility and market as professions? Since the ultimate success of a profession depends on its negotiation of varied relationships within a society, this analysis emphasizes the relational aspects of sexology's development. That is, it views sexology as dynamic, acting and reacting in a shifting political, cultural, and economic context in which resistance, particularly in the form of sociopolitical movements, has been a major factor in the process of professionalization.

Broad resistance to the very notion of studying sex scientifically has largely shaped sexology's professional strategies. Its early alignment with science and medicine, for example, was made in the hope of drawing on the authority already accorded to both. Sexology has also had to compete against groups as varied as religious authorities, political groups, and the sex industry. Through a public presentation of empirical, and particularly biomedical, expertise, sexologists succeeded in edging out a number of competitors. In the early days of sex therapy, for example, Masters and Johnson eliminated prostitutes as competitors by providing surrogate partners for their male clients. In their roles as "medical authorities," they claimed that "so much more is needed and demanded from a substitute partner than effectiveness of purely physical sexual performance that to use prostitutes would have been at best clinically unsuccessful and at worst psychologically disastrous."[3] Since both involved the exchange of sex for money, it was important to establish a scientific distinction between surrogacy and prostitution.

Creating a market entails the attraction of a clientele, not only by establishing credibility and eliminating competitors, but also by persuading the public that they have needs that the profession can meet. Often these tasks overlap, and the profession can be most successful by responding to existing social and cultural needs. By addressing ongoing cultural concerns about heterosexual sex, marriage and the family, and gender roles, sexology tapped into a ready market of sexually confused or troubled individuals. The task for sexology was to redefine sexual problems as sexual diseases and dysfunctions and to offer solutions in the form of therapy, drugs, or surgery. By offering scientific and medical expertise for disruptive social problems, sexology established legitimacy while building a market.

While sexology's professional development has been problematic, its accomplishments are noteworthy. As the scientific study of sex burgeoned and the mantle of authority over sexual issues shifted away from religion, some of the mystification of sexuality diminished. Sexologists equated sexuality with other bodily processes like eating and digestion, and, using a biomedical lexicon, they attempted to neutralize it as an appropriate topic both for scientific study and for public discourse. Undeniably, this demystification has been a factor in the increased openness about sex. And sexologists have taken a further step as sexual enthusiasts. Sex therapy can offer permission to be sexual and provide assistance regarding certain sexual problems. Sex research has increased information about the body, physiological sexual response, and certain patterns of sexual behavior. Moreover, sexology's status has improved over the decades. The blatant harassment experienced by Kinsey and Masters and Johnson has dissipated. Professional organizations, although often financially precarious, are enduring centers of research and development. Individual sexologists have achieved professional success and credibility; some author columns in popular magazines or star in educational programs aired on cable channels.

Sexology has, however, largely failed to achieve its goal of cultural authority over sexual knowledge and values, comparable to, for example, the medical profession's dominance over health and illness. This is manifest, on the structural level, in the lack of a power base and of a state mandate in the form of licensing. Of greater significance, however, is sexology's inability to chart the terms of sexual discourse. Although sex researchers and therapists have constructed many of our contemporary concepts and definitions, these are far from being the only ones current in debates over sexual mores. In a recent article Donald Mosher decries sexology's limitations:

> A common media metaphor for science is that it is a national resource of great importance. . . . Yet, sexual science is not well represented in government or the media. Furthermore, sexual science does not speak to legislators, administrators, or citizens with a voice of scientific authority.[4]

Most recently, this failure is evidenced by sexology's inability to orchestrate a swift and effective response to the AIDS crisis. Other constituencies, notably the gay community, mobilized with grass-roots epidemiological research and innovative outreach and education. Public health and medicine, not typically noted for expertise in sexual issues, have provided the major professional players in AIDS research and education. When some sexologists eventually articulated a response to the disease, the most prominent, such as Helen Singer Kaplan, Theresa Crenshaw, William Masters, and Virginia Johnson, chose politically reactionary and medically unsound positions that were derided by both the public and health officials.

Structurally, sexology remains a fragmented, diffuse, and defensive field. As Paul Abramson so aptly notes, the professional stakes are high for those who would choose a career in the field of human sexuality. And sexologists themselves are often the first to admit that "misconceptions and bad jokes" plague the field.[5] Sexologist Don Mosher has complained that the profession has not been afforded the esteem which it deserves, and he notes, "Sexual science also remains invisible, in part, because sexual scientists (and organizations devoted to sexual science) have not actively facilitated their legitimate place in the pantheon of science, and they have failed to educate and cultivate the necessary opinion-leaders of society."[6]

Why is this so, when there is clearly a need for information, education, and assistance regarding sexual matters? The overwhelming demand for advice books, and even the more academic texts of Kinsey and Masters and Johnson, speaks to a desire for knowledge and guidance in sexual issues. On an individual level, people search for answers and for reassurance that they are "normal." On the social level, the values and meanings of sexuality are hotly contested. It is all the more striking, then, in an era characterized by professional dominance, that scientific sex experts have not achieved wholesale recognition and acceptance.

The factors that account for sexology's failure to fully consolidate and establish professional dominance are both specific to its internal strategies of professional development and related to culture and politics. For example, the difficulty of locating sexuality in the sphere of public discourse has limited sexology. Since the nineteenth century, sexual issues have increasingly shifted from the private arena to the public realm of politics and the market. Historians have noted the collapse of "the division between public reticence and private actions," and sexuality's current centrality "to our economy, our psyches, and our politics."[7] Yet tensions remain about which sexual issues are suitable for public discussion and how explicitly this can be undertaken. Shame, stigma, and moralism about sex underpin the cultural ambivalence over the free, public discussion of sexuality. Despite growing support, the appropriateness of sex education in the public schools is still questioned. A comprehensive nationwide survey recently revealed more support and more programming for AIDS education than for sex education.[8] This is not surprising, given historical ambivalence and resistance to teaching about issues such as pregnancy and birth control in the school system. Instruction about AIDS is acceptable because it can reinforce a message of fear and abstinence. Public discussion of sexuality then becomes a discourse of disease.

In fact, the response to the AIDS epidemic is another marker of this tension over public sexual discourse. Widespread dissemination of safer sex information coexists with prohibitions that constrain some state agencies from distributing condoms or publishing literature with explicit language and graphics.[9] Further, the Helms Amendment codifies a sexual hierarchy in which federal dollars can be used only to discuss certain behaviors, most notably abstinence and monogamous marital heterosexuality. And when researchers developed a new sex survey to update the Kinsey data on sexual behavior and attitudes, the White House delayed funding after two conservative legislators complained that the research constituted "an invasion of privacy."[10] The success of a field dealing with sexual issues is limited by the tenuous and contested presence of sexual discourse in the public domain. Sexology confronts institutional obstacles such as lack of funding and recognition from both the government and the academy, and market obstacles such as the belief on the part of potential clients that sexual issues are private and sexual problems are personal.

Cultural factors aside, sexology is ultimately impeded most dramatically by its internal strategies. Its empirical and biomedical methodology has prompted tensions that have disrupted professionalization. The incongruity, for example, between science and the sexual marketplace has been a factor in sexology's fragmented internal identity. In terms of research directions, methodology, and modes of clinical intervention, those who would attract a clientele and bolster the market oppose those who would perpetuate a staid, scientific public presentation. In short, what sells is often not what is most rigorously empirical and scientific. Overall, sexology suffers from a narrow professional vision, constrained, in part, by the rigidity of the biomedical model. Sexologists' claims to a scientific rationality that emphasizes objectivity and individual solutions has rendered them ineffective in truly grappling with issues of sex and gender, which are profoundly embedded in political conflict and social structures. This failure of scientific sexology to address power and social relations and to explore diversity in sexual meanings has cleared a path for challenge and resistance by feminism and gay liberation.

The application of the scientific method to issues of sexuality and gender must be reassessed, not with the moralistic fervor characteristic of the Kinsey era, but in light of evidence of its limitations. We must ask not whether it is "wrong" to study sex scientifically, but whether this methodology can address sex and gender issues in any but the most superficial ways. The biomedicalized view of sexuality largely as a physiological response obscures social relations and the fact that definitions and categories of sexuality and sexual behavior are socially constructed. Yet sexology as an institution seems impervious to critiques of the limitations of science. Individual sexologists speak as though future success depended upon even more rigorous "state of the art, highly technical mathematical work that is specific to the area of sexuality."[11] As long as sexologists' overriding goal is professional respectability, they will retreat in this way from confronting difficult issues involving their own internal methods and biases.

Ultimately, of course, it is not a question of *whether* politics can infuse sexual science, but of what kinds of politics *do* underpin the field. Emerging professions have the best chance at success if their values coincide with the dominant ideology, and we have seen how sexology typically speaks with a voice that supports mainstream cultural values about sexuality and gender.[12] Yet the increased drift toward biological determinism —the search for physiological bases for gender and sexual behavior— is defended even by sexologists who consider themselves progressive, on the grounds that "groups that have been discriminated against can receive special legal protection if the trait for which they are stigmatized is an immutable one (such as race)."[13] Underlying this strategy is the belief that sexuality and different sexual lifestyles will become acceptable not through political struggle, but through the accrual by sexual science of data proving that they are biologically "natural." Scientific rationality is irresistibly compelling for those who view it as the source of both social progress and professional success.

An unremitting commitment to science will continue to circumscribe sexology's participation in the complex cultural negotiations around sexuality and gender. This raises the question of the relationship between sexology and other social actors, such as progressive political movements. Feminists have taken basic sexological data on sexuality and recontextualized it more broadly and analytically; on the other hand, feminism and gay liberation have disrupted sexology's professionalization and challenged its hegemony over sexuality and gender issues by generating an alternative world view. The lesbian/gay movement disputes the perspective that would pathologize "sissy boys" and subject them to clinical treatment. Women with sexual problems are apt to encounter a different analysis in a feminist support group than in a sex therapist's office. These challenges have pushed sexology to expand its focus, so that, for example, conferences now often include presentations on AIDS, feminist issues in sex therapy, and challenges to homophobia along with the traditional scientific and biomedical offerings.

Although the resistance to sexology is largely external, a small cohort of feminist and gay sexologists is attempting political change from within the field. How appropriate or effective is such a strategy? Some critics would eschew any such connection, cautioning that a profession's vested interest in the dominant social order renders its practice irrelevant to groups that seek radical change.[14] Further, there is the danger of cooptation, should the dominant profession superficially accommodate political groups and thus mask its repressive underpinnings. These cautions are apt, and significant professional transformation seems unlikely in light of sexologists' recent energetic attempts to revitalize logical positivism within the field. However, internal opposition is important, if only to hold sexologists accountable for the ramifications of their positions on such issues as AIDS, "sissy boys," and women's sexual

behavior. In the absence of both internal and external opposition, sexologists' attempts to consolidate as the cultural experts on sexuality and
gender would go unchallenged.

Challenge, conflict, and contradiction are ultimately the most salient
themes of this book. An analysis of sexology reveals nothing so much
as the complexities inherent in any enterprise involving sexuality and
gender. For sexology's fortunes do not rise and fall simply according
to its strategic effectiveness; they depend on the complicated terrain of
metaphors and symbols that make up our sex/gender system. Sexology's
hopes for professional dominance represent a promise as yet unfulfilled.
After more than a century of effort, those prospects are unlikely to
change. Its failure, however, speaks to the need for a more powerful
vision and a multiplicity of voices in the cultural discourse on sex.

Notes and Index

Notes

INTRODUCTION

1. Sponsored by the World Association for Sexology, the congress was organized by the United States Consortium for Sexology—an Illinois-based nonprofit corporation comprising representatives from various sexological organizations in the United States. Four large associations of sex professionals collaborate through the Consortium—the American Association of Sex Educators, Counselors, and Therapists (AASECT), the Sex Information and Education Council of the United States (SIECUS), the Society for Sex Therapy and Research (SSTAR), and The Association of Sexologists (TAOS). Although it was not a sponsor of the 1983 World Congress, the Society for the Scientific Study of Sex (SSSS) was also a noticeable presence there.

2. Philip Boffey, "Sexology Struggling to Establish Itself Amid Wide Hostility," *New York Times*, May 31, 1983.

3. James Lardner, "Only One Thing on Their Minds," *Washington Post*, May 28, 1983.

4. The phrase "cultural authority" is used to describe the role of physicians by Paul Starr, *The Social Transformation of American Medicine* (New York: Basic Books, 1982).

5. Program of the sixth World Congress of Sexology, May 23–27, 1983.

6. Edwin Haeberle, "Sexology: Conception, Birth and Growth of a Science," paper presented at the sixth World Congress of Sexology, May 23, 1983.

7. Shirley Zussman, "Emerging Dimensions of Sexology," paper presented at the sixth World Congress of Sexology, May 23, 1983.

8. Howard Ruppel, "Self-Perceptions of Orgasmic Response Among Women," paper presented at the sixth World Congress of Sexology, May 23, 1983.

9. Quoted in Lardner, "Only One Thing."

10. Charles Mosher, "The Iatrogenic Problems of Incest," paper presented at the sixth World Congress of Sexology, May 24, 1983. See also *Off Our Backs*, July 1983, p. 9.

11. Quoted in Lardner, "Only One Thing."

12. Quoted in Boffey, "Sexology Struggling to Establish Itself."

13. In 1908, Magnus Hirschfeld began editing the first journal committed to the scientific study of sex, *Zeitschrift für Sexualwissenschaft*. In 1913, in Berlin, Iwan Bloch founded the field's first professional association, the Medical Society for Sexology and Eugenics, and some months later Albert Moll founded a second organization, the International Society for Sex Research, also in Berlin.

14. Edwin Haeberle, "The Birth of Sexology: A Brief History in Documents" (n.p.: World Association for Sexology and U.S. Consortium for Sexology, 1983).

15. Myron Sharaf, *Fury on Earth: A Biography of Wilhelm Reich* (New York: St. Martin's Press, 1983). Ch. 13.

16. Atina Grossman, "The New Woman and the Rationalization of Sexuality in Weimar Germany," in *Powers of Desire: The Politics of Sexuality*, ed. Ann Snitow, Christine Stansell, and Sharon Thompson (New York: Monthly Review Press, 1983), pp. 153–171.

17. Haeberle, "Birth of Sexology." See also Jeffrey Weeks, *Sex, Politics and Society: The Regulation of Sexuality since 1800* (New York: Longman, 1981).

18. See, for example, the historical surveys of Edwin Haeberle, such as "The

Birth of Sexology," "Swastika, Pink Triangle, and Yellow Star: The Destruction of Sexology and the Persecution of Homosexuals in Nazi Germany," *Journal of Sex Research* 17 (1981): 270–287.

19. See Nathan Hale, *Freud and the Americans: The Beginning of Psychoanalysis in the United States, 1876–1913* (New York: Oxford University Press, 1971), for a discussion of early research on sexual issues. Also see Weeks, *Sex, Politics and Society*, for a discussion of more mystical sex reformers such as Edward Carpenter.

20. See, for example, Eliot Friedson, *Profession of Medicine: A Study of the Sociology of Applied Knowledge* (New York: Harper & Row, 1970); Magali Sarfatti Larson, *The Rise of Professionalism: A Sociological Analysis* (Berkeley: University of California Press, 1977); Starr, *Social Transformation of American Medicine*.

21. Starr, *Social Transformation of American Medicine*, p. 4.

22. See, for example, A. M. Carr-Saunders and P. A. Wilson, *The Professions* (Oxford: Clarendon Press, 1933); Friedson, *Profession of Medicine*; Larson, *Rise of Professionalism*.

23. Starr, *Social Transformation of American Medicine*, p. 16.

24. Friedson, *Profession of Medicine*, p. 187.

25. Michel Foucault, *The History of Sexuality*, vol. 1: *An Introduction* (New York: Pantheon, 1978).

26. See, for example, Sheila Jeffreys, *The Spinster and Her Enemies: Feminism and Sexuality 1880–1930* (London: Pandora Press, 1985); Edward Brecher, *The Sex Researchers* (New York: Signet, 1969); Margaret Jackson, "Sex Research and the Construction of Sexuality: A Tool of Male Supremacy," *Women's Studies International Forum* 7, no. 1 (1984): 43–51; Thomas Szasz, *Sex by Prescription* (New York: Anchor Press/Doubleday, 1980); Christian Defense League, "Sex Education: The Assault on Christian Morals," Special Report no. 6. Exceptions to the above are the fine analyses of sexology by Carole Vance ("Gender Systems, Ideology, and Sex Research," in Snitow, Stansell, and Thompson, *Powers of Desire*, pp. 371–384), and by Jeffrey Weeks (*Sexuality and Its Discontents: Meanings, Myths and Modern Sexualities* [London: Routledge & Kegan Paul, 1985]).

27. See, for example, Cindy Patton, *Sex and Germs: The Politics of AIDS* (Boston: South End Press, 1983).

28. Vern Bullough, "Problems of Research on a Delicate Topic: A Personal View," *Journal of Sex Research* 21 (1985): 375–386.

29. See Foucault, *History of Sexuality*; Weeks, *Sex, Politics and Society*; John

D'Emilio and Estelle Freedman, *Intimate Matters: A History of Sexuality in America* (New York: Harper & Row, 1988), for historical changes in sexuality.

30. Sandra Harding, *The Science Question in Feminism* (Ithaca, N.Y.: Cornell University Press, 1986), p. 16.

31. Rue Bucher, "Pathology: A Study of Social Movements Within a Profession," in *Medical Men and Their Work: A Sociological Reader*, ed. Eliot Friedson and Judith Lorber (New York: Aldine, 1972), pp. 113–127.

32. See, for example, John D'Emilio, "Capitalism and Gay Identity," in Snitow, Stansell, and Thompson, *Powers of Desire*, pp. 100–113; Kathy Peiss, "'Charity Girls' and City Pleasures: Historical Notes on Working-Class Sexuality, 1880–1920," ibid., pp. 74–87; Eli Zaretsky, *Capitalism, The Family, and Personal Life* (New York: Harper and Row, 1976).

33. See, for example, various texts by members of the Frankfort School: for example, Herbert Marcuse, *One-Dimensional Man: Studies in the Ideology of Advanced Industrial Society* (Boston: Beacon Press, 1964).

34. See Linda Gordon and Ellen DuBois, "Seeking Pleasure on the Battlefield: Danger and Pleasure in Nineteenth-Century Feminist Sexual Thought," in *Pleasure and Danger: Exploring Female Sexuality*, ed. Carole S. Vance (Boston: Routledge & Kegan Paul, 1984). See also Laura Lederer, *Take Back the Night: Women on Pornography* (New York: William Morrow, 1980); Kathleen Barry, *Female Sexual Slavery* (Englewood Cliffs, N.J.: Prentice Hall, 1979); Andrea Dworkin, *Pornography: Men Possessing Women* (New York: G. P. Putnam's Sons, 1981); Susan Griffin, *Pornography and Silence: Culture's Revolt Against Nature* (New York: Harper and Row, 1981).

35. On feminist views about the complicated nature of pornography, see FACT Book Committee, *Caught Looking: Feminism, Pornography and Censorship* (New York: Caught Looking, Inc., 1986); Varda Burstyn, ed., *Women Against Censorship* (Vancouver, B.C.: Douglas & McIntyre, 1985). See also Frederique Delacoste and Priscilla Alexander, *Sex Work: Writings by Women on the Sex Industry* (Pittsburgh: Cleis Press, 1987), and Laurie Bell, *Good Girls/Bad Girls: Feminists and Sex Trade Workers Face to Face* (Toronto: Seal Press, 1987).

36. For an instance of the idealization of science, see Derek Price, "The Nature of Science," in *Biology*, ed. R. Goldsby (New York: Harper and Row, 1976), p. 1; for criticism of it, see Rita Arditti, Pat Brennan, and Steve Cavrak, *Science and Liberation* (Boston: South End Press, 1980).

37. Ruth Bleier, *Feminist Approaches to Science* (New York: Pergamon Press, 1988), p. 5.

38. John Costello, *Virtue Under Fire: How World War II Changed Our Social and Sexual Attitudes* (Boston: Little, Brown, 1985).

39. Harding, *Science Question in Feminism.*

40. Bernie Zilbergeld, *Male Sexuality* (Boston: Little, Brown, 1978), p. vii.

41. See Eric Berne, *Games People Play* (New York: Grove Press, 1964), for an early description of script theory. This theory has been applied to issues of sexuality by, for example, John Gagnon and William Simon, *Sexual Conduct* (Chicago: Aldine, 1973).

42. Wendy Stock, "Sex Roles and Sexual Dysfunction," in *Sex Roles and Psychopathology*, ed. Cathy S. Widom (New York: Plenum Press, 1984), pp. 249–275.

43. Thomas Ruble, "Sex Stereotypes: Issues of Change in the 1970s," *Sex Roles* 9 (1983): 397–401.

44. Barbara Ponse, *Identities in the Lesbian World: The Social Construction of Self* (Westport, Conn.: Greenwood Press, 1978).

45. Discussed in Linda Murray, "Sexual Destinies," *Omni*, April 1987. See also G. Doerner, W. Rohde, F. Stahl, L. Krell, and W. Masius, "A Neuro-endocrine Predisposition for Homosexuality in Men," *Archives of Sexual Behavior* (1975): 1–8.

46. For example, see Gagnon and Simon, *Sexual Conduct*. For a review of the research tradition of the Chicago School of sociology, see Ken Plummer, "Symbolic Interactionism and Sexual Conduct: An Emergent Perspective," in *Human Sexual Relations: Towards a Redefinition of Sexual Politics*, ed. Mike Brake (New York: Pantheon, 1982), pp. 223–241.

47. Gayle Rubin, "The Traffic in Women: Notes on the 'Political Economy' of Sex," in *Toward an Anthropology of Women*, ed. Rayna R. Reiter (New York: Monthly Review Press, 1975), pp. 157–210.

48. Gayle Rubin, "Thinking Sex: Notes for a Radical Theory of the Politics of Sexuality," in Vance, *Pleasure and Danger*, p. 282.

49. Ibid.

50. Tucker Pamella Farley, "Lesbianism and the Social Function of Taboo," in *The Future of Difference*, ed. Hester Eisenstein and Alice Jardine (New Brunswick, N.J.: Rutgers University Press, 1980), p. 268.

51. Bleier, *Feminist Approaches to Science*, p. 147.

52. See Harding, *Science Question in Feminism*.

53. Nancy Miller, quoted by Alice Jardine, "Prelude: The Future of Difference," in Eisenstein and Jardine, *Future of Difference*, p. xxv.

54. See, for example, Bonnie Kreps, "Radical Feminism 1," in *Radical Feminism*, ed. Anne Koedt, Ellen Levine, and Anita Rapone (New York: Quadrangle, 1973), pp. 234–239.

55. Donald Mosher, quoted in Kim McDonald, "Out of the Closet Now, but Misunderstood: Research on Sex," *Chronicle of Higher Education*, November 10, 1987.

PART ONE: THE EMERGENCE OF SCIENTIFIC SEXOLOGY

1. Paul Robinson, *The Modernization of Sex* (New York: Harper & Row, 1976).

CHAPTER ONE: TOWARD A "VALUE-FREE" SCIENCE OF SEX

1. Peter Gabriel Filene, *Him/Her/Self* (New York: Harcourt Brace Jovanovich, 1974), p. 143.

2. Quoted ibid., p. 149.

3. Quoted in Susan Ware, *Holding Their Own: American Women in the 1930s* (Boston: Twayne, 1982), p. 62.

4. John D'Emilio and Estelle Freedman, *Intimate Matters: A History of Sexuality in America* (New York: Harper & Row, 1988).

5. Filene, *Him/Her/Self*, p. 184.

6. Michelle Perrot, "The New Eve and the Old Adam: Changes in French Women's Condition at the Turn of the Century," in *Behind the Lines: Gender and the Two World Wars*, ed. Margaret Randolph Higonnet, Jane Jenson, Sonya Michel, and Margaret Collins Weitz (New Haven: Yale University Press, 1987), p. 57.

7. See, for example, Michael Delli Carpini, *Stability and Change in American Politics: The Coming of Age of the Generation of the 1960s* (New York: New York University Press, 1986); Paul C. Light, *Baby Boomers* (New York: Norton, 1988); Pamela Reynolds, "What Lies Ahead for Baby Boomers," *Boston Globe*, June 15, 1987.

8. Personal conversation, Michael Bronski, June 12, 1987.

9. Linda Gordon, *Woman's Body, Woman's Right: Birth Control in America* (New York: Penguin Books, 1974).

10. Diana Long Hall, "Biology, Sex Hormones, and Sexism in the 1920s," in *Women and Philosophy: Toward a Theory of Liberation*, ed. Carol Gould and Marx Wartofsky (New York: G. P. Putnam's Sons, 1979), pp. 81–96.

11. Diana Long Hall, "The Social Implications of the Scientific Study of Sex," paper presented at the Barnard Conference, 1976.

12. Quoted ibid., p. 14.

13. Ibid., pp. 14–16, quotation at p. 14.

14. Sexual consciousness has changed so much that a researcher who attempted this mode of questioning with his female students in the 1990s would likely be vulnerable to accusations of sexual harassment.

15. Alfred C. Kinsey, Wardell B. Pomeroy, Clyde E. Martin, and Paul H. Gebhard, *Sexual Behavior in the Human Female* (New York: Pocket Books, 1953), pp. 9, 8; hereafter cited as *SBHF*.

16. Alfred C. Kinsey, Wardell B. Pomeroy, Clyde E. Martin, and Paul H. Gebhard, *Sexual Behavior in the Human Male* (Philadelphia: W. B. Saunders, 1948), p. 5; hereafter cited as *SBHM*.

17. Wardell D. Pomeroy, *Dr. Kinsey and the Institute for Sex Research* (New York: Harper & Row, 1972), p. 21.

18. *SBHM*, pp. 11–12.

19. *SBHF*, p. 264.

20. *SBHF*, p. 20.

21. Edwin Sutherland, "The Diffusion of Sexual Psychopath Laws," *American Journal of Sociology* 56 (1950): 142–48; Estelle Freedman, "'Uncontrolled Desires': The Response to the Sexual Psychopath, 1920–1960," *Journal of American History* 74 (1987): 83–106.

22. Kinsey's opposition to sex laws seems clearly resonant with his admiration for those with rich and varied sex lives. He saw sex laws as simply another impediment to sexual realization. In this respect, Kinsey frequently pits males against females, males being pursuers of sexual gratification and females reluctant gatekeepers. His texts are peppered with examples of lusty, male adolescents unjustly chastened by rigid female authorities who lack the capacity to empathize with them. He goes even further, in his criticism of sex laws, by asserting that often young girls misunderstand sexual advances made by older men. In

SBHM, he writes, "Many small girls reflect the public hysteria over the prospects of 'being touched' by a strange person; and many a child, who has no idea at all of the mechanics of intercourse, interprets affection and simple caressing, from anyone except her own parents, as attempts at rape. In consequence, not a few older men serve time in penal institutions for attempting to engage in a sexual act which at their age would not interest most of them, and of which many of them are undoubtedly incapable" (p. 238). This is one of several instances of his denial of the possible validity of girls' claims of sexual abuse.

23. Peter Jackson, "The Tender Trap," *Mattachine Review*, February 1957, p. 9.

24. Pomeroy, *Dr. Kinsey*, p. 395.

25. See, for example, Elizabeth Hall, "New Directions for the Kinsey Institute," *Psychology Today*, June 1986, pp. 33–39.

26. Letter, Lester Kirkendall to Mary S. Calderone, January 4, 1965, SIECUS Library, New York.

27. *SBHF*, p. 7.

28. *SBHM*, p. 153.

29. Ibid., p. 147.

30. Ibid., p. 19.

31. *SBHF*, p. 67.

32. *SBHM*, p. 42.

33. Ibid., p. 47. See Elliot G. Mishler, *Research Interviewing: Context and Narrative* (Cambridge: Harvard University Press, 1986).

34. *SBHM*, p. 6.

35. Pomeroy, *Dr. Kinsey*, p. 102.

36. Ibid., p. 101.

37. Ibid., p. 103.

38. *SBHM*, p. 157.

39. *SBHF*, p. 8.

40. *SBHM*, p. 202.

41. Ibid., p. 201.

42. Ibid., p. 263.

43. Quotations from *SBHF*, pp. 230–232.

44. Ibid., p. 283.

45. Ibid., p. 365.

46. Ibid., p. 412.

47. Ibid., p. 436.

48. *SBHM*, p. 666.

49. Ibid., p. 203.

50. *SBHF*, p. 102.

51. *SBHM*, p. 207.

52. Ibid., p. 209.

53. Ibid., p. 327.

54. Ibid., p. 158.

55. *SBHF*, p. 46.

56. *SBHM*, p. 650.

57. Alan Bell, Martin Weinberg, and Sue Hammersmith, *Sexual Preference: Its Development in Men and Women* (Bloomington: Indiana University Press, 1981).

58. *SBHM*, p. 639.

59. Sandra Gilbert, "Soldier's Heart: Literary Men, Literary Women, and the Great War," in Higonnet et al., *Behind the Lines*, p. 201.

60. Allan Berube, "Marching to a Different Drummer: Lesbian and Gay GIs in World War II," in *Powers of Desire: The Politics of Sexuality* ed. Ann Snitow, Christine Stansell, and Sharon Thompson (New York: Monthly Review Press, 1983), p. 89.

61. Valerie Taylor, "Five Minority Groups in Relation to Contemporary Fiction," *The Ladder* 5, no. 4 (January 1961): 10.

62. See, for example, Michael Bronski, *Culture Clash: The Making of Gay Sensibility* (Boston: South End Press, 1984); John D'Emilio, *Sexual Politics, Sexual Communities: The Making of a Homosexual Minority in the United States, 1940–1970* (Chicago: University of Chicago Press, 1983).

63. I am grateful to Michael Bronski for pointing out this connection to me. See Nora Sayre, *Running Time: Films of the Cold War* (New York: Dial Press, 1982), p. 81.

64. *SBHM*, p. 375.

65. Ibid., p. 389.

66. See *SBHF*, pp. 685–689, for this discussion of men, women, and social conditioning.

67. Ibid., p. 641.

68. Ibid.

69. Ibid., p. 642.

70. *SBHM*, p. 209.

71. Ibid.

72. Ibid.

73. Ibid., p. 177.

74. Pomeroy, *Dr. Kinsey*, p. 172.

75. This notion was challenged in the early 1980s by sexologists who proclaimed the existence of a highly sensitive area in the vagina, which they named the G-spot after sex researcher Ernst Grafenberg. Grafenberg's research is noted by Kinsey in *SBHF*, pp. 576, 580, 587, 635.

76. Ibid., p. 171.

77. Ibid., p. 346.

78. Ibid., p. 347.

79. Ibid.

80. Ibid., p. 358.

81. Ibid., p. 13.

82. *Herald Tribune*, May 16, 1958.

83. Paul Robinson, *The Modernization of Sex* (New York: Harper & Row, 1976), p. 116.

84. *Catholic News*, July 10, 1954.

85. *New York Mirror*, August 27, 1953.

86. "Sex vs. America," *Newsweek*, September 7, 1953, p. 20.

87. Lionel Trilling, "The Kinsey Report," in *The Liberal Imagination* (New York: Harcourt Brace Jovanovich, 1957).

88. Pomeroy, *Dr. Kinsey*, p. 380.

89. Quoted in "Repairing the Conjugal Bed," *Time*, May 25, 1970, pp. 49–52.

CHAPTER TWO: SCIENCE, MEDICINE, AND A MARKET

1. William Masters, "Three Decade Retrospective of the Masters and Johnson Institute," Society for the Scientific Study of Sex, November 18, 1983.

2. Albert Rosenfeld, "Inside the Sex Lab," *Science Digest Special*, November–December 1980, p. 70.

3. Albert Rosenfeld, "They Dared to Document Sex," *Science Digest Special*, September–October 1980, p. 70.

4. Marion K. Saunders, "The Sex Crusaders from Missouri," *Harpers*, May 1966, p. 53.

5. "Playboy Interview: Masters and Johnson," *Playboy*, November 1979, p. 88.

6. Rosenfeld, "Inside," p. 124.

7. Masters, "Three Decade Retrospective."

8. "Morals: The Second Sexual Revolution," *Time*, January 24, 1964.

9. Marty Jezer, *The Dark Ages: Life in the United States, 1945–1960* (Boston: South End Press, 1982), p. 223.

10. Andrew Cherlin, *Marriage, Divorce, Remarriage* (Cambridge: Harvard University Press, 1981), p. 40.

11. Mary Jo Bane, *Here to Stay: American Families in the Twentieth Century* (New York: Basic Books, 1976), p. 27.

12. Philip Wylie, *Generation of Vipers* (New York: Rinehart and Winston, 1942).

13. Mrs. L. R. Maxwell, "Just Between Us Mothers," *Mattachine Review*, June 1957, p. 21.

14. Barbara Ehrenreich, *The Hearts of Men* (New York: Anchor Press, 1983), p. 42.

15. "The New American Domesticated Male," *Life*, January 4, 1954, pp. 42–45.

16. "Morals: The Second Sexual Revolution."

17. Lily Tomlin, *On Stage*, Arista Records, 1977.

18. Winifred Breines, "Sexual Puzzles: Sex, Romance and Teenage Girls in the 1950s," paper presented at the seventh Berkshire Conference on the History of Women, June 21, 1987.

19. Linda Gordon, *Woman's Body, Woman's Right: Birth Control in America* (New York: Penguin Books, 1974), pp. 361–362.

20. "Sex Manuals: How Not To . . . ," *Newsweek*, October 18, 1965, pp. 100–101.

21. Ibid.

22. Lois Pemberton, *The Stork Didn't Bring You* (New York: Hermitage Press, 1948), quoted in Patricia Campbell, *Sex Education Books for Young Adults, 1892–1979* (New York: R. R. Bowker, 1979), p. 98.

23. Ibid.

24. Ibid., p. 101.

25. Jezer, *Dark Ages*, p. 233.

26. Cherlin, *Marriage, Divorce, Remarriage*, p. 44.

27. "Morals: The Second Sexual Revolution."

28. "I Hate Women," *The Ladder* 9, nos. 5–6 (February–March), p. 7.

29. Campbell, *Sex Education Books*, p. 116.

30. "Morals: The Second Sexual Revolution."

31. Ibid.

32. Edward Herold and Marnie Foster, "Changing Sexual References in Mass Circulation Magazines," *Family Coordinator*, January 1979, pp. 21–25.

33. "Morals: The Second Sexual Revolution."

34. "Why the Furor Over Sex Education," *U.S. News and World Report*, August 4, 1969, pp. 44–46.

35. "Sex: How to Read All About It," *Newsweek*, August 24, 1970, pp. 38–43.

36. "Sex Manuals."

37. Ibid. References are to Dutch gynecologist Th. H. van de Velde, who wrote *Ideal Marriage*, one of the first marriage manuals; urologist Abraham Stone and his wife, Hannah, who wrote *Marriage Manual*; and English psychologist Eustace Chesser, who wrote *Love Without Fear*.

38. "Sex: How to Read All About It."

39. Ibid.

40. Edward Brecher, *The Sex Researchers* (New York: Signet, 1969), p. 326.

41. H. W. Magoun, "John B. Watson and the Study of Human Sexual Behavior," *Journal of Sex Research* 17 (1981): 368–378.

42. Brecher, *Sex Researchers*, pp. 326–330.

43. For critiques of Masters and Johnson's research, focusing on the graphing of their findings, their understanding of physiology, inadequate equipment, and shoddy conceptualization, see Paul Robinson, *The Modernization of Sex* (New York: Harper and Row, 1976), and Patrick M. McGrady, *The Love Doctors* (New York: Macmillan, 1972).

44. McGrady, *Love Doctors*, p. 290.

45. Masters, "Three Decade Retrospective."

46. Rosenfeld, "They Dared to Document," p. 71.

47. Mary Harrington Hall, "A Conversation with Masters and Johnson," *Medical Aspects of Human Sexuality* 3, no. 12 (December 1969): 43.

48. Edward Brecher, "A New Way to Help Troubled Marriages," *Redbook*, March 1968, pp. 76–145.

49. William Masters and Virginia Johnson, "The Scientist and His Interpreters," *Bulletin of the American Medical Writers Association* 17, no. 5 (November–December 1967): 4–9.

50. Rosenfeld, "They Dared to Document," p. 72.

51. Leslie H. Farber, "I'm Sorry, Dear," *Commentary*, November 1964.

52. Rosenfeld, "They Dared to Document," p. 70.

53. Masters and Johnson, "The Scientist and His Interpreters."

54. Fred Belliveau and Lin Richter, *Understanding Human Sexual Inadequacy* (New York: Bantam Books, 1970), p. 59.

55. William Masters and Virginia Johnson, *Human Sexual Response* (New York: Bantam Books, 1966), p. 10; hereafter cited as *HSR*.

56. Brecher, *Sex Researchers*, p. 333.

57. *HSR*, p. 11.

58. Ibid., pp. 10, 12.

59. Nat Lehrman, *Masters and Johnson Explained* (Chicago: Playboy Press, 1970), p. 140.

60. William Masters and Virginia Johnson, *Human Sexual Inadequacy* (New York: Bantam Books, 1970), p. 347; hereafter cited as *HSI*.

61. Helen Singer Kaplan, *The New Sex Therapy* (New York: Brunner/Mazel, 1974), p. 13.

62. Ruth Brecher and Edward Brecher, eds., *An Analysis of Human Sexual Response* (New York: Signet, 1966), p. 60.

63. *HSR*, p. 16.

64. Shirley Zussman, "Emerging Dimensions of Sexology," paper presented at the sixth World Congress of Sexology, May 23, 1983.

65. Belliveau and Richter, *Understanding Human Sexual Inadequacy*, pp. 19–20.

66. Robinson, *Modernization of Sex*, p. 130.

67. *HSR*, p. v.

68. Hall, "Conversation," p. 55.

69. *HSR*, pp. 4–6.

70. Hall, "Conversation," p. 46.

71. This would be challenged in the 1980s by other sexologists (see Chapter Five).

72. *HSR*, p. 131.

73. Ibid., p. 64.

74. Ibid., p. 131.

75. William Leach, *True Love and Perfect Union* (New York: Basic Books, 1980), pp. 10, 12, 47; Alice Echols, "The New Feminism of Yin and Yang," in *Powers of Desire: The Politics of Sexuality*, ed. Ann Snitow, Christine Stansell, and Sharon Thompson (New York: Monthly Review Press, 1983), pp. 439–459.

76. McGrady, *Love Doctors*, p. 292.

77. Philip Sarrel and William Masters, "Sexual Molestation of Men by Women," *Archives of Sexual Behavior* 2, no. 2 (1982): 117–131; William Masters, "Clinical Management of Men Raped by Women," paper presented at the AASECT Conference, March 1982.

78. Boston Women's Health Book Collective, *Our Bodies, Ourselves*, 3d ed. (New York: Simon and Schuster, 1984), p. 99.

79. *HSI*, p. 9.

80. Masters, "Three Decade Retrospective."

81. *HSI*, p. 211.

82. See, for example, "Playboy Interview," p. 120.

83. *HSR*, p. vi.

84. Arthur Snider, "Sex Study Raises Ruckus," *Science Digest*, July 1966, p. 29. Although Masters and Johnson invoked the specter of marriages collapsing as a result of sexual dysfunction, researchers discovered that reported dysfunction in relationships was not correlated with satisfaction. It appeared, according to these data, that couples who experienced sexual problems overwhelmingly reported sexual satisfaction in the marriage nevertheless. See E. Frank, C. Anderson, and D. Rubinstein, "Frequency of Sexual Dysfunction in 'Normal' Couples," *New England Journal of Medicine* 299 (July 20, 1978): 111–115.

85. *HSR*, p. 16.

86. Robinson, *Modernization of Sex*, p. 126.

87. Anne Koedt, "The Myth of the Vaginal Orgasm," in *Radical Feminism*, ed. Anne Koedt, Ellen Levine, and Anita Rapone (New York: Quadrangle, 1973), pp. 198–207.

88. Ibid.

89. Natalie Shainess, "How Sex Experts Debase Sex," *World of Research*, January 2, 1973, pp. 21–25.

90. Rosenfeld, "Inside."

PART TWO: SEXOLOGY AT A CROSSROAD

1. William Masters, "Phony Sex Clinics—Medicine's Newest Nightmare," *Today's Health*, November 1974, pp. 22–26.

2. Patrick M. McGrady, *The Love Doctors* (New York: Macmillan, 1972), p. 344.

3. Statement of the Society for the Scientific Study of Sex.

4. SIECUS newsletter, Spring 1967.

5. Carol Cassell, "A Perspective on the Great Sex Debate," in *Challenges in Sexual Science*, ed. Clive Davis (Lake Mills, Iowa: Graphic Publishing, 1983), p. 91.

6. Ibid., pp. 85–108.

7. "Street Corner Clinics," *Time*, May 14, 1973.

8. Linda Wolfe, "The Question of Surrogates in Sex Therapy," in *Handbook of Sex Therapy*, ed. Joseph LoPiccolo and Leslie LoPiccolo (New York: Plenum Press, 1978), p. 492.

9. Masters, "Phony Sex Clinics."

10. Ibid.

11. Robert J. Levin, "Most Sex Therapy Clinics are Frauds," *Physician's World* 3, no. 1 (January 1975): 17–21.

12. Masters, "Phony Sex Clinics."

13. Albert Ellis, "Certification for Sex Therapists," in *Progress in Sexology*, ed. Robert Gemme and Connie Wheeler (New York: Plenum Press, 1976), p. 252.

14. Masters, "Phony Sex Clinics."

15. Ibid.

16. Ibid.

CHAPTER THREE: THE HUMANISTIC THEME IN SEXOLOGY

1. *SAR guide for a Better Sex Life* (San Francisco: National Sex Forum, 1975), p. 15.

2. Ibid., p. 15.

3. Sally Quinn, "Sex Counselors: They're No Laughing Matter," *Boston Evening Globe*, April 6, 1978.

4. Ibid.

5. For history and theory of humanistic psychology, see Charlotte Buhler and Melanie Allen, *Introduction to Humanistic Psychology* (Monterey, Calif.: Brooks/ Cole, 1972); Irvin Child, *Humanistic Psychology and the Research Tradition: Their Several Virtues* (New York: John Wiley and Sons, 1973); Brewster Smith, "Humanism and Behaviorism in Psychology: Theory and Practice," *Journal of Humanistic Psychology* 18, no. 1 (Winter 1978): 26–36.

6. Brochure of the Association of Humanistic Psychology, as quoted in Buhler and Allen, *Introduction*, pp. 1–2.

7. William H. Whyte, *The Organization Man* (New York: Anchor, 1957).

8. Herbert Otto, "The Human Potentialities Movement: An Overview," *Journal of Creative Behavior* 8, no. 4, pp. 258–264.

9. Myron Sharaf, *Fury on Earth: A Biography of Wilhelm Reich* (New York: St. Martin's Press, 1983), p. 94.

10. Ibid., pp. 129–131.

11. Mildred Brady, "The Strange Case of Wilhelm Reich," *New Republic*, May 26, 1947.

12. For more on Wilhelm Reich, see Sharaf, *Fury*; W. Edward Mann and Edward Hoffman, *The Man Who Dreamed of Tomorrow: A Conceptual Biography of Wilhelm Reich* (Boston: Houghton Mifflin, 1980); David Boadella, *Wilhelm Reich: The Evolution of His Work* (Chicago: Henry Regnery, 1973).

13. See Walter Truett Anderson, *The Upstart Spring: Esalen and the American Awakening* (Reading, Mass.: Addison-Wesley, 1983). The following account of the human potential movement draws on Anderson's description.

14. Ibid., p. 95.

15. Ibid., p. 157.

16. Ibid., p. 185.

17. Quoted ibid.

18. Robert B. Sipe, "False Premises, False Promises: A Re-Examination of the Human Potential Movement," *Issues in Radical Therapy* 12, no. 4 (1987): 27.

19. Ellen Willis, *Beginning to See the Light: Pieces of a Decade* (New York: Alfred A. Knopf, 1981), p. xix.

20. Sipe, "False Premises," p. 28.

21. Anderson, *Upstart Spring*, p. 291.

22. Buhler and Allen, *Introduction*, p. 85.

23. Interview with Ted McIlvenna, July 21, 1987.

24. Interview with Phyllis Lyon, July 22, 1987.

25. McIlvenna interview.

26. Lyon interview, July 22, 1987; telephone interview with Gina Ogden, August 1, 1987.

27. Lyon and Ogden interviews.

28. Lyon interview.

29. McIlvenna interview.

30. See Richard Blasband, "Genitality: Myth or Reality," *Journal of Orgonomy* 21, no. 2 (November 1987): 154–158.

31. Richard Blasband, "Clinical Implications of Wilhelm Reich's Concept of Genitality," paper presented to the Society for the Scientific Study of Sex, November 11, 1988.

32. William Hartman and Marilyn Fithian, *Treatment of Sexual Dysfunction: A Bio-Psycho-Social Approach* (Long Beach, Calif.: Center for Marital and Sexual Studies, 1972), p. 205.

33. Ibid., pp. 29–65.

34. Ibid., pp. 151–154.

35. Ibid., p. 4.

36. Ibid., p. 80.

37. Interview with Marilyn Fithian, November 21, 1988.

38. William Hartman and Marilyn Fithian, "Desert Retreat," in *An Analysis of Human Sexual Inadequacy*, ed. Jhan and June Robbins (New York: Signet, 1970), pp. 154–160.

39. Hartman and Fithian, *Treatment*, p. vii.

40. Ibid., p. 208.

41. William Masters, "Phony Sex Clinics-Medicine's Newest Nightmare," *Today's Health*, November 1974, p. 24.

42. Robert J. Levin, "Most Sex Therapy Clinics Are Frauds," *Physician's World* 3, no. 1 (January 1975): 17–21.

43. Linda Wolfe, "The Question of Surrogates in Sex Therapy," in *Handbook of Sex Therapy*, ed. Joseph LoPiccolo and Leslie LoPiccolo (New York: Plenum Press, 1978), p. 496.

44. Ibid., p. 493.

45. Ibid., p. 495.

46. McIlvenna interview.

47. Personal communication, Gina Ogden, March 9, 1989.

48. *Kristan Bagley* v. *James Hoopes*, Civil Action no. 81-1126-2, United States District Court, District of Massachusetts. Settled out of court, May 1986.

49. See, for example, Billie W. Dziech, *The Lecherous Professor* (Boston: Beacon Press, 1984); Catherine MacKinnon, *Sexual Harassment of Working Women* (New Haven: Yale University Press, 1979); Lin Farley, *Sexual Shakedown: The Sexual Harassment of Women on the Job* (New York: McGraw-Hill, 1978).

50. McIlvenna interview.

51. "Beyond Masters and Johnson," paper presented to the Society for the Scientific Study of Sex, November 19–22, 1981.

52. Robert T. Francoeur, "Sex Films," *Society* 14, no. 5 (July–August, 1977): 33–37.

53. Quinn, "Sex Counselors."

54. Michael Carrera and Charon Lieberman, "Evaluating the Use of Explicit Media in a Human Sexuality Course," *SIECUS Report* 3, no. 6 (July 1975): 1.

55. Ibid.

56. Francoeur, "Sex Films," p. 33.

57. Ibid.

58. Ibid., p. 34.

59. John Money and Harvey Alexander, "Films for Sex Education," *Journal of Sex Education and Therapy* 2 (Fall–Winter 1975): 30–34.

60. Carole Vance, "Gender Systems, Ideology, and Sex Research," in *Powers of Desire: The Politics of Sexuality*, ed. Ann Snitow, Christine Stansell, and Sharon Thompson (New York: Monthly Review Press, 1983), pp. 371–384.

61. Bernie Apfelbaum, "Negative Effects of Sex Films in Sex Therapy," sixth World Congress of Sexology, May 25, 1983.

62. Joseph LoPiccolo, "Evolving Issues in Sex Therapy and Counseling," Society for the Scientific Study of Sex, November 11, 1988.

63. Telephone interview with Helen Singer Kaplan, October 20, 1983.

CHAPTER FOUR: SEXUAL SCIENCE AND SEXUAL POLITICS

1. Boston Women's Health Book Collective, *Our Bodies, Ourselves* (New York: Simon and Schuster, 1971), p. 24.

2. Barrie Thorne with Marilyn Yalom, *Rethinking the Family: Some Feminist Questions* (New York: Longman, 1982), p. 2.

3. Susan Harding, "Family Reform Movements: Recent Feminism and Its Opposition," *Feminist Studies* 7, no. 1 (Spring 1981): 67.

4. Thorne, *Rethinking*, p. 5.

5. William Leuchtenburg, "The Revolution in Morals," in *The American Sexual Dilemma*, ed. William O'Neill (New York: Holt, Rinehart and Winston, 1972).

6. John D'Emilio, *Sexual Politics, Sexual Communities: The Making of a Homosexual Minority in the United States, 1940–1970* (Chicago: University of Chicago Press, 1983).

7. Ibid.

8. See Ronald Bayer, *Homosexuality and American Psychiatry: The Politics of Diagnosis* (New York: Basic Books, 1981).

9. Nancy Wechsler, "The Lesbian and Gay Movements Today: We Must Still Fight for Liberation," *Changes: Socialist Monthly* 5, no. 3 (April 1983): 29.

10. Judith Stacey and Barrie Thorne, "The Missing Feminist Revolution in Sociology," *Social Problems* 32 (1985): 301–316.

11. Sheryl Burt Ruzek, *The Women's Health Movement* (New York: Praeger, 1979), p. 53.

12. "Repairing the Conjugal Bed," *Time*, May 25, 1970.

13. William Masters and Virginia Johnson, *Human Sexual Inadequacy* (New York: Bantam Books, 1970), p. 187.

14. "Playboy Interview: Masters and Johnson," *Playboy*, November 1979, pp. 87–121.

15. See, for example, William Masters and Virginia Johnson, *The Pleasure Bond* (New York: Bantam Books, 1975); hereafter cited as *PB*.

16. Ibid.

17. Ibid., p. 8.

18. Lonnie Barbach, *For Yourself: The Fulfillment of Female Sexuality* (New York: Doubleday, 1975).

19. Ibid., p. xv.

20. Ibid., p. xviii.

21. Jerome Wakefield, "The Negative Influence of Group Sex Therapy on Marital Relationships," paper presented at the sixth World Congress of Sexology, May 25, 1983.

22. Lonnie Barbach, *For Each Other: Sharing Sexual Intimacy* (New York: Anchor Books, 1983).

23. Carol Pollis, "Feminism, Feminist Scholarship on Sexuality, and Sexual Science: An Assessment and Agenda for Change," paper presented at the annual meeting of the Society for the Scientific Study of Sex, November 1986.

24. Interview with David McWhirter, September 21, 1987.

25. Letter, Wendy Stock of the Feminist Perspectives on Sexual Science Interest Group, to FPSS members, May 22, 1987.

26. McWhirter interview.

27. Telephone interview with Paul Abramson, December 16, 1988.

28. Stock letter.

29. Interview with Leonore Tiefer, September 17, 1987.

30. See Alice Echols, "The Taming of the Id: Feminist Sexual Politics, 1968–83," in *Pleasure and Danger: Exploring Female Sexuality*, ed. Carole S. Vance (Boston: Routledge & Kegan Paul, 1984), pp. 50–72; Ann Snitow, "Retrenchment Versus Transformation: The Politics of the Antipornography Movement," in *Women Against Censorship*, ed. Varda Burstyn (Vancouver, B.C.: Douglas & McIntyre, 1985), pp. 107–120.

31. Snitow, "Retrenchment," p. 112.

32. Echols, "Taming."

33. Sheila Jeffreys, "The Eroticization of Submission: From Havelock Ellis to Gayle Rubin," paper presented at the Five College Symposium on Feminism, Sexuality, and Power, October 30, 1986; Andrea Dworkin, *Intercourse* (New York: Free Press, 1987).

34. A Southern Women's Writing Collective, "Women Against Sex" (n.p., 1987).

35. See, for example, John Money, "Pornography in the Home: A Topic in Medical Education," in *Contemporary Sexual Behavior: Critical Issues in the 1970s*, ed. Joseph Zubin and John Money (Baltimore: Johns Hopkins University Press, 1973), pp. 409–440.

36. Richard Green, *The "Sissy Boy Syndrome" and the Development of Homosexuality* (New Haven: Yale University Press, 1987), p. ix; see also foreword by Christie Hefner (of Playboy Enterprises, Inc.) in *Sexuality and Medicine*, vol. 2, ed. Earl E. Shelp (Norwell, Mass.: Reidel, 1987), pp. ix–xi.

37. *Off Our Backs*, July 1983, p. 9.

38. Ibid.

39. John Money, "Lovemaps and Pornography," paper presented at the ninth annual meeting of the Eastern Region of the Society for the Scientific Study of

Sex, April 12, 1986; Donald Mosher, "Threat to Sexual Freedom," paper presented at the thirtieth annual meeting of the Society for the Scientific Study of Sex, November 6, 1987.

40. Letter, President Joseph LoPiccolo to the membership of the Society for the Scientific Study of Sex, undated.

41. Margaret Nichols, "Lesbian Sexuality: Issues and Developing Theory," in *Lesbian Psychologies: Explorations and Challenges*, ed. Boston Lesbian Psychologies Collective (Urbana: University of Illinois Press, 1987), p. 108.

42. There is an extensive and diverse literature on gender and science. See, for example, Ruth Bleier, *Feminist Approaches to Science* (New York: Pergamon Press, 1988); Sandra Harding, *The Science Question in Feminism* (Ithaca, N.Y.: Cornell University Press, 1986); Sandra Harding and Jean O'Barr, *Sex and Scientific Inquiry* (Chicago: University of Chicago Press, 1987); Ruth Bleier, *Science and Gender: A Critique of Biology and Its Theories on Women* (New York: Pergamon Press, 1984).

CHAPTER FIVE: CONFLICT AND ACCOMMODATION

1. Shere Hite, *The Hite Report: A Nationwide Study on Female Sexuality* (New York: Macmillan, 1976), p. xi.

2. Norma Swenson and the Judith Collective, "Toward a Feminist Sexuality," *Sister Courage*, February 1977.

3. Hite, *Hite Report*, pp. 197–198.

4. Both from Shere Hite, *The Hite Report on Male Sexuality* (New York: Alfred A. Knopf, 1981), pp. 328–329.

5. See, for an analysis of the nasty media coverage of *Women and Love*, Lisa Duggan, "Shere Hite and America's Fed-Up Women," *Ms.*, December 1987. See also Fox Butterfield, "Hite's New Book Is Under Rising Attack," *New York Times*, November 13, 1987, for allegations that Hite strangled her chauffeur and engaged in other "bizarre" behavior.

6. See "Back Off, Buddy," *Time*, October 12, 1987.

7. Ibid.

8. See, for example, Arlie Russell Hochschild, "Why Can't a Man Be More Like a Woman," *New York Times Book Review*, November 15, 1987.

9. See Pamela Reynolds, "The Hite Report Card," *Boston Globe*, October 22, 1987.

10. Hochschild, "Why Can't."

11. Linda Gordon, "The Hite Report: The Myths Keep Coming," *Seven Days*, February 14, 1977, pp. 34–35; Barbara Melosh, "The Hites of Ecstasy: The Politics of Orgasm Unveiled," *Socialist Review* 8, no. 1 (January–February 1978): 143.

12. Melosh, "Hites of Ecstasy."

13. Gordon, "Hite Report," p. 34.

14. Melosh, "Hites of Ecstasy," p. 150.

15. "The Hite Report Scrapbook," unpublished compilation of international press clippings filed in the SIECUS archives.

16. Swenson, "Feminist Sexuality."

17. Wardell Pomeroy, "The Hite Report: Two Professional Views," *SIECUS Report* 5, no. 2 (November 1976).

18. Sally Quinn, "Sex Counselors: They're No Laughing Matter," *Boston Evening Globe*, April 6, 1978.

19. Ibid.

20. Ibid.

21. Leah Schaefer, "The Hite Report: Two Professional Views," *SIECUS Report* 5, no. 2 (November 1976).

22. Pomeroy, "Hite Report," p. 1.

23. Press packet released by Hite Research, New York.

24. Jane Gallop, *Thinking Through the Body* (New York: Columbia University Press, 1988), p. 81.

25. The health activists of the Federation of Feminist Women's Health Centers simply incorporated the G-spot into their already greatly expanded definition of the clitoris. In this view, the G-spot is the urethral sponge. See *A New View of a Woman's Body* (New York: Touchstone Books, 1981).

26. See Thomas Kuhn, *The Structure of Scientific Revolutions* (Chicago: University of Chicago Press, 1962), and Michael Mahoney, *Scientist as Subject: The Psychological Imperative* (Cambridge: Ballinger, 1976), for a perspective on the development of science.

27. Alice Ladas, Beverly Whipple, and John Perry, *The G-Spot and Other Recent Discoveries About Human Sexuality* (New York: Holt, Rinehart and Winston, 1982).

28. Beverly Whipple, paper presented to the Society for the Scientific Study of Sex, November 19–22, 1981.

29. Alan Abbey, "Researchers Make Discoveries About Women and Sex," *Burlington Free Press* (Vt.), January 7, 1981.

30. William Masters, annual conference of the American Association of Sex Educators, Counselors, and Therapists, 1981.

31. Zwi Hoch, letter to the editor, "G-Spot," *Journal of Sex and Marital Therapy* 9, no. 2 (1983): 166.

32. See, for example, Zwi Hoch, "The Female Orgasmic Reflex—Its Sensory Arm," in *Proceedings of the IX World Congress of Gynecology and Obstetrics* ed. Sakamoto, Congress Series no. 512 (Amsterdam: Excerpta Medica International, 1980); G. Zwang, "La Fonction Erotique" (Paris: Laffont, 1972); S. Fisher, *Understanding the Female Orgasm* (Harmondsworth, England: Penguin Books, 1973).

33. See M. Zaviacic, Zaviacicova, et al., "Female Urethral Expulsions," *Journal of Sex Research* 24 (1988); Heli Alzate, "Vaginal Eroticism: A Replication Study," *Archives of Sexual Behavior* 14, no. 6 (1985); H. Alzate and Z. Hoch, "The 'G-Spot' and 'Female Ejaculation': A Current Appraisal," *Journal of Sex and Marital Therapy* 12, no. 3 (Fall 1986): 211–220.

34. J. Sevely and J. W. Bennett, "Concerning Female Ejaculation and the Female Prostate," *Journal of Sex Research* 14, no. 1 (February 1978): 1–20.

35. Zaviacic et al., "Female Urethral Expulsions"; F. Addiego, E. Belzer, et al., "Female Ejaculation: A Case Study," *Journal of Sex Research* 17 (1981): 13–21.

36. E. Belzer, B. Whipple, W. Moger, "On Female Ejaculation," *Journal of Sex Research* 20 (1984): 403–406.

37. Jeanne Warner, review of *The G-Spot*, *SIECUS Report*, January 1983, p. 17.

38. Bernie Zilbergeld, "Pursuit of the Grafenberg Spot," *Psychology Today*, October 1982, pp. 82–83.

39. "In Search of the Perfect G," *Time*, September 10, 1982.

40. Warner, review, p. 18.

41. Telephone interview with Helen Singer Kaplan, October 20, 1983.

42. Alzate, "Vaginal Eroticism," p. 531.

43. "In Search of the Perfect G."

44. Ladas, Whipple, and Perry, *G-Spot*, p. 151. Also "Models of Female Orgasm," American Association of Sex Educators, Counselors and Therapists, March 11–15, 1982.

45. Warner, review, p. 17.

46. Interview with Beverley Whipple, October 23, 1987.

47. Ibid.

48. Abbey, "Discoveries About Women and Sex."

49. For a discussion of mandatory testing, see Ronald Bayer, Carol Levine, and Susan Wolf, "HIV Antibody Screening: An Ethical Framework for Evaluating Proposed Programs," *New England Journal of Public Policy* (Winter/Spring 1988): 173–187. For a report on the Centers for Disease Control conference that opposed mandatory testing, see the CDC document, "Recommended Additional Guidelines for HIV Antibody Counseling and Testing in the Prevention of HIV Infection and AIDS," April 30, 1987, Atlanta, Ga. For a critique of quarantine, see David Musto, "Quarantine and the Problems of AIDS," *Milbank Quarterly* 64, suppl. 1 (1986): 97–117.

50. See, for example, Chris Bull, "Congress Guts AIDS Education," *Gay Community News*, October 25–31, 1987; Jill Lawrence, "Helms Wins Bid to Limit Material in AIDS Teaching," *Boston Globe*, October 15, 1987; Bruce Mohl, "Furor Builds on Hill over Safe-Sex Brochure," *Boston Globe*, November 18, 1987. See also the lawsuit challenging the Helms Amendment: *Gay Men's Health Crisis, Hetrick Martin Institute, Horizons Community Services, San Antonio Tavern Guild AIDS Foundation, and the Fund for Human Dignity v. Otis R. Bowen or his successor, Secretary of Health and Human Services; and James O. Mason or his successor, Director of the U.S. Centers for Disease Control,* filed in the U.S. District Court for the Southern District of New York.

51. Cindy Patton, "Resistance and the Erotic: Reclaiming History, Setting Strategy as We Face AIDS," *Radical America*, 20, no. 6 (November–December 1987): 68–74.

52. See, for example, Warren Winkelstein, Jr., James Wiley, Nancy Padian, Michael Samuel, Stephen Shiboski, Michael Ascher, and Jay Levy, "The San Francisco Men's Health Study: Continued Decline in HIV Seroconversion Rates Among Homosexual/Bisexual Men," *American Journal of Public Health* 78 (1988): 1472–1474; Warren Winkelstein, Michael Samuel, Nancy Padian, James Wiley, William Lang, Robert Anderson, and Jay Levy, "The San Francisco Men's Health Study: III—Reduction in Human Immunodeficiency Virus Transmission Among Homosexual/Bisexual Men, 1982–86," ibid., 76 (1987): 685–689; Ronald Valdiserri, David Lyter, Laura Leviton, Catherine Callahan, Lawrence Kingsley, and Charles Rinaldo, "AIDS Prevention in Homosexual

and Bisexual Men: Results of a Randomized Trial Evaluating Two Risk Reduction Interventions," *AIDS* 3, no. 1 (1989): 21–26.

53. Patton, "Resistance," p. 69.

54. Theresa Crenshaw, AIDS plenary, American Association of Sex Educators, Counselors and Therapists, May 2, 1987.

55. Telephone interview with Michael Shernoff, September 23, 1987.

56. Helen Singer Kaplan, editorial, *Journal of Sex and Marital Therapy* 2, no. 4 (Winter 1985): 211–212.

57. Letters, James Harrison to Helen Singer Kaplan, November 14, 1985, and December 4, 1985.

58. The existing test is performed to detect the presence of HIV antibody, which indicates infection by the human immunodeficiency virus. There is no test for AIDS, which is a syndrome, not a specific disease.

59. Edwin Haeberle, "AIDS and the Sex Therapist: A Rebuttal," *Sexuality Today* 9, no. 18 (February 17, 1986).

60. James Harrison, "On the Scope and Method of 'AIDS and the Sex Therapist,'" manuscript, December 1985.

61. Crenshaw, AIDS plenary.

62. Michael Shernoff, AIDS plenary, American Association of Sex Educators, Counselors, and Therapists, May 2, 1987.

63. Margaret Nichols, AIDS plenary, ibid.

64. William Masters, Virginia Johnson, and Robert Kolodny, *Crisis: Heterosexual Behavior in the Age of AIDS* (New York: Grove Press, 1988), p. 7, hereafter cited as *Crisis*.

65. Ibid., p. 1.

66. See Paul Cleary, Michael Barry, Kenneth Mayer, Allan Brandt, Larry Gostin, and Harvey Fineberg, "Compulsory Premarital Screening for the Human Immunodeficiency Virus," *Journal of the American Medical Association* 258 (1987), for a critique of this practice.

67. *Crisis*, p. 94.

68. Ibid., p. 154. Priscilla Alexander, "Prostitutes Are Being Scapegoated for Heterosexual AIDS," in *Sex Work: Writings by Women in the Sex Industry*, ed. Frederique Delacoste and Priscilla Alexander (Pittsburgh: Cleis Press, 1987), questions the evidence that prostitutes are transmitting HIV infection to heterosexual men. Alexander extrapolates, for example, that if perhaps 5 percent of the 20,000 prostitutes in New York City were infected in 1978, then:

4,000 prostitutes times 1,500 customers times 3 years (incubation period) times 20 percent (one estimate of the female-to-male transmission rate) = 360,000 diagnosed cases of AIDS. By contrast, only 70 men diagnosed with AIDS as of 1987 claimed contact with a prostitute as their sole risk factor. See also Allan Brandt, *No Magic Bullet: A Social History of Venereal Disease in the United States Since 1800* (New York: Oxford University Press, 1987) for historical documentation of the scapegoating of prostitutes for the spread of venereal disease.

69. B. D. Colen, "Masters and Johnson in the AIDS Age," *Newsday*, March 8, 1988.

70. "Koop Blasts AIDS Book's 'Scare Tactics,'" *Boston Globe*, March 10, 1988.

71. Constance Wofsy, keynote speech, Women and AIDS Conference, Boston, April 9, 1988.

72. Ellen Bartlett, "Scientists Condemn Findings in AIDS Book," *Boston Globe*, March 8, 1988.

73. Edward Kaplan, "Crisis? A Brief Critique of Masters, Johnson and Kolodny," *Journal of Sex Research* 25 (1988): 317–322.

74. *Crisis*, p. 169.

75. See Jan Zita Grover, "A Matter of Life and Death," *Women's Review of Books*, March 1988; Janet Saevita, "Safety First," *The Sentinel*, June 10, 1988. For an example of pop culture dissemination, see Helen Singer Kaplan, "No Sex This Year," *New Woman*, January 1988, p. 81.

76. Helen Singer Kaplan, *The Real Truth About Women and AIDS: How to Eliminate the Risks Without Giving Up Love and Sex* (New York: Fireside Book, 1988), p. 15.

77. Ibid., p. 19.

78. Ibid., especially pp. 110–113.

79. Crenshaw, AIDS plenary.

80. "Safe Love International," brochure, West Bethesda, Md., n.d.

81. Edwin Haeberle, quoted in "AIDS and the Sex Therapist: A Rebuttal."

82. Helen Singer Kaplan, AIDS plenary, American Association of Sex Educators, Counselors and Therapists, May 2, 1987.

83. Interview with David McWhirter, September 21, 1987.

84. Shernoff interview.

85. Telephone interview with Ted McIlvenna, October 30, 1987.

86. Josh Getlin, "Reagan's AIDS Panel Takes Heat at Meeting," *Boston Globe*, September 10, 1987.

87. Sandra Boodman, "AIDS Panel Recommends Law Banning Discrimination," *Washington Post*, June 18, 1989.

88. This accusation was made by Crenshaw in the AASECT AIDS plenary. As the epidemic progresses, more sexologists are beginning to address AIDS issues within the context of their education and research. Some are careful to insist that strategies for the prevention of HIV infection need not spell the demise of an active sex life: see, for example, the book for women that G-spot researcher Beverly Whipple co-authored: Beverly Whipple and Gina Ogden, *Safe Encounters* (New York: McGraw-Hill, 1988).

89. Theresa Crenshaw, press conference, annual AASECT Conference, May 2, 1987.

PART THREE: THE PRACTICE OF SCIENTIFIC SEXOLOGY

1. John Gagnon and William Simon, *Sexual Conduct* (Chicago: Aldine, 1973), p. 5.

2. Michel Foucault, *The History of Sexuality*, vol. 1: *An Introduction* (New York: Pantheon, 1978).

CHAPTER SIX: REPAIRING THE CONJUGAL BED: THE CLINICAL PRACTICE OF MODERN SEX THERAPY

1. Edwin Haeberle, "Sexology: Conception, Birth and Growth of a Science," sixth World Congress of Sexology, May 23, 1983.

2. Vern Bullough, "Sex Research and Therapy," in *Sexuality and Medicine*, vol. 1, ed. Earl E. Shelp (Norwell, Mass.: Reidel, 1987), pp. 73–85.

3. See, for example, Marie Stopes, *Married Love* (London: G. P. Putnam's Sons, 1918).

4. Helen Singer Kaplan, *The New Sex Therapy* (New York: Brunner/Mazel, 1974), p. 388. The use of the vibrator was introduced into American gynecological practice by Robert Latou Dickinson early in the twentieth century.

5. Susan D. Toliver, "20/20 Vision: A Perspective on Women's Changing

Roles and the Structure of American Families, Past and Future," *Frontiers: A Journal of Women Studies* 9, no. 1 (1986): 27–31.

6. Lillian Rubin, *Intimate Strangers: Men and Women Together* (New York: Harper & Row, 1983), p. 2.

7. Nancy Chodorow, *The Reproduction of Mothering: Psychoanalysis and the Sociology of Gender* (Berkeley: University of California Press, 1978).

8. Morton Hunt, *Sexual Behavior in the 1970s* (New York: Dell, 1974).

9. Patrick McGrady, *The Love Doctors* (New York: Macmillan, 1972), p. 310.

10. Irving K. Zola, "In the Name of Health and Illness: On Some Socio-Political Consequences of Medical Influence," *Social Science and Medicine* 9 (February 1975): 83–87.

11. See Paul Starr, "The Politics of Therapeutic Nihilism," in *The Sociology of Health and Illness*, ed. Peter Conrad and Rochelle Kern (New York: St. Martin's Press, 1981), pp. 434–448.

12. Sheryl Ruzek, "The Women's Self-Help Movement," ibid., pp. 563–569.

13. Ivan Illich, "Medical Nemesis," ibid., pp. 426–433. See also Irving Zola, "Medicine as an Institution of Social Control," ibid., pp. 511–526.

14. "Sexology on the Defensive," *Time*, June 13, 1983.

15. J. Wolpe, "Reciprocal Inhibition as the Main Basis of Psychotherapeutic Effects," in *Behavior Therapy and the Neuroses: Readings in Modern Methods of Treatment Derived from Learning Theory*, ed. H. J. Eysenck (New York: Pergamon Press, 1960), pp. 88–113.

16. William Masters and Virginia Johnson, *Human Sexual Inadequacy* (New York: Bantam Books, 1970), p. 1; hereafter cited as *HSI*.

17. Lenore Tiefer, "In Pursuit of the Perfect Penis: The Medicalization of Male Sexuality," *American Behavioral Scientist* 29 (1986): 579–599.

18. In 1989, the average fee was $6,000 plus the costs of laboratory tests and the living expenses incurred over the two weeks. The Institute's sliding-fee scale ranges from $0 to $10,000, depending on the problem.

19. *HSI*, pp. 10, 15.

20. See, for example, ibid., p. 130.

21. Ibid., p. 349.

22. See Nat Lehrman, *Masters and Johnson Explained* (Chicago: Playboy Press, 1970), p. 222; Alvin Cooper, "Sexual Enhancement Programs: An Examination of Their Current Status and Directions for Future Research," *Journal of Sex Research* 21 (1985): 387–404.

23. See, for example, Leslie Farber, "I'm Sorry, Dear," in *An Analysis of Human Sexual Response*, ed. Ruth Brecher and Edward Brecher (New York: Signet, 1966), pp. 291–311. Also see Natalie Shainess, "How Sex Experts Debase Sex," *World of Research*, January 2, 1973, pp. 21–25.

24. Vivian Cadden, "The Psychiatrists versus Masters and Johnson," in *Handbook of Sex Therapy*, ed. Joseph LoPiccolo and Leslie LoPiccolo (New York: Plenum Press, 1978), pp. 485–490.

25. *HSI*, p. 9.

26. Ibid., p. 197.

27. Ibid., pp. 63, 210.

28. Ibid., p. 210.

29. Ibid., p. 211.

30. Ibid., p. 211.

31. Ibid., p. 81.

32. Fred Belliveau and Lin Richter, *Understanding Human Sexual Inadequacy* (New York: Bantam Books, 1970), pp. 237–238.

33. Baley, "Massage Parlors or Psychotherapy," quoted in Robert Meyners, "Sex Research and Therapy: On the Morality of the Methods, Practices and Procedures," in *Sexuality and Medicine*, vol. 2, ed. Earl E. Shelp (Norwell, Mass.: Reidel, 1987), pp. 171–195.

34. *HSI*, p. 14.

35. As noted earlier, research indicates no correlation between sexual satisfaction and marital satisfaction.

36. *HSI*, p. 14.

37. Bernie Zilbergeld and Michael Evans, "The Inadequacy of Masters and Johnson," *Psychology Today*, August 1980, pp. 29–43.

38. Peter Wyden and Barbara Wyden, *Inside the Sex Clinic* (New York: World Publishing Co., 1971), p. 101.

39. See Wendy Stock, "Sex Roles and Sexual Dysfunction," in *Sex Roles and Psychopathology*, ed. Cathy S. Widom (New York: Plenum Press, 1984), pp. 249–275.

40. See Douglas Hogan, "The Effectiveness of Sex Therapy: A Review of the Literature," in LoPiccolo and LoPiccolo, *Handbook of Sex Therapy*.

41. Ibid.; see also William Hartman and Marilyn Fithian, *Treatment of Sexual Dysfunction: A Bio-Psycho-Social Approach* (Long Beach, Calif.: Center for Marital and Sexual Studies, 1972).

42. Zilbergeld and Evans, "Inadequacy."

43. *Sexuality Today*, June 20, 1983.

44. Zilbergeld and Evans, "Inadequacy," p. 29.

45. Quoted in "Sexology on the Defensive."

46. "The *Forum* Interview: Dr. Bernie Zilbergeld," *Forum*, June 1983.

47. "Sexology on the Defensive."

48. Ibid.

49. See Kaplan, *New Sex Therapy*, p. 197; Joseph LoPiccolo, "The Professionalization of Sex Therapy: Issues and Problems," in LoPiccolo and LoPiccolo, *Handbook of Sex Therapy*, pp. 511–526; Linda Wolfe, "The Question of Surrogates in Sex Therapy," ibid.; William Masters, "Phony Sex Clinics—Medicine's Newest Nightmare," *Today's Health*, November 1974, pp. 22–26.

50. Telephone interview with Helen Singer Kaplan, October 20, 1983.

51. Kaplan, *New Sex Therapy*, p. 136.

52. Helen Singer Kaplan, *The Evaluation of Sexual Disorders* (New York: Brunner/Mazel, 1983).

53. Kaplan interview.

54. Kaplan, *New Sex Therapy*, p. 5.

55. Diane Klein, "Interview: Helen Singer Kaplan," *Omni*, August 1981, p. 74.

56. Ibid.

57. Ibid., p. 77.

58. Ibid., p. 92.

59. Kaplan, *New Sex Therapy*, p. 45.

60. Ibid., p. 137.

61. Ibid., p. 131.

62. Ibid., p. 359.

63. Ibid., pp. 191–192.

64. See, for example, George Herbert Mead, *Mind, Self, and Society: From the Standpoint of a Social Behaviorist*, ed. Charles Morris (Chicago: University of Chicago Press, 1964); Eric Berne, *Games People Play* (New York: Grove Press, 1964).

65. William Simon and John Gagnon, "Sexual Scripts: Permanence and Change," *Archives of Sexual Behavior* 15, no. 2 (1986): 97.

66. Leonore Tiefer, "A Feminist Critique of the Sexual Dysfunction Nomenclature," paper presented to the Society for the Scientific Study of Sex, November 14, 1986.

67. Stock, "Sex Roles and Sexual Dysfunction."

68. Ibid., p. 270.

69. Helen Singer Kaplan, *Disorders of Sexual Desire, and Other New Concepts and Techniques in Sex Therapy* (New York: Brunner/Mazel, 1979).

70. Harold Lief, "Disorders of Sexual Desire," paper presented to the American Association of Sex Educators, Counselors and Therapists, March 13, 1982.

71. Carl Degler, "What Ought to Be and What Was: Women's Sexuality in the Nineteenth Century," in *Women and Health in America*, ed. Judith Walzer Leavitt (Madison: University of Wisconsin Press, 1984), pp. 40–56.

72. Nancy Cott, "Passionlessness: An Interpretation of Victorian Sexual Ideology, 1790–1850," ibid., pp. 57–69.

73. Kaplan, *Disorders*, p. 141.

74. Klein, "Interview with Kaplan," p. 92.

75. Kaplan, *Disorders*, p. 9.

76. John Gagnon and William Simon, quoted in Raymond Rosen and Sandra Leiblum, "Current Approaches to the Evaluation of Sexual Desire Disorders," *Journal of Sex Research* 23, no. 2, p. 143.

77. Barry Bass, "The Myth of Low Sexual Desire: A Cognitive Behavioral Approach to Treatment," *Journal of Sex Education and Therapy* 2, no. 2 (Fall/Winter 1985).

78. Ibid., p. 62.

79. Bernard Apfelbaum, "An Ego-Analytic Perspective on Desire Disorders," in *Sexual Desire Disorders*, ed. Sandra Leiblum and Raymond Rosen (New York: Guilford Press, 1988), p. 78.

80. Sandra Leiblum and Raymond Rosen, "Conclusion: Conceptual and Clinical Overview," in Leiblum and Rosen, *Sexual Desire Disorders*, p. 457.

81. AASECT news release on Wellbrutin, undated, Washington, D.C.

82. Harold Lief, quoted ibid.

83. Leiblum and Rosen, "Conclusion," p. 457.

84. Sandra Leiblum, "Evolving Issues in Sex Therapy and Counseling," paper presented to the Society for the Scientific Study of Sex, November 11, 1988.

85. Donahue transcript no. 04297.

86. Perhaps the most famous Dora in psychoanalysis was the infamous patient who terminated treatment with Sigmund Freud. Her complex case has been the subject of much speculation and discussion and raises issues of sexual desire, exploitation, and patriarchal assumptions about female sexuality. The

feminist Helene Cixous has noted that Dora "is the core example of the protesting force of women"; see Catherine Clement and Helene Cixous, *La Jeune nee* (Paris: 10/18, 1975), p. 283.

87. Kaplan, *Disorders*, p. 92.

88. Ibid., p. xvi.

89. John D'Emilio and Estelle Freedman, *Intimate Matters: A History of Sexuality in America* (New York: Harper & Row, 1988).

90. The historical, economic, and ideological rootedness of ISD is even more striking when one considers the relative lack of success of the obverse diagnosis—sexual addiction. Like ISD, sexual addiction appeared as a diagnosis in the early 1980s. After a brief flurry of attention, it faded through lack of interest. Critiques dubbed it "conceptually flawed . . . , subjective and value laden." See Martin Levine and Richard Troiden, "The Myth of Sexual Compulsivity," *Journal of Sex Research* 25 (1988): 347–363.

91. Kaplan, *Disorders*, p. 90.

92. Freida Stuart, D. Corydon Hammond, and Marjorie Pett, "Inhibited Sexual Desire in Women," *Archives of Sexual Behavior* 16, no. 2 (1987): 91–106. See also Stock, "Sex Roles and Sexual Dysfunction," and Tiefer, "Feminist Critique."

93. William Masters, "Three Decade Retrospective of the Masters and Johnson Institute," paper presented to the Society for the Scientific Study of Sex, November 18, 1983.

94. Jessica Benjamin, *The Bonds of Love: Psychoanalysis, Feminism, and the Problem of Domination* (New York: Pantheon Books, 1988); see also Jade McGleughlin, "The Freedom to Want Passionately: A Theoretical Exploration of Women's Desire," MSW thesis, Smith School of Social Work, 1987. I am grateful to Jade McGleughlin and Carolyn Stack for our discussions about feminism, psychoanalysis, and desire.

95. McGleughlin, "Freedom."

96. Kaplan, *New Sex Therapy*, p. 410.

97. Ibid., p. 373.

98. See, for example, Jessie Bernard, *The Future of Marriage* (New York: World Publishing, 1972), pp. 16–17; Leo Srole et al., *Mental Health in the Metropolis* (New York: McGraw-Hill, 1962), pp. 177–178.

99. Stock, "Sex Roles and Sexual Dysfunction," p. 265.

100. See LoPiccolo, "Professionalization"; Wolfe, "Question of Surrogates"; Tiefer, "Feminist Critique."

101. Joseph LoPiccolo and Julia Heiman, "Cultural Values and the Therapeutic Definition of Sexual Function and Dysfunction," *Journal of Social Issues*, 33, no. 2 (1977): 181.

102. Catherine Kohler Riessman, "Women and Medicalization: A New Perspective," *Social Policy*, Summer 1983, pp. 3–18; and Zola, "Medicine as an Institution of Social Control."

103. Peter Conrad and Joseph Schneider, *Deviance and Medicalization* (St. Louis, Mo.: C. V. Mosby, 1980), p. 35.

104. American Psychiatric Association Task Force on Nomenclature and Statistics, *Diagnostic and Statistical Manual on Mental Disorders*, 3d ed. (Washington, D.C.: APA, 1980).

105. Kaplan, *Evaluation*, p. 25.

106. Joseph Gusfield, *The Culture of Public Problems: Drinking-Driving and the Symbolic Order* (Chicago: University of Chicago Press, 1981).

107. Betsy Hermance, "The Satisfied Customer," *Boston Magazine*, November 1982.

108. Tiefer, "In Pursuit."

109. Interview with Leonore Tiefer, November 25, 1988.

110. Kaplan, *Evaluation*, p. 48.

111. Raymond Rosen and J. Gayle Beck, *Patterns of Sexual Arousal: Psychophysiological Processes and Clinical Applications* (New York: Guilford Press, 1988).

112. Edward Brecher, *The Sex Researchers* (New York: Signet, 1969).

113. Albert Ellis, "An Informal History of Sex Therapy," *Counseling Psychologist* 5, no. 1 (1975): 9–13.

114. Shirley Zussman, "Emerging Dimensions of Sexology," sixth World Congress of Sexology, May 23, 1983.

CHAPTER SEVEN: BOYS WILL BE GIRLS

1. John Money, *Love and Love Sickness: The Science of Sex, Gender Difference, and Pair-Bonding* (Baltimore: Johns Hopkins University Press, 1980), pp. xi, xii.

2. See Suzanne J. Kessler and Wendy McKenna, *Gender: An Ethnomethodological Approach* (New York: John Wiley & Sons, 1978); Deborah Feinbloom, *Transvestites and Transsexuals: Mixed Views* (New York: Delacorte Press, 1976).

3. John Money and Patricia Tucker, *Sexual Signatures: On Being a Man or a Woman* (Boston: Little, Brown, 1975), p. 8.

4. My experience, in teaching many semesters of college-level courses on sexuality, has been that despite protestations that times have changed and people "don't really behave that way anymore," students can readily recite gender stereotypes.

5. See Money and Tucker, *Sexual Signatures*; John Money and Anke Ehrhardt, *Man and Woman: Boy and Girl* (Baltimore: Johns Hopkins University Press, 1972).

6. Joseph Pleck, "The Theory of Male Sex-Role Identity: Its Rise and Fall, 1936 to the Present," in *The Making of Masculinities: The New Men's Studies*, ed. Harry Brod (Boston: Allen and Unwin, 1987), p. 27.

7. Rosalind Rosenberg, *Beyond Separate Spheres: Intellectual Roots of Modern Feminism* (New Haven: Yale University Press, 1982).

8. Lewis Terman and Catherine Miles, *Sex and Personality* (New York: McGraw-Hill, 1936).

9. Ibid., p. v.

10. Ibid., p. 451.

11. Ibid., pp. 1–2.

12. Ibid., p. 8.

13. Pleck, "Theory of Male Sex-Role Identity," p. 24.

14. Talcott Parsons and R. F. Bales, *Family Socialization and Interaction Process* (Glencoe, Ill.: Free Press, 1955).

15. Tim Carrigan, Bob Connell, and John Lee, "Toward a New Sociology of Masculinity," in Brod, *Making of Masculinities*, p. 68.

16. See, for example, Ann Snitow, Christine Stansell, and Sharon Thompson, *Powers of Desire: The Politics of Sexuality* (New York: Monthly Review Press, 1983); Carole S. Vance, *Pleasure and Danger: Exploring Female Sexuality* (Boston: Routledge & Kegan Paul, 1984); Jane Flax, "Postmodernism and Gender Relations in Feminist Theory," *Signs* 12 (1987): 621–643.

17. Barbara Ponse, *Identities in the Lesbian World: The Social Construction of Self* (Westport, Conn.: Greenwood Press, 1978).

18. Gayle Rubin, "Thinking Sex: Notes for a Radical Theory of the Politics of Sexuality," in Vance, *Pleasure and Danger*, pp. 267–319.

19. See, for example, ibid.; Carole Vance, "Introduction," in Vance, *Pleasure and Danger*, pp. 1–28; Ann Snitow, Christine Stansell, and Sharon Thompson, "Introduction," in Snitow et al., *Powers of Desire*, pp. 9–47.

20. Rubin, "Thinking Sex," p. 287.

21. Ibid., p. 287.

22. Esther Newton and Shirley Walton, "The Misunderstanding: Toward a More Precise Sexual Vocabulary," in Vance, *Pleasure and Danger*, pp. 242–250.

23. Joan Nestle, "Butch-Fem Relationships," *Heresies: Sex Issue*, issue 12 (1981): 21–24.

24. George Gilder, *Sexual Suicide* (New York: Quadrangle/New York Times, 1973).

25. Sarah Snyder, "Gender Selection Kit Selling Despite Criticism from FDA," *Boston Globe*, May 19, 1987.

26. John Money, "Propaedeutics of Diecious G-I/R: Theoretical Foundations for Understanding Dimorphic Gender-Identity/Role," in *Masculinity/Femininity: Basic Perspectives*, ed. June M. Reinisch, Leonard A. Rosenblum, and Stephanie A. Sanders (New York: Oxford University Press, 1987), pp. 13–28.

27. John Money, *Gay, Straight, and In-Between: The Sexology of Erotic Orientation* (New York: Oxford University Press, 1988), pp. 59–63.

28. John Money, "Gender-Transposition Theory and Homosexual Genesis," *Journal of Sex and Marital Therapy* 10, no. 2 (1984): 81.

29. Money and Tucker, *Sexual Signatures*, p. 231.

30. Frank Beach, "Alternative Interpretations of the Development of G-I/R," in Reinisch, Rosenblum, and Sanders, *Masculinity/Femininity*, p. 31.

31. Richard Green, *The "Sissy Boy Syndrome" and the Development of Homosexuality* (New Haven: Yale University Press, 1987), pp. 80–81.

32. See, for example, Lynda Birke, *Women, Feminism and Biology* (Brighton, Sussex: Harvester Press, 1986).

33. Lesley Rogers and Joan Walsh, "Shortcomings of the Psychomedical Research of John Money and Co-Workers into Sex Differences in Behavior: Social and Political Implications," *Sex Roles* 8 (1982): 270.

34. Money, *Gay, Straight*, p. 50.

35. Quoted in Elizabeth Hall, "New Directions for the Kinsey Institute," *Psychology Today*, June 1986, p. 34.

36. Green, *"Sissy Boy,"* p. 12.

37. Jeffrey Weeks, *Sex, Politics and Society: The Regulation of Sexuality Since 1800* (New York: Longman, 1981).

38. Eve Kosofsky Sedgwick, *Between Men: English Literature and Male Homosocial Desire* (New York: Columbia University Press, 1985).

39. Alan Bell, Martin Weinberg, and Sue Hammersmith, *Sexual Preference: Its Development in Men and Women* (Bloomington: Indiana University Press, 1981), see "Introduction."

40. Dwight Billings and Thomas Urban, "The Socio-Medical Construction of Transsexualism: An Interpretation and Critique," *Social Problems* 29 (1982): 266–282.

41. See Michel Foucault, *The History of Sexuality*, vol. 1: *An Introduction* (New York: Pantheon, 1978); Weeks, *Sex, Politics, and Society*; Diane Richardson, "The Dilemma of Essentiality in Homosexual Theory," *Journal of Homosexuality* 9, no. 2–3 (Winter 1983/Spring 1984): 79–90.

42. See, for example, Esther Newton, "The Mythic Mannish Lesbian: Radclyffe Hall and the New Woman," *Signs* 9 (1984): 557–575; George Chauncey, Jr., "From Sexual Inversion to Homosexuality: Medicine and the Changing Conceptualization of Female Deviance," *Salmagundi* 58–59 (Fall 1982–Winter 1983): 114–146; John D'Emilio and Estelle Freedman, *Intimate Matters: A History of Sexuality in America* (New York: Harper & Row, 1988); Lillian Faderman, *Surpassing the Love of Men* (New York: William Morrow, 1981); Carroll Smith-Rosenberg, *Disorderly Conduct: Visions of Gender in Victorian America* (New York: Alfred Knopf, 1985).

43. Phyllis Grosskurth, *John Addington Symonds* (London: Longman, 1964), p. 273.

44. For a more detailed exegesis of early sex research on homosexuality, see Jeffrey Weeks, *Coming Out: Homosexual Politics in Britain, from the Nineteenth Century to the Present* (London: Quartet Books, 1977); Carroll Smith-Rosenberg, "The New Woman as Androgyne: Social Disorder and Gender Crisis, 1870–1936," in *Disorderly Conduct*, pp. 245–296.

45. Smith-Rosenberg, "The New Woman."

46. Esther Newton argues convincingly that "mannish lesbians" or "butches" were not simply victims of sexological medical discourse; in fact, the identity was useful to them as a signifier of explicit sexuality. See Newton, "The Mythic Mannish Lesbian."

47. Quoted in Smith-Rosenberg, "The New Woman," p. 271.

48. Ibid., p. 272.

49. Richard von Krafft-Ebing, *Psychopathia Sexualis*, 12th (revised and enlarged) ed. (1902), trans. Franklin Klaf (New York, 1965), pp. 222–368.

50. Havelock Ellis, "Sexual Inversion with an Analysis of Thirty-three New Cases," *Medico-Legal Journal* 13 (1895–96).

51. See, for example, Richard Green, "Navigating the Straits of Oedipus," *New York Times*, December 11, 1988.

52. See Jeffrey Weeks, *Sexuality and Its Discontents: Meanings, Myths and Modern Sexualities* (London: Routledge & Kegan Paul, 1985); Weeks, *Sex, Politics and Society*; and Linda Murray, "Sexual Destinies," *Omni*, April 1987.

53. Notions of acquired etiology, because they introduce the role of culture, are sometimes confused with social construction theory. Yet there are important differences. Although social factors are stressed in theories of acquired etiology, these influences are seen as molding a stable sexual drive or energy that, under developmentally "normal" circumstances, is heterosexual. There is, therefore, a tendency within such theories to pathologize homosexuality, although some social learning theorists espouse a liberal tolerance for diversity. Unlike social learning theories, social construction theory avoids the medicalized nomenclature of disease and cure. Constructionism does not see gay people as hapless members of a fixed and deviant sexual category, but examines how the meaning of same-gender sexual behavior has emerged and changed in different eras and cultures. It acknowledges social, political, historical, and economic factors as essential to the development of homosexual identity and community. The gay individual is positioned as an empowered social actor. Because of this, social construction theory is sometimes misconstrued as implying that sexuality is flexible and easily changed. This implication may be upsetting to a gay person who does not experience sexuality as a "choice" or mere "preference." But the critique of stable categories of meaning that social constructionism offers does not suggest that sexuality is quixotic or that different configurations of desire and expression can be easily interchanged. Rather, by refusing to accept traditional ideas of sexuality as a transcendent force, the theory allows for imaginative questions that probe for more sophisticated analyses of the development of sexual desire and behavior.

I am grateful to Lisa Duggan and Carole Vance for discussions on this topic.

54. Alan Bell and Martin Weinberg, *Homosexualities: A Study of Diversity Among Men and Women* (New York: Simon and Schuster, 1978), p. 14.

55. See, for example, John Kitsuse, "Societal Reaction to Deviant Behavior," in *Deviance: The Interactionist Perspective*, ed. Earl Rubington and Martin Weinberg (New York: Macmillan, 1968), pp. 19–29.

56. Telephone interview with Martin Weinberg, October 7, 1988.

57. Martin Weinberg and Colin Williams, *Male Homosexuals: Their Problems and Adaptations* (New York: Oxford University Press, 1974), p. 8.

58. Bell, Weinberg, and Hammersmith, *Sexual Preference*, p. xii.

59. Ibid.; Weinberg and Williams, *Male Homosexuals.*

60. Alfred C. Kinsey, Wardell B. Pomeroy, Clyde E. Martin, and Paul H. Gebhard, *Sexual Behavior in the Human Male* (Philadelphia: W. B. Saunders, 1948), p. 639.

61. Bell, Weinberg, and Hammersmith, *Sexual Preference*, p. 189.

62. Bell and Weinberg, *Homosexualities*, p. 230.

63. Weinberg interview.

64. See, for example, Robert Etherington, "A Monumental Study: Less Than Monumental Results," *Gay Community News*, September 30, 1978, pp. 10–11; Nancy Walker, "Nothing New About Lesbians," *Gay Community News*, September 30, 1978, p. 13.

65. Larry Goldsmith, "Science vs. Real Life," *Gay Community News*, February 6, 1982, p. 6.

66. Bell, Weinberg, and Hammersmith, *Sexual Preference*, p. 216.

67. Hall, "New Directions for the Kinsey Institute."

68. Bell, Weinberg, and Hammersmith, *Sexual Preference*, p. 218.

69. "Playboy Interview: Masters and Johnson," *Playboy*, November 1979, pp. 87–121.

70. Ibid., p. 104; William Masters and Virginia Johnson, *Homosexuality in Perspective* (New York: Bantam, 1979); hereafter cited as *HIP*.

71. Quoted in "Sex and the Homosexual," *Newsweek*, April 30, 1979.

72. *HIP*, p. 411.

73. Ibid., p. 227.

74. Ibid., pp. ix, 403.

75. Ibid.

76. Noted in "Playboy Interview," p. 87.

77. Richard Bayer, *Homosexuality and American Psychiatry: The Politics of Diagnosis* (New York: Basic Books, 1981).

78. Ibid., p. 37.

79. *HIP*, p. 357.

80. Ibid., p. 377.

81. Diane Klein, "Interview with Helen Singer Kaplan," *Omni*, August 1981, p. 92.

82. Helen Singer Kaplan, *Disorders of Sexual Desire, and Other New Concepts and Techniques in Sex Therapy* (New York: Brunner/Mazel, 1979), p. 64.

83. Ibid.

84. Quoted in Lawrence Mass, "Shrinking Homophobia: AMA Report Echoes the Same Old Prejudices," *New York Native*, April 12–25, 1982.

85. *Sexuality Today*, March 8, 1982.

86. David P. McWhirter and Andrew Mattison, *The Male Couple: How Relationships Develop* (Englewood Cliffs, N.J.: Prentice Hall, 1984), p. 292.

87. Edwin Haeberle, "Swastika, Pink Triangle and Yellow Star—The Destruction of Sexology and the Persecution of Homosexuals in Nazi Germany," *Journal of Sex Research* 17 (1981): 270–287.

88. McWhirter and Mattison, *Male Couple*, p. xii.

89. Quoted in Thomas Szasz, *Sex by Prescription* (New York: Anchor Press/Doubleday, 1980), p. 44.

90. Bell, Weinberg, and Hammersmith, *Sexual Preference*, p. 219.

91. Ibid., p. 221.

92. Billings and Urban, "Construction of Transsexualism," p. 266.

93. Ibid., p. 267.

94. For further information on Benjamin, see "Memorial for Harry Benjamin," *Archives of Sexual Behavior* 17, no. 1 (February 1988): 3–31.

95. Jon Meyer and Donna Reter, "Sex Reassignment: Follow-Up," *Archives of General Psychiatry*, 36 (1979): 1010–1015.

96. Billings and Urban, "Construction of Transsexualism," p. 269.

97. See Rene Dubos, *Mirage of Health: Utopias, Progress, and Biological Change* (New York: Harper & Row, 1959).

98. Alonzo L. Plough, *Borrowed Time* (Philadelphia: Temple University Press, 1986), p. 4.

99. "Memorial for Harry Benjamin," p. 6.

100. See Eliot Friedson, *Profession of Medicine: A Study of the Sociology of Applied Knowledge* (New York: Harper & Row, 1970).

101. Quoted in David Leff, "Genes, Gender and Genital Reversal," *Medical World News*, April 18, 1977, p. 46.

102. Anne Bolin, *In Search of Eve: Transsexual Rites of Passage* (South Hadley, Mass.: Bergin & Garvey, 1988), p. 3.

103. Leff, "Genes," p. 51.

104. Katherine Ellison, "Transsexual Surgery, Counseling Results Said Equal," *Washington Post*, August 11, 1979.

105. Fifth International Gender Dysphoria Symposium, February 10–13, 1977.

106. Quoted in Billings and Urban, "Construction of Transsexualism," p. 275.

107. Personal conversation, Deborah Feinbloom, January 1977.

108. Quoted in Bolin, *In Search of Eve*, p. 54.

109. Dianne Dumanoski, "Gender Identity Service Services the Transsexual," *Boston Phoenix*, November 25, 1975, p. 27.

110. David Barlow, Joyce Mills, N. Stewart Agras, and Debra Steinman, "Comparison of Sex-Typed Motor Behavior in Male-to-Female Transsexuals and Women," *Archives of Sexual Behavior* 9 (1980): 245–252.

111. Quoted in Bolin, *In Search of Eve*, p. 107.

112. Ibid., p. 52.

113. Billings and Urban, "Construction of Transsexualism," p. 273.

114. Quoted in "Hopkins Halts Sex-Change Surgery," *Evening Capital*, August 10, 1979.

115. See, for example, Michael Fleming, Carol Steinman, and Judy Bocknick, "Methodological Problems in Assessing Sex Reassignment Surgery: A Reply to Meyer and Reter," *Archives of Sexual Behavior* 9 (1980): 450–456; letters, *Psychology Today*, April 1980.

116. Leslie Lothstein, "The Role of Expressive Psychotherapy in the Treatment of Transsexualism," paper presented at the sixth World Congress of Sexology, May 24, 1983.

117. Leslie Lothstein, *Female-to-Male Transsexualism: Historical, Clinical, and Theoretical Issues* (Boston: Routledge & Kegan Paul, 1983), p. 294.

118. Leslie Lothstein, "Theories of Transsexualism," in *Sexuality and Medicine*, vol. 1, ed. Earl E. Shelp (Norwell, Mass.: Reidel, 1987), p. 55.

119. Quoted in Billings and Urban, "Construction of Transsexualism," p. 275.

120. Lothstein, "Theories," p. 70.

121. See Feinbloom, *Transvestites and Transsexuals*; Bolin, *In Search of Eve*.

122. Quoted in Bolin, *In Search of Eve*, p. 137.

123. Ira Pauly and Milton Edgerton, "The Gender Identity Movement: A Growing Surgical–Psychiatric Liaison," *Archives of Sexual Behavior* 15 (1986): 315–329.

124. See Marcia Yudkin, "Transsexualism and Women: A Critical Perspective," *Feminist Studies* 4, no. 3 (October 1978); Ira Reiss, *Journey Into Sexuality: An Exploratory Voyage* (Englewood Cliffs, N.J.: Prentice Hall, 1986), p. 85.

125. Quoted in Billings and Urban, "Construction of Transsexualism," p. 276.

126. Bolin, *In Search of Eve*, p. 62.

127. Quoted in Janice Raymond, *The Transsexual Empire: The Making of the She-Male* (Boston: Beacon Press, 1979), p. 103.

128. *Sojourner*, October 1978.

129. Amy Hoffman, letter to the editor, *Sojourner*, January 1979.

130. Alice Echols, "The Taming of the Id: Feminist Sexual Politics 1968–83," in *Pleasure and Danger: Exploring Female Sexuality*, ed. Carole S. Vance (Boston: Routledge & Kegan Paul, 1984), pp. 50–72.

131. Raymond, *Transsexual Empire*, p. xvii.

132. Karen Lindsay, letter to the editor, *Sojourner*, November 1978.

133. Esther Newton, *Mother Camp: Female Impersonators in America* (Chicago: University of Chicago Press, 1972).

134. Pat Califia, "Gender-Bending: Playing with Roles and Reversals," *The Advocate*, September 15, 1983.

135. Quoted in Leff, "Genes," pp. 45–58.

136. George A. Rekers, "Atypical Gender Development and Psychosexual Adjustment," *Journal of Applied Behavior Analysis* 10 (1977): 559–571.

137. Ibid., p. 562.

138. Richard Green, *Sexual Identity Conflict in Children and Adults* (Baltimore: Penguin Books, 1974), p. 193.

139. Ibid., p. 276.

140. Ibid., p. 279.

141. Ibid., p. 282.

142. Ibid., p. 289.

143. Green, "*Sissy Boy*," p. 12.

144. Ibid.

145. Lawrence Mass, "A Symposium on Homosexuality: More Psychiatric Shenanigans," *New York Native*, January 16–21, 1982.

146. Quoted in Green, "*Sissy Boy*," pp. 261–262.

147. Ibid., p. 11.

148. Ibid., p. 318.

149. Ibid., p. 319.

150. Green, *Sexual Identity Conflict*, p. 245.

151. Green, "*Sissy Boy*," pp. 189–190.

152. Mel Horne, "Once I Was a Sissy, Now I'm a Gender Discord Boy," *Gay Community News*, March 3, 1979.

153. Weinberg interview.

154. Green, "*Sissy Boy*," p. 12.

CONCLUSION

1. Sandra Leiblum, "Evolving Issues in Sex Therapy and Counseling," paper presented to the Society for the Scientific Study of Sex, November 11, 1988.

2. Joseph LoPiccolo, "Evolving Issues in Sex Therapy and Counseling," paper presented to the Society for the Scientific Study of Sex, November 11, 1988.

3. William Masters and Virginia Johnson, *Human Sexual Inadequacy* (New York: Bantam Books, 1970), p. 141.

4. Donald Mosher, "Advancing Sexual Science: Strategic Analysis and Planning," *Journal of Sex Research* 26, no. 1 (February 1989): 2.

5. See Kim McDonald, "Out of the Closet Now but Misunderstood: Research on Sex," *Chronicle of Higher Education*, November 18, 1987.

6. Mosher, "Advancing Sexual Science," p. 3.

7. John D'Emilio and Estelle Freedman, *Intimate Matters: A History of Sexuality in America* (New York: Harper & Row, 1988).

8. Asta Kenney, Sandra Guardado, and Lisanne Brown, "Sex Education and AIDS Education in the Schools: What States and Large School Districts Are Doing," *Family Planning Perspectives* 21, no. 2 (March–April 1989).

9. The Department of Public Health in Massachusetts, for example, cannot finance the distribution of condoms, and state educators are limited in how explicit they can be in educational programs. The AIDS ACTION Committee of Massachusetts, Inc., was threatened with the termination of state funding when state legislators discovered that the organization had developed and printed an explicit brochure directed to gay men.

10. "White House Has Delayed National Survey on Sex," *Boston Globe*, March 29, 1989.

11. Telephone interview with Paul Abramson, December 16, 1988. See also Mosher, "Advancing Sexual Science."

12. Magali Sarfatti Larson, *The Rise of Professionalism: A Sociological Analysis* (Berkeley: University of California Press, 1977).

13. Richard Green, "Navigating the Straits of Oedipus," *New York Times*, December 11, 1988.

14. Rueschemeyer, in *Professions and Power*, ed. Terence Johnson (London: Macmillan, 1972), p. 25.

Index

		DATE DUE	